That Reminds Me of the Time...

An anthology
by the

Arizona Highway Patrol Coalition of DPS Retirees

D1546502

CLC Publishing,
Books with Purpose

Published by CLC Publishing, LLC.
Mustang, OK 73064

Edited by Jamie Beasley

Photographs used with permission.

Printed in the United States of America
Book Design by Shannon Whittington

Cover Design by Naeem Khan

ISBN: 978-1-7363318-0-4

Biography/Autobiography/Law Enforcement Biography/
Autobiography/Personal Memoir

Coalition of DPS Retirees, Inc.

The Coalition of DPS Retirees proudly presents this book for your reading pleasure. It is comprised of true stories and experiences written and compiled by members and their families of our Coalition.

ACKNOWLEDGMENTS

The Coalition of DPS Retirees wishes to thank the following DPS retirees and their families for contributing their stories to this book. Without their experiences and their humor, this book would not have been possible. Many of the authors' stories were written prior to their passing and kept for this book.

Dysart Murphy, Harley Thompson, Chick Lawwill, Jim Phillips, Paul Palmer, Hank Shearer, Bud Richardson, Rick Ulrich, Dennis McNulty, Dick Shafer, John Kennedy, Colin Peabody, Frank Glenn, Jim Knapp, Greg Eavenson, Bill Chewning, Don Uhles, Bob Osborn, Larry Burns, Ralph Shartzer, Gamble Dick, B.C. Irwin, Craig Williamson, Gregg Girard, Norm Jones, Rick Tannehill, Dave Denlinger, Jeff Trapp, Jack Bell, Larry Jensen, Jim Carroll, Doug Kluender, Don Williams, Kevin Williams, Vern Andrews, Brad Butler, Steve Page, Anthony Dees, Jim Eaves, Herschel Eaves, Scott Lane, Ernest Tofani, Tom Ticer, Jim Berry, Jeff Raynor, Mike Denney, T.K. Waddell, John Hale, Dennis McMillen, Linda Rouillard, Bill Whitlow, Carolyn Barnett, Tomie Lee, Steve Gendler, Jim Daugherty, Larry Thompson, Bill Hansen, Alan Whitney, Ron Bruce, Ron Cox, Travis Qualls, Beverly Jones, Ben Hancock.

Those contributing their stories especially wish to thank the Coalition of DPS Retirees for their full support of this book.

DEDICATION

This book would not have been possible without the input from some of the finest people you could ever meet. These people are the men and women of the Arizona Highway Patrol/Department of Public Safety who have honorably served and retired from this great agency. This book is dedicated to our current retirees, retirees who have passed, and to future retirees. You are a fantastic group, and it is an honor to have served with you.

INTRODUCTION

The first thing that you are going to notice about this book is that it has no chapters.

The second thing you are going to notice is that the stories are not always grammatically correct. They are real stories told by real people. The stories fall in place with no literary structure. Think of this book as if you were sitting down for coffee with friends. You know how it is when you meet fellow retirees for breakfast. Before the coffee is served, the stories start. One guy will tell a story and another will say, "That reminds me of the time...." The stories continue through breakfast, through after-breakfast coffee, and into the parking lot as you make your way to your cars. These are stories told by the people who lived them. They are from retired officers who have a deep love for and great pride in the Arizona Highway Patrol/Department of Public Safety and the men and women they worked with. Now, grab a cup of coffee and sit back and relive these stories with us. Some stories will leave you laughing, and some may bring a tear to your eye. But I can't help but think that it will make your day a little bit better.

Paul Palmer 342
Colin Peabody 481

How do I begin describing a 43-year love affair with the Arizona Highway Patrol, Arizona Department of Public Safety? I'm starting to warm up to this Trooper thing, but it hasn't been easy for me. I was always impressed by how professional the patrolman looked and presented themselves. When I came home from the military, I began classes at NAU.

While at NAU, I met and became friends with a fellow classmate (who I later learned was a Highway Patrolman). Given our developing friendship, I went on a ride-along and instantly knew this was what I wanted to spend my professional life doing. While I went on to finish my degree, I never really had any interest in putting it to use.

One of the things I most enjoyed about joining the Highway Patrol was the family-like atmosphere of nearly everyone in the agency. It didn't matter what you did in the agency, sworn or civilian, it was always like being part of the family.

Something else that became apparent to me very early on was I would have to both earn the title and accept the responsibilities of being an Arizona Highway Patrolman.

When I initially applied, I did not meet the vision requirements. I was finally accepted, nearly 18 months later, when my eyesight was waived.

During this 18-month period, I became employed as an Officer with the Flagstaff Police Department. While I am grateful for this experience and the many friends I have there, my true ambition was to be a member of the Highway Patrol.

What I liked and enjoyed most as a Highway Patrolman was having the opportunity to help people from all walks of life, and I do mean from all walks of life. It seemed that most of the people I encountered over the years were very appreciative of the help.

The people in the agency were really what made it a fantastic place to work, once you were accepted into this amazing family (with the primary responsibility of keeping the Arizona highways safe).

The next 40 some years seemed to go by in the blink of an eye. There were very few days where I didn't want to go to work, and those were days when I was going on vacation.

All in all, I often tell people that I was one of the luckiest people around, in that I had a job I absolutely enjoyed performing every day. Not to mention that I was receiving a paycheck every two weeks just for doing it.

To this day, I still thank GOD for the opportunity to serve others, especially those in need or in trouble. If I had to do it all over again, I would still jump at the chance.

As I traversed these 43 years in the profession, I met some pretty amazing people. Some of my closet friends are people that I met during this journey – one in particular I married! We are now celebrating our 44th year of marriage.

I can only hope I've earned the right and privilege to call myself an Arizona Highway Patrolman.

Col Bobby Halliday
DPS Director Ret

When my old friend Paul Palmer told me he and Colin Peabody were putting together a book on the reminisces of retired DPS officers, it was welcome news. Their stories need to be told.

I served on the Arizona Peace Officer Memorial Board for more than 30 years, and during that time, I made a lot of friends at DPS.

Reading these stories, many of their names are familiar, including Gordon Selby, who was the model for the Arizona Peace Officer Memorial in the Wesley Bolin Plaza at the state capitol. Gordon and I have seen much of Arizona from the back of a horse.

Paul Palmer and Ruben Chavez, filming Eddie Sydney at Walpi, Hopi First Mesa.

I've known Doug Kleunder since he was a kid and served with Colonel Dusty Coleman and Lt. Ron Young on the APOMB.

My cousin, DPS Sgt. Bill Rogers, retired just a few years ago.

Listening to their stories and those of other officers, I've often said, "You should be writing these stories down for your children, grandchildren, and their children," or,

"You've got a book inside that's chomping at the bit to get out."

As a kid growing up in the Route 66 town of Ash Fork between 1947 and 1955, my mother was a waitress in one of the local cafés, and the Highway Patrolmen along 66 and 89 were always stopping in for a cup of coffee. They shared their stories with her, and she then passed them along to me.

World War II was still a recent memory, and I grew up with great respect for men in uniform, and that respect carried over to the Highway Patrolmen. Highway 66 was a narrow, two-lane road with some dangerous curves between Ash Fork and Williams in those days before Interstate 40.

So, naturally there were some horrific accidents and some pretty tough characters to deal with, especially when they've been seduced by Nancy Whiskey.

One day, Les McMahon, a Highway Patrolman stationed in Williams, stopped in and said, "I stopped Charlie for speeding on Ash Fork Hill this afternoon."
Charlie was my older brother. He was always getting into mischief.

"He's pretty salty. I hope he didn't give you any smart talk."
He laughed and said, "I pulled him over and asked, 'Who do you think you are, Barney Oldfield?'"
"He gave me a funny look and said, 'Who's he?'"
We weren't very worldly in Ash Fork in those days before television.

By the time he was 13, Charlie could hot wire our mom's 1936 Ford while she was working and take it for a joy ride.

One day, Officer McMahon walked into the café with a big grin and said "Juanita, I just saw your old car speeding down 66 and there was no driver."

Charlie was short and skinny for his age. She paused and said, "Charlie! I hope you busted him."

He grinned again.

Charlie was stopped again for speeding on 66, but this time he was hauled before Judge Patterson in Prescott. He smarted off, so the judge let him spend the night in the Prescott pokey.

Charlie turned out okay. When he was 17, with a little encouragement from Judge Patterson, he joined the Air Force, received a couple of medals during the Korean War, and came home pretty squared away.

Among the many reminisces in this book, I got the most chuckles from those of the small town justices of the peace and magistrates. Ash Fork's JP was Jack Slamon who owned the dime store on main street.

There was only one paved road in Ash Fork, and that was Route 66. When a highway patrolman cited a speeder, and most were Californians, they would follow the patrolman into town. Then, they would travel into Judge Slamon's dime store where he dealt justice from the candy counter.

The judge had an uncanny instinct for knowing just how much a violator could afford, and he fined accordingly. During the 40s and early 50s, he was the stuff of legends on Route 66. Locals lovingly referred to him as the "Roy Bean of Route 66."

One story had the judge patrolling 66 in a panel wagon. When a highway patrolman stopped a speeder, the judge would drive up and open up the back (where he had a desk installed). He'd hold court, fine 'em on the spot, and save 'em a trip into town. I cannot vouch for the veracity of that story; it may have originated in the fertile mind of a Californian.

During the 1970s, I was flying down US 80 west of Gila Bend heading to Yuma to give a speech in my 1955 Oldsmobile Hardtop Convertible when I saw flashing red lights in my rearview mirror. Busted! I was ticketed and escorted to Sonny Winsor's court in Gila Bend.

The first thing I told him was that I was from Ash Fork and had played high school baseball against Gila Bend. He paused, looked at my ticket, paused again, and finally said, "Okay, Marshall. This one's on me. The next one's on you."

Among the fascinating stories is that of Everett Bowman from Wickenburg. He was a World Champion Rodeo Cowboy during the 1930s, and he had nearly two dozen championship buckles to prove it. Bulldogging was one of his specialties.

He was also a highway patrolman and sometimes his rodeo skills came in handy with the highway patrol.

Harley Thompson told a story of the time he and Bowmen were cruising a street in Williams after a rodeo parade at the 1946 Labor Day Rodeo when a horse shied and threw its rider, then took off down the road at a gallop. Everett climbed out on the running board and told Thompson to speed up and get close to the runaway.

When the patrol car pulled up beside the horse, he made a flying leap, grabbed the horse around its neck, and bulldogged it. He then mounted, rode back, and returned the horse to its grateful owner.

Thompson tells of another time when Everett ran down a speeder in his airplane and gave him a ticket. He'd been in hot pursuit out west of Wickenburg but couldn't catch the car, so he drove to his ranch, fired up his airplane, took to the air and caught up with the car. He landed his plane, flagged the driver down and gave him a ticket. He then got in his plane and flew back to his ranch.

You can't make up stories this good.

Reading these "war" stories from retirees is like sitting around a pot-bellied stove on a snowy day or attending an old timer's picnic on a warm summer afternoon and listening to one storyteller after another painting a picture with words of life as a highway patrolman.

These stories are important, as they give the DPS retires a chance to fondly remember those days of yesteryear when highway patrolmen had to be able to improvise when a situation went south; when a backup might be hours away.

To use a term that's almost become a cliché but still one I love; they bonded together like a band of brothers.

Marshall Trimble
Arizona State Historian

I left the Arizona Highway Patrol on a military leave of absence when I was commissioned a 2nd Lt in the United States Marine Corps and had an opportunity to become a Marine pilot. As a newly trained AV-8B Harrier pilot, I joined my first tactical jet squadron and was soon given the personal call sign "Lawman." Every Marine, Navy, and Air Force jet pilot is given a call sign (or essentially a nickname that everyone calls you by). You can't pick it yourself, and the more you hate it, the more it sticks.

I got lucky with "Lawman," and I thank the Highway Patrol for that. Now I could have been called "Barney" or "Festus" or whatever, as my Marine squadron mates were determined to give me a call sign that was related to law enforcement work, because I told them stories about my time with the Arizona Highway Patrol. They loved the stories just as much as I loved the experiences, I had that gave me those stories.

I served just barely four years with the Highway Patrol, but those were four very rewarding and exciting years. I went on to fly many different jets and aircraft in the Marine Corps and was also lucky enough to be selected to fly with U.S. Navy Blue Angels as the #2 pilot for two years. Years earlier when I left the Highway Patrol for the Marines, I asked if I could keep my badge, #2676.

I had worn that badge every day in uniform, and like my aviator call sign of Lawman, I was simply known by most other patrolmen and dispatchers as "2676." I was told by headquarters that I would have to turn the badge in, but they would hold it for me in some special drawer in Phoenix until I returned from the Marine Corps. I thought I would never see that badge again.

After spending 11 years in the Marines (including a combat tour flying Harriers off a Navy ship in Desert Storm), I found myself back in the US Southwest at El Centro, California, where the Blue Angels train in the winter. I was contacted by Paul Palmer, who told me that the AHP wanted to do some Public Service Announcements with the Blue Angels because of my association with both.

So, several folks from the Highway Patrol came out to El Centro where we filmed commercials, and as a complete surprise to me, Bob Holliday presented me with my old badge, #2676. Mine to keep.

That badge, and the time I served with it pinned .to my chest, still brings me a lot of pride and good memories of serving the people of the State of Arizona. Those who transited through it, but mostly those who I served with.

I remember my time with the Highway Patrol as if it were just yesterday. Yes, I wrote a lot of tickets, arrested a lot of drunk drivers, had some great high-speed chases, put some bad guys in jail, but I also helped countless folks driving through the vast Arizona desert and changed flat tires, did some basic car repairs to keep them moving on, got some folks gas to make it to the next town, and gave immediate first aid to those who were injured in car accidents.

As a patrolman in some of the remote parts of Arizona, you were often the first one at the scene of a serious accident, and people were counting on you to save them. People counted on you to help and make a difference. And countless troopers for decades have done just that – made a difference enforcing the laws of Arizona or helping the motoring public along their way.

Usually a one-person unit, driving by themselves, sometimes with no backup or the nearest backup 20 minutes away. As one of the Highway Patrol's most well-known training officers, JD Buck Savage, used to say, our job was to "Fight crime, save lives, and place fear in the hearts of evildoers."

I think most Arizona state troopers did just that and served well and honorably. Some gave their lives wearing that uniform and badge. Just like in the Marine Corps, where you never forget those you served with that did not come home from war alive, we remember those law enforcement officers that did not come home alive from a shift.

Good men I knew and served with in the Arizona Highway Patrol like Skip Fink. A big man with a big heart and a great guy to have as a backup. I treasure my time with troopers like Skip and thousands of others like him. I am proud to still be known as both Lawman and 2676.

Col Ben Hancock USMC Ret
2676/Lawman

As a teenager, I had the opportunity to work at the YMCA summer camp, which is located out on the old Senator Highway south of Prescott. In doing so, I made several trips on SR69 and I17 to and from Phoenix each summer.

I had fond memories seeing the "patrolman" of the Highway Patrol in action (driving their Mercury Marquis). I dreamed about being a Highway Patrolman stationed out of Prescott when I grew up. At the age of 20, I applied for my dream job with the Arizona Highway Patrol.

At the same time, I applied for the Phoenix Police Department. I was successful in both application processes.

The Highway Patrol offered me a trainee position out of the Country Club Station, and the Phoenix Police Department offered me a position in the police academy, allowing me to be a police officer at the age of 20 (my mom had to buy my bullets for my service weapon if I wanted practice on my own). I asked my Highway Patrol background investigator, Patrolman Pebler what I should do. He suggested I go through the Phoenix Police Department academy, get a year's experience on the streets as an officer and lateral over to the Patrol.

Well, I got through the academy and my year probation as an officer and really didn't want to go through that probationary year again, so I just stayed with the PD.

But as fate would have it, my next 35 plus years in law enforcement, I would have the coolest, most rewarding, and memorable opportunities to work with the men and women of the Arizona Highway Patrol and the Arizona Department of Public safety.

My dream of being given a DPS vehicle came true when I was assigned to the Arizona Governor's Office of Highway Safety as the State Coordinator of the DUI alcohol and drug programs to include the HGN and DRE training programs. The men and women of the Arizona Highway Patrol had and continue to have a very positive influence on many of us from other agencies.

One of the unique cultural environments of the Highway Patrol was the inclusion and support of other agencies throughout the state to accomplish our common goal of making our communities, roadways, and highways the safest they could be.

In my early years with the Phoenix Police Department, my first exposure to this collaborative culture of the Highway Patrol was during the development of the Standardized Field Sobriety Testing to include horizontal gaze nystagmus (HGN) training program. A statewide steering committee was developed to implement the new protocol.

Every agency was included with equal importance and participation in the steering committee and throughout the training process. Shortly thereafter, the Drug Recognition Expert (DRE) program was implemented in the same manner.

Once again, the Highway Patrol played a key role in the successful implementation. Officers from other agencies throughout the country marveled at the fact that officers from the Highway Patrol, county sheriffs, and local departments sat together at the same table, also including criminalists from the state DPS crime lab and prosecutors.

Because of this collaborative culture, Arizona became the model for other states throughout the country.

This collaborative culture was not just contained to the Highway Patrol in the DUI programs, but it was also evident in the gang enforcement arena and other major criminal investigations as well.

Training and support staff from DPS enhanced the National HGN and DRE training programs through (then novel) action training videos. All of this, once again, made Arizona (as a state) and the Highway Patrol (as one of the leading agencies) stand out as one of the leaders in the field nationally.

This collaboration also was evident in the Mark Goudeau serial killer case. It was the proactive expansion of DNA at the Department of Public Safety's crime lab that was able to break the case through the new advances made in their lab.

It would be very easy to go on for pages and pages and list names and names of members of the Arizona Highway Patrol and the Arizona Department of Public Safety and the true impact they have had on making Arizona and our local communities safer places to live, as well as the personal relationships that were formed due to their unselfishness and collaborative culture.

Many of us in the Phoenix Police Department can say our careers, the successes we had, and accomplishments we enjoyed were enhanced and benefited from the members of Arizona Highway Patrol.

Joe Klima, Ret. Commander
Phoenix Police Department

Since the inception of the Arizona Highway Patrol in 1931, most patrolmen (at some point in time in their career) have considered or wished they had started writing a book.

This book would contain anecdotes of the life that they lead while on duty in situations that are sometimes perilous, at other times extremely humorous, and everything in between.

Most people have very little concept of the things that law enforcement officers deal with on a day-to-day basis. This book is a compilation of stories, as told by the individual officers involved, that will shed some light into those activities.

Please enjoy just a few of the true stories presented by the actual officers involved, and remember that many, if not most of them, involve activities that occurred in the last century.

Lynn Ideus Capt DPS Ret
Chairman, AHP/DPS Legacy Museum

ROLL CALL
Paul Palmer #342

It is a special place in Heaven that God has set aside for only the bravest. It is reserved for those men and women who paid the ultimate sacrifice, giving their lives to protect us. Today the street is lined with all of the officers who have fallen in the line of duty. Men and women, all in various uniforms, razor-sharp creases in their uniforms, with shoes shined to a high gloss. At the head of the line are the tan uniforms of the officers of the Arizona Highway Patrol. Today, 29 officers stand ready to accept a new member. Louie Cochran, badge 59, EOW 12-22-58 steps forward at the head of the line and calls the officers to attention. Louie's voice booms out.

"Paul Marston, badge 138, EOW 6-9-69." "HERE SIR," is the response.
Gib Duthie, badge 143, EOW 9-5-70. —HERE SIR.
Jim Keeton, badge 310, EOW 2-5-71. —HERE SIR.
Don Beckstead, badge 409, EOW 2-7-71. —HERE SIR.
Alan Hansen, badge 204, EOW 7-19-73. —HERE SIR.
Greg Diley, badge 1442, EOW 12-2-77. —HERE SIR.
Mac Merrill, badge 695, EOW 12-11-78. —HERE SIR.
John Walker, badge 150, EOW 11-30-79. —HERE SIR.
Bill Murie, badge 721, EOW 11-19-80. —HERE SIR.
Tom McNeff, badge 1758, EOW 10-2-83. —HERE SIR.
Rick Stratman, badge 1622, EOW 10-2-83. —HERE SIR.
Bruce Petersen, badge 3536, EOW 10-20-87. —HERE SIR.
Ed Rebel, badge 233, EOW 6-28-88. —HERE SIR.
Johnny Garcia, badge 3572, EOW 10-14-89. —HERE SIR.
Dave Gabrielli, badge 1231, EOW 8-31-90. —HERE SIR.
John Blaser, badge 2916, EOW 8-31-90. —HERE SIR.
Manny Tapia, badge 1409, EOW 1-8-91. —HERE SIR.

Dave Zesiger, badge 1848, EOW 7-3-92. —HERE SIR.
Mark Dryer, badge 9764, EOW 7-3-93. —HERE SIR.
Mike Crowe, badge 2729, EOW 7-4-95. —HERE SIR.
Bob Martin, badge 474, EOW 8-15-95. —HERE SIR.
Doug Knutson, badge 3818, EOW 1-2-98. —HERE SIR.
Juan Cruz, badge 3111, EOW 12-9-98. —HERE SIR.
Skip Fink, badge 940, EOW 2-18-2000. —HERE SIR.
Brett Buckmister, badge 5548, EOW 3-21-2000. —HERE SIR.
Bruce Harrolle, badge 5669, EOW 10-13-2008. —HERE SIR.
Chris Marano, badge 6759, EOW 12-17-2009. —HERE SIR.
Tim Huffman, badge 5430, EOW 5-6-13. —HERE SIR.

Louie then does a slow about-face as the gates of Heaven open and in walks a young officer with a somewhat bewildered look on his face. Louie's voice booms again as he orders, "RIGHT HAND SALUTE."

The arms of 29 officers begin a slow rise to the brim of their hats as the young man, now with a slight smile on his face, walks through the line of officers. The 29 officers think, *this young man could be my son*, or *this young man could be my grandson*. The young officer reaches the end of the line and takes his place among these heroes. The officers' arms slowly drop from the brim of their hats. Louie's voice booms again. "Tyler Edenhofer, badge 10449, EOW 7-25-18."

Tyler stands a little taller and responds, "HERE SIR." Louie dismisses the men, and they all gather around Tyler to welcome him to this special place in Heaven. Louie looks over the scene as a tear rolls down his cheek because he knows in his heart that this will not be the last time he assembles this group of heroes to welcome a new hero into their midst.

THE BEGINNING
Dysart Murphy #906

Note: Dysart Murphy wore badge number 906. He came on the department in 1938 and retired well before the badge number changes. He had a badge number in the 900's which were reserved for captains and above. At retirement he held the rank of Inspector. He wore his hat cocked at an angle on his head and could give a look that would strike the fear of God into any man. Here is his story.

Under Governor Osborne in January 1931, Capt. Ellis Watt conducted a month-long training program which almost the entire patrol attended. World War II became a big issue, and no more training was then conducted until Hathaway became in 1950 under the merit system. In the interim, the 35-year age was waived, and most patrolmen were retired police officers or old men who knew nothing about police work. Their training was much like mine was when I joined in 1938.My first day I went to work at 5:00 in the afternoon, and at 6:00 I was helping Corporal Ed Brastelein investigate an accident. No, he wasn't impressed with my assistance either. I was still wondering about the way I was sworn in by Superintendent Tom Rumens when he asked me back into his middle office which was located in the Highway Department building on West Jackson.

He laid his cigar down long enough to say, "Raise your right hand and swear after me."

He started out on every subject I could think of. My hand was getting heavy, and he concluded with, "Do you solemnly swear that you have nothing to do with no women?"

I swore and then I was a Highway Patrolman. And that's about the way they were trained in those days, except for the cigar and the mandate concerning females. For example, we sent a new man out to Salome, and he hadn't been there a week before he had slot machines in one of the garages. When it was brought to his attention, he said, "Well, that's what I thought I was supposed to do." Then there was another young man when asked for his driver's license, he said he didn't have one.

"Well, what experience do you have driving a car?"

"Well," he said, "I used to have to drive my dad home when he got drunk." No, the FBI didn't check them out in those days. They had other things to do. When the pressure from the war began to ease up, they got a week's training with Riley Brian but nothing like a training school. Nevertheless, there were some good men that came to the patrol that way. Men like Kratzberg, Tyra, Kimmler, Thompson, Dick Raymond, Whitlow, and Bob Cochran. I never thought of it before, but I can't think of a single one that came on in that period that turned out bad. It wasn't until we went under the merit system that each applicant was carefully screened by the FBI. Then, it was with the formal school that the misfits began to show up. So almost 10 years went by before there was a training department. As long as Osborn was governor, the patrol was his department. and he wanted it to stay out of politics. But when he realized that he wouldn't be able to run for governor again, he allowed us to take the situation to the voters of Arizona, and they voted in the merit system by about 3 to 1. And that was the beginning of job security. And after it was implemented, Greg Hathaway became superintendent. Hathaway told me that I reminded him of an old white-haired professor, so he established the Plans and Training Department. He thought the Western District could get along without me for a while, and I became that department. At the time, we were still limited by law to one patrolman for every 3,500 registered vehicles. When they checked up on it, they found out we could have 59 patrolmen instead of 57, and we began looking for two new patrolmen.

Someone discovered Harold Johnson. His age was okay because the age ceiling was still 35. But the clearance between his head and the top of the door was a problem. So we measured him again and, with a little stooping, he made it. Rose Perica, now known as Governor Rose, used to work at the Arizona Highway's Magazine Department. She saw to it that members of the patrol around the office there were regularly supplied with copies of the magazine. One day I got a call from her, and she said, "I've done the patrol a few favors, and now I want you to do one for me."

I said, "Okay, what's his name?"

She said, "Leslie Raymond McMahan."

She said, "You can't go wrong with him," and she was right.

The first training class since 1941 began. We didn't have a classroom anywhere, but that big conference table in the Highway Commissioner's office was used only about one day a month. It was a big, old table that would seat 20-25 people. So, the old white-haired professor sat at one end of the table, and Harold and Les sat at the other end where they learned how to become highway patrolmen and the old white-haired professor learned about teaching.

And that is where your department got its start. I don't know if that teacher graduated, but those two men did. They became the last two hired where the age limit was 35, and I might add that both of them retired from the patrol with a long and commendable service record.

Sometime after that, Greg went to the Legislature and got them to realize how ridiculous the system was that only allowed one patrolman per 3,500 registered vehicles. So, they allowed him to exceed his budget. He hired 20 new patrolmen, and the conference table in the Highway Commissioner's office was completely surrounded by 20 new patrolmen.

By that time the Merit System Council had drawn up rules and regulations and so forth, and one of those changes was to reduce the age ceiling to age 25, as well as recognize a preference for servicemen. And that's what that first class was. We had Merit System rules and working under politics. Then I added two new subjects: Arizona geography and the story of Communism. Since Greg was a strong commie fighter, he approved the additions. It isn't done anymore. but for a time there, all the mail that went out from the patrol office carried a slogan on the outside of the envelope that was anti-communist.

After that first class, there was another one about the same size. But there was too much time between classes, which made the Western District look better by the day. During this time. we moved from the Highway Department at 1701 West Jackson to Encanto, and in that same year, 1953, Kratzberg went back to Northwestern for the long course. Inspector Whitlow and five captains went back for a six-week course. After this, I went back to the Western District, and Kratzberg took over training. I still came back and taught Arizona Geography and anti-communism.

HUMBLE BEGINNINGS
Harley Thompson #6

I had spent the last three Christmas seasons floating around out in the South Pacific on a Fletcher Class Destroyer, the USS Conway DD507. I was due to get out of the Navy and had more than enough points to rotate back to the states, but I was stuck out on the high seas. We were on a clean-up process at the end of the war. Now, for a boy from Cottonwood this was an exciting time for me, but in all reality, I just about had as much of this fun as I could stand. But here I was, February 1946, and I was finally getting out of the Navy and returning to my beloved Arizona.

When I got back home to Cottonwood, I had absolutely no idea about what my future was going to be, but as good as it was to be home, I knew my future did not involve Cottonwood.

After I had been home about two weeks my father asked me to take a two-wheel trailer he had just made down to the local jail on a day when the Motor Vehicle Division agent would be there and have a serial number assigned to the trailer and get it registered. While I was talking to the MVD agent, he asked me if I knew Joe Mulcaire. I told him that I did and that, in fact, Joe and I and his two brothers went to Clarkdale High School together. He told me that Joe was working for the Arizona Highway Patrol.

Well, that got me to thinking. Hell, if Joe can do it, so can I. So I asked the agent if he would give me an address to write to so I could get an application.

"Here it is," he said. "The address is 1701 W. Jackson, and you'll want to address it to Superintendent Horace Moore."

That very night I wrote to Superintendent Moore and asked for an application.

A couple of days later I went to work for a friend of my father's who was building houses in the Verde Heights addition. I was hired to dig footings for the foundation using a pick and shovel. This was long before backhoes came into use. I made 85 cents an hour.

About a week later I received an answer to my inquiry into the Highway Patrol saying there were no openings at the present, but I could go ahead and submit an application for future reference. I returned the application and continued to dig footings in that hard old caliche dirt, winding up with blisters that had blisters. That caliche was hard as rocks.

It wasn't long, maybe two weeks, and I received a letter from Superintendent Moore advising me that Merritt Chaffey, a patrolman from Prescott, would be in

Cottonwood the following week. I was to meet him at an appointed time at the local jail for an interview.

I met with patrolman Chaffey and rode around with him for about an hour or so. He asked me about my background and why I was interested in becoming a Highway Patrolman.

At this point in time, I had absolutely no idea that the job was highly political. I was 21 years old, not a registered voter, and had no party affiliation. I didn't know anyone who had political influence nor anyone who knew anyone who did. I told Patrolman Chaffey that I thought it was a worthwhile job and that maybe I could help make the highways a little safer. I also told him that I had always admired Patrolman Vidrene who used to be stationed in Cottonwood and that I had been friends with his son. Patrolman Chaffey left that same day, and I heard no more for about another week. Back to digging footings!

One day my mother drove up to the subdivision where I was working and told me that I was to call a Mr. Moore in Phoenix right away. She took me back home, which was only about a half mile away, and I called Mr. Moore. He asked me how soon I could get to Phoenix and asked if I was interested in a job as a radio dispatcher. I told him I could catch the Santa Fe Trailways bus down to Phoenix the next day and that, yes, I would take the dispatching job. My ticket out of Cottonwood! I returned to the jobsite and dug footings for the rest of the day and then quit my job that evening.

The next day I caught the Trailways bus and waved goodbye to Cottonwood. I arrived in Phoenix at around 5:00 PM, got a room at the Adams Hotel ,and the next morning took off on foot for 1701 W. Jackson. That didn't seem too far for an old country boy, only 17 blocks. I had on my new loafers and on the 26th day of May, 1946, that 17 blocks turned out to be longer than I thought. By the time I reached the patrol office, I had blisters on my heels to match the blisters on my hands.

Superintendent Moore greeted me and said that they had filled the dispatcher job yesterday. He said that they had hired Cecil McCormick, but they had a patrolman position open up and asked if I would take it. I told him that would be just fine. Hell, I didn't care. I needed a job!

I filled out some more paperwork, and the Superintendent introduced me to Patrolman Jack Hirsch and told me that he would take me back to the hotel and I was to meet another patrolman out front of the hotel at 1630 hours. I would be working from 1700 to 0200 and would be riding with that officer. I found out about this time that I would be earning $200 a month for the first three months and then be accelerated to $220 a month and finally top out at $240 forever!

At the appointed time I was out in front of the Adams and was picked up by Patrolman Archie Tufts. Patrolman Tufts took me back to the patrol office and got me a code book with the traffic codes and said, "This is your Bible. Memorize it!"

We headed out east on Baseline Road and worked our way out towards Chandler. During the first couple of hours, I kept hearing what I thought at the time were all these references to 10 this and 10 that until I finally asked Archie what that meant. He laughed and told me about the 10 codes. He also told me that he would get me a printed copy of the codes so that I could memorize them.

We made a couple of stops, and I watched him as he did his thing. Somewhere around 0130, he took me back to the hotel and told me that he would pick me up at the same time the next afternoon.

I spent most of the next day studying the traffic codes and trying to memorize them. I took Patrolman Tufts at his word.

The following couple of days were no different, except I was told that Patrolman Hirsch would pick me up at 1300 hours on the third day and take me to a store where I could order some uniforms, (called officer pinks) and then take me to N. Porter & Co. and be measured up for a gun belt.

After five days with Patrolman Tufts, he said that the following day was his day off and that another officer would pick me up at the usual time. This was Patrolman Fred Gittner, and he was not happy with me riding with him as he seemed more interested in procuring some items for some rental houses that he had.

Then it was back with Archie for the next six days. We made a stop over by Tempe as I recall for a headlight out, or something like that, and he told me to write the repair order. I recall vividly that as I took the license from the violator, my hands were shaking so badly. So badly, in fact, the violator laughed and asked if I was new at this, to which I replied, "This is my very first time."

He said, "Don't worry, this is my first time being stopped."

Something happened at that very moment when he said what he did. I stopped shaking, and it never, ever bothered me again.

Six more days with Patrolman Tufts and I was picked up by Patrolman John Perica. Now, I liked John. He was different than Gittner. John made me feel welcome. He also showed me how to investigate an accident. We had a minor 961 out east towards Tempe, and John went through the entire procedure very carefully with me and he let me fill out the entire accident report. I was beginning to feel now that I was a real part of the Highway Patrol.

Back to working with Patrolman Tufts for the next five days after which time I was being sent to Yuma. I now had all of my uniforms and equipment. I remember when I was given ammunition for my gun, Claude Emery asked how many rounds for the gun and how many rounds it took for the cartridge holder, and he counted out just exactly that number of shells.

The superintendent told me that patrol vehicle Z-199 was my assigned unit and that I was going to Yuma that night. Now, for those of you who don't know, the national speed limit of 35 mph was still in effect. That was the war-time limit. If you have never driven to Yuma in the middle of the night, some 200 miles, at 35 mph, that is an experience in itself!

To Yuma I went and checked into the Lee Hotel in the wee hours of the morning. I had been instructed to meet Patrolman Norman Cole at the Sheriff's office at 1000 hours and to work with him and that he would help me find a place to live. I met Patrolman Cole at the appointed time, and he was quick to inform me that he was in charge down there and I would follow his orders. He also told me that he would work days and I would work nights. In the absence of air conditioning that was OK with me! Now here it was in June and it was pretty hot already, so I figured that I had the better end of the deal.

Three weeks had gone by, and I had still not had a day off and didn't know which day I should take. With Patrolman Cole saying he was in charge, I asked him what day I should take, and he assigned me a day four or five days away. And so it was!

My training period left just a whole lot to be desired. Frankly, in my opinion, I was not ready to be an officer at all, but I thought I would just tough it out, go carefully, ask a lot of questions and take it one step at a time.

Patrolman Cole showed me some places to rent, none of which I found suitable, mostly crappy, run-down, dirty hovels. So, I continued to live at the hotel.

About two weeks later, Cole informed me that he was being transferred to Coolidge and being promoted to Captain. (Patrolman Cole never rose above the rank of patrolman) He advised me that two more patrolmen were coming down to Yuma. Cole left a couple of days later and Patrolman Lee Shepard and another officer, whose name I don't recall, arrived. I had now been there about a month, and I was instructed to return to Phoenix for reassignment.

During my time in Yuma, I was allowed six days of expenses at $8.00 per day. I had never received any instruction in filling out an expense account, so again I was in the dark there. When I got back to Phoenix, I asked Mr. Claude Emery, the chief clerk, how to go about filing out an expense form, and I learned something here. If you asked Claude to help you, you were in like Flynn and were paid very quickly.

The superintendent called me into his office and told me that I was being transferred to Williams and would be working for Captain Jack Powell. I'm here to tell you that going to Williams was just like dying and going to Heaven! Wow!! That was a choice assignment!

My whole point in this story is to point out how totally untrained I was during my "break-in period" as compared to how patrolmen are trained now. To survive those early days was nothing short of a miracle. To work for and with Captain Jack Powell was a real revelation. He was such a great help and guiding power.

YESTERYEAR
Harley Thompson #6

I was just thinking about my very first winter upon the Mother Road, US 66, and what life was like back then in 1946. Several things come to mind.

While stationed in Williams, I had completed my first six months on probation and was at the top of the pay scale. I was making $240 per month before taxes, and I was still pretty shaky about what law enforcement really entailed. Thanks to the able tutoring by Captain Jack Powell, I was beginning to get my feet a little more firmly on the ground. I was fat, dumb, and happy. Well, not fat.

As I thought about those days, I began to recall some of the things we did not have. First and foremost was the lack of adequate radio communications. The unit in my vehicle was powered by a motor generator in the trunk that had to be wound up pretty tight before it would transmit, and at night the headlights would go dim or go out when you used the radio. The unit transmitted on a frequency of 2430 kcs, and the only time I was able to talk to anyone was when I would be close to Flagstaff or Prescott, generally about 10 or 15 miles. The ability to talk to another patrol unit did not exist. If I wanted a wrecker or ambulance, it was necessary to stop a motorist, tell him what I wanted, and give him a piece of paper with the necessary phone number. I would ask them to make the call and then wait hopefully.

My patrol unit was a '42 Ford, made in 1941, with the old flathead engine cranking out a gut-twisting 90 mph going downhill and aided by a tail wind. It rattled, wheezed, and banged, It lacked power steering and power brakes, but it was road worthy.

I was always alone on patrol and never had a back-up unit available. At accident scenes I always did the first aid to the injured as best I could with a limited supply of first aid materials.

Bulletproof vests did not exist. The only red light was a spotlight mounted on the left front pillar post. Flashers did not exist. I had no cell phone, of course, Fire departments never left the city limits, and most firemen were volunteers at that. I never had tire chains or snow tires during the winter months.

We had a pretty severe winter in 1946-47, and since we didn't have a specific uniform coat for winter wear, I asked my captain what I should wear, He said, "Whatever will keep you warm and look presentable." Well, I still had my US Navy-issued peacoat, which did not see any action in the South Pacific theater. It had been in storage for nearly three years. I broke it out, and that is what I wore. Very comfy!

The heat in the patrol vehicles was provided by a Southwind Heater and had two heats, hot and hotter. When they were working! The big disadvantage in those heaters was the fact that they burned gas which was provided through a vacuum. When you were driving code 2 or 3, the fact that you were accelerating took the vacuum away and the heater did not work, blowing only cold air. Brrrrrr!

It was about that time, two weeks before Thanksgiving, that my good captain told me that all days off were cancelled until further notice. The captain gave the explanation for this action as follows: He said that, since nearly all those that had been in the military service during World War II were now discharged, there would be more people traveling during the holiday season. He said we needed to be out there on the road providing a deterrent to violators and keeping the accident rate down the best we could. Unfortunately, this no-days-off period lasted until about ten days after New Year's. Back then we did not complain because we all figured that it was just a condition of employment.

Even so, it was good to have a job that truly turned out to be the most satisfying I ever had in my life. I have said this many times. It was the only job I ever had that I did not care what day it was or what time it was, and I mean that from the bottom of my heart.

NAVY COMMANDO
Chick Lawwill #35

In 1941 I dropped out of high school and joined the Navy with three of my buddies. After boot camp I was assigned to the Navy Commando Unit. (In 1946 Navy Commandos and Navy Frogs became known as Navy Seals). MY unit fought on many Islands in the Pacific, and we were present at the landing of General MacArthur when he walked ashore to fulfill his promise of "I shall return." We stood in a line and saluted the general as he made his way onto the beach to make his famous speech.

From there I went to Manila. After a couple of weeks in Manila, I had earned enough points to return stateside. While still stateside the war ended. I did not have to go back to the Pacific!

I went on to earn my GED and then completed two years at Phoenix College. My career with the Arizona Highway Patrol would follow.

FAILED TESTS
Chick Lawwill #35

After several unfulfilling jobs, my wife, Faye, encouraged me to go into law enforcement. I put in applications to the Border Patrol, Phoenix Police Department, and the Arizona Highway Patrol. I did not pass the test for the Border Patrol, and the Phoenix Police Department rejected me because my physical revealed a spot on my lung. My doctor said it would clear up, but Phoenix didn't want to take a chance.

While waiting to hear from the Border Patrol and Phoenix, Arizona Highway Patrolman Gibson kept showing up at my door. He urged me to join the patrol saying I was just the kind of guy they were looking for. I finally gave in and said yes. He said I would get a provisional appointment, and I could take the test later. Tests and me do not get along. I freeze up. I said I wanted to take the test first.

Jim Phillips was working at Reynolds Aluminum and had also applied to the patrol. He and his wife and little girls lived in Arizona Park. His wife worked as a telephone operator. He would come by the house, and we would study together. Years later, when I was transferred from Yuma to Phoenix, Jim was transferred to Yuma to take my place as District Commander.

SELIGMAN
Chick Lawwill #35

I joined the Highway Patrol on March 24, 1952. My first badge number was 17. When I first came on the patrol, you were dispatched by your unit number, which was the number of the vehicle you were assigned. You best not forget to advise the dispatcher if you were driving a swing car! My first car was a 1949 Ford with 170,000 miles, car number Z499. It was previously assigned to Lt. Kratzberg.

I first went to Seligman, leaving my family in Phoenix until I found a place to live and got settled in. John Gantt was my coach. The only place I could find to rent was a room-and-board with a husband and wife with two small children. My room was a converted chicken pen.

Two weeks later John Gantt was transferred to Phoenix, and I inherited his duplex. The walls were paper thin, and there were railroad tracks just behind the duplex and just in front was the highway.

I had no phone. The phone was at a 24-hour service station across the street. A loud bell on the outside of the building would signal an incoming call. If the patrol was calling, he would run across the street and wake me up. I would then get in the car and check for traffic. I had been in Seligman for 7-8 months when an opening in Yuma became available. Everyone thought I was crazy when I jumped at the chance to transfer to Yuma.

YUMA
Chick Lawwill #35

When I first arrived in Yuma from Seligman, there were only two patrolman assigned to Yuma. Louie Cochran and myself. The patrol was very generous and understanding when it came to the family being in the patrol car and the use of the patrol car for personal business. Being on call 24 hours a day and for the most part having no phone, I could not leave the house without the patrol car. Our home was not far from the highway, and many times I would hit the siren as I drove past letting Faye know I was taking a call and would be late for dinner.

We had both county and state highways to patrol, and we were dispatched out of the sheriff's office. We were on call 24 hours a day and no days off. When we did start to get one day off a week, we were still on call. If you were called out on a day off, tough. There was no overtime or comp time. Our reports were done on our own time in our homes since there was no patrol office in Yuma.

You were expected to put in 8 hour a day on the highway and had to work all holidays. You can forget about sick leave. If you were sick, you still had to work because there was no one else to work the road. We received sick leave at a rate of 1/4, not a day per month, and the most you could accumulate was 5 days. It was later increased to one day per month with a maximum accumulation of 15 days. Anything over 15 days, you lost.

I was earning $235 a month, and to supplement my income, I drove a melon truck. I believe that, throughout the years, every patrolman in Yuma drove the melon trucks for added income.

Our area started from San Luis, Mexico, on south Highway 95, to Stone Cabin, a little over halfway between Yuma and Quartzsite. It was a gravel road. We had US80 from Yuma to Sentinel.

CALL ME JIM
Jim Phillips #36

My badge number is 36. I came on the Arizona Highway Patrol in 1952 and retired in 1975. I came on the department making $250 with a $10-a-month clothing allowance. I had to furnish my own equipment, including gun, flashlight, batteries, and just about anything I needed to get the job done. We didn't have department-issued shotguns. I carried an old Marine Corps carbine for added protection. (I am one of the few Arizona USMC WWII vets still alive). We patrolmen worked alone. A backup? What was that?

I am a Charter member of the Arizona Highway Patrol Association and have been paying dues and supporting the Association since 1958. Almost 60 years now.

My first duty assignment was in Gila Bend where my area was north to 51st Avenue and US80, east on US84 to Stanfield, west to the Yuma county line, and south to the Mexico border. There were times I might get called out to an accident and not get home before my next shift or the one after. I worked six days a week. The pay was low, and there was no such thing as overtime pay or a 20-year retirement. But I loved my job. I was an Arizona Highway Patrolman!

Over the years, I transferred to different locations. Bert Zambonini, badge 60, and I were the first patrolmen assigned to the state legislature. Later I was assigned to protect Governor Paul Fannin. This was before Governor Security Detail was formed. I was a Lieutenant and District Commander in District Seven, Globe. I retired as a Captain, and after retiring I was a member of the State Legislature representing Yuma County.

Early in my career, we didn't have an employee support group. Superintendent Greg Hathaway worked closely with the legislature. Some have said he demeaned himself and made the department a political animal. But everything he did was for the department. He never personally benefitted from the favors given to members of the legislature. Yes, we transported members of the legislature around, something that would be unheard of today. But we got the money we needed from the legislature. A different time indeed!

It may sound like we were totally political, but Superintendent Greg Hathaway, a wonderful man, actually got the department out of politics and out from under the control of the Arizona Highway Department. He was a true leader of men. This was a time before managers!

I wish I could claim ownership of a great idea to get air conditioning in our patrol cars, but it arose from a group discussion. We decided that in the summer, while we were waiting to transport a member of the legislature, especially when his wife was involved, we would run the patrol car's heater wide open. Just before they got into the car, we would lower the fan to the lowest setting.

Usually, it was the wife who commented on how hot the car was. "Officer, do you always have to put up with this awful heat?"

"Yes, ma'am, it gets rough at times."

The Arizona Highway Patrol was one of the first law enforcement agencies in the nation to have air-conditioned vehicles. It was a unit mounted under the dash, but it was cool! It was the way we did business.

In 1958 the Arizona Highway Patrol Association was formed. We all worked hard to make it a success. Each year the Association would hold the Highway Patrolmen's Ball. Patrolmen would work after a shift and on days off to sell tickets to the Ball. Patrolmen would be given a certain area, and they would pound the pavement stopping at businesses to sell tickets. It was a way for guys to not only help the Association but to also put a little extra money in their wallets. They would also talk to friends or places where they did business and get them to advertise in the magazine.

We all worked hard to promote and support the Association. This dedication and support continued though our years with the department and during our retirement. It was this dedication and hard work that assisted in getting our 20-year retirement.

My badge number is 36. But I'm not just a number. Please call me Jim.

MY HEROES
Paul Palmer #342

I have been thinking an awful lot about my heroes lately. No, they are not famous and you haven't seen their names in headlines. They are the old-timers of the department. Some retired, and some of them are still with the department, nearing retirement. Some have been killed in the line of duty, and some have left us far too early due to illness or accident. I have always hesitated writing about these friends and heroes because, when you start naming names, you are bound to leave someone out, and the last thing I want to do is to fail to honor someone who has meant a lot to me. But I'm going to try it, and if I missed you, I apologize; but remember, your friendship is cherished.

We use the term heroes pretty loosely, and I'm probably guilty of that now. To me, these people are heroes, not for something courageous they did, but just for being themselves and influencing my life and the lives of others. Men who made the Arizona Highway Patrol one of the most respected state law enforcement agencies in the nation and paved the way for the Department of Public Safety.

Some of you are probably thinking, *here we go again. Some old retiree telling us about the good old days and how bad they had it and how easy we have it.* No, not gonna do that.

The people I am talking about are ordinary folks going about their daily lives, suffering from conditions of age and, for some, the loss of lifetime partners. People forgotten by the department. People who retired and, as they left, never heard the words "Thank you" from the department. People who, in their own minds, are somehow still attached to the department but realize that they are the forgotten ones. People who, whether they will admit it or not, are hurt by this shun.

Growing up in the state yard in Gila Bend, I was always in contact with Highway Patrolmen. As a young kid I looked up to them and worshiped them. Men like Ed Shartzer. He taught me how to shake hands. When I first met him and he extended his hand for a handshake, I reached out and placed my small hand in his big paw. I remember him telling me that men don't shake hands like that. You have to grip a man's hand firmly he said. A lesson I never forgot.

Later, when I was dispatching in Holbrook and working the graveyard shift, you would hear a voice over the radio. "Whatcha doing? Let's get a cup."

Here it was, one or two o'clock in the morning and Inspector Shartzer was out and about meeting with his men. And I would know that it was only a matter of time when I would hear that same voice asking if the coffee was on as his black Oldsmobile pulled into the Holbrook office parking lot.

His son, Ralph, became the first officer in St. George, Utah. His patrol area was the Virgin River Gorge, and being the only patrolman in St. George earned him the nickname "Lonesome George of the gorge". Ralph helped pave the way for future officers being assigned in St. George.

Another son, Chuck, worked in TCD. Always with a quick smile and a laugh, he personally made sure that officers' radio needs were taken care of. As a supervisor, he was in on many of the radio improvements over the years.

Norman Cole, Dick Shafer, Ken Forgia, Norm Jackson, Jim Phillips, Ed Rebel, and J.R. Ham were a few of the officers I remember from Gila Bend.

Lt. Vern Fugat who used to stop at the state yard and visit my dad. As they stood outside and talked, Vern would launch a stream of tobacco juice clear across the road, kicking up dust on the other side. Now, who wouldn't admire that?

Lt. Chick Lawwill, District Commander in Yuma. I was in the Navy, missed a bus, and was stranded in Gila Bend. Chick gave me a ride to Yuma in his patrol car and arranged a flight with the Marine Corps to take me to Twenty-Nine Palms. Chick kept me from being AWOL and out of the Marine Corps brig.

Lt. Bud Kratzburg and Louie Cochran were visitors to the Gila Bend state yard.

Inspector Dysart Murphy was feared by many, but to me he was a kind, old family friend who gave me a bible as a high school graduation gift and urged me to read it. Many years later, a few years before his death, he sent me a package containing 16 audio cassette tapes. On the first tape he spoke of my mother and father and then began telling stories of his early days on the Arizona Highway Patrol. On the remaining 15 tapes was Dysart's voice narrating the bible.

G.O. Hathaway was Superintendent of the Patrol when I came on the department. Hathaway flew the bomber immediately behind the Enola Gay when the atomic bomb was dropped on Hiroshima. A man with a military bearing and stern looks that could instill fear in any man. Later, however, I learned that he was actually not that stern at all; just a man who had learned to keep his emotions in check.

Major Jack Monschein was an inspiration to me. He was in charge of communications, and after meeting with him, he offered me a job as dispatcher in Holbrook. It was a provisional job he explained, and he needed someone in Holbrook right away. I would have to be in Holbrook within a week, and I would have to test for the position later to become a permanent employee. After accepting, he took me down the hall and introduced me to Superintendent Hathaway. To say I was in awe is an understatement. Thus began my career with the department. Major Monschein led the way, making operational communications what it is today. He was also instrumental in locating NLETS at state headquarters in Phoenix.

When I came on the patrol and was stationed in Holbrook, the district commander was Lt. Don Naval. You would be hard-pressed to find anyone who was so fit and looked as great as he did in a uniform. He exuded confidence and authority, and he scared me to death. He knew it and enjoyed it. But that didn't keep him from inviting this bachelor to his home for dinner and later offering me fatherly advice when I told him I wanted to transfer to Phoenix.

Sgt. John Consoni, a father figure who passed away as his medical transport plane lifted off from the Holbrook airport en route to a Phoenix hospital for treatment of a critical lung condition.

Sgt. Ray Dahm, a short feisty man who seemed to rule the White Mountains.

Sgt Bob Harvey who, it seemed, personally knew and was respected by almost every Indian on the Navajo reservation.

Some of the finest officers in the state patrolled the highways of District Three. I wish I could name each of them individually, but names would mean nothing unless you knew the men. We were a close group and I miss them all.

As you read this, if you are a retiree, it will bring back memories of officers with single-digit badge numbers or at least double-digit numbers. Officers you worked with and who are now leaving us as old age and illness consume their bodies. Officers you worried over as they lay in a hospital bed from an on-duty injury. Officers you mourned as you watched the superintendent or director place a folded flag in the hands of a grieving widow.

If you are a young officer, you are concerned about today and how to feed a family on an officer's pay. You are concerned about getting home safely to your families after each shift. The old-timers have no place in most of your thoughts. That is not wrong.

I am not trying to place blame. How can you think of these people when you have never heard of them or their influence on the department or heard the hilarious stories of some of their antics? In your busy daily lives, you have enough to do without worrying about the old-timers who have gone before you.

But if you come across a retiree, don't brush him off. Take the time to listen. Let them know that you care. If you hear of a retiree in the hospital, stop by and say hello. You may not have known him, but let him know you care. Attend his funeral. Honor him. It will mean so much to his family and fellow retirees.

Remember, time goes by fast, and one day you will be in his shoes.

SAD NIGHT IN THE OLD PUEBLO
Hank Shearer #122

It was December 20, 1959. The telephone rang in the middle of the night from the Highway Patrol dispatcher. I was told to respond to a serious accident just east of Tucson on the Wilmot overpass (I-10 under construction) and that additional help was needed. When I arrived at the scene, it was horrific. Many emergency vehicles were already there with their red and yellow lights flashing. Officers and other emergency responders were scurrying around the scene.

A Greyhound bus and a loaded cattle truck had collided head-on the overpass. Cattle had been catapulted up and out of the truck, some landing on top of the bus and others on the pavement. I had never heard a more distressing sound from the animals, a complete crescendo of noise. A mixture of blood and diesel fuel was everywhere.

My Sergeant, Jim Hart #706, intercepted me with a list of various tasks that needed attention. At this time, I was a new recruit with only a couple of weeks in District 8, Tucson. The aid and removal of the dead and injured was already being attended to. I performed whatever needed doing. I can't remember all that I did, but I do vividly remember that, when I returned home, there was blood above the soles of my boots.

After the scene was somewhat cleared, Sgt. Hart and I went to the mortuary on follow-up. I recall a middle-aged woman, a victim of the accident, laying there with her long hair straight back with no visible injuries. So sad.

The next day Sgt. Hart and I went to the wrecking yard to inspect the cab of the truck. As I was pawing through the matter on the driver's floorboard, I collected a number of small white pills. I didn't know what they were. I had my suspicions, but I never heard the results.

Patrolman Jimmy Williams #29 was the investigating officer. He used a single roll of butcher paper to diagram the scene, and when unrolled, it stretched the length of the office squad room.

This accident, some 61 years ago, turned out to be the worst scene I was involved with in my 32 years with the department. There was a total of 9 fatalities, multiple injuries, and many dead and injured animals.

MY WORST FATALITY
Baldy Velasco #18

I was called out to the Greyhound bus and cattle truck accident and when I got there, I began giving officers their assignments. Officer Jimmy Williams badge 29 was the investigator and Sgt. Hart was the follow-up investigator.

En route to the accident I had been told that three people had been killed. At the scene I was told that the number was six killed. A few minutes later someone said they had found another. Seven. Then someone hollered from the back of the bus that he had found another. The final total was nine killed. The children get to you. The biggest shocker was the number of children on the bus.

As I crawled through the wreckage, diesel fuel was running down and soaking everything. I was afraid there would be a fire and that we wouldn't be able to get to the people. I had been told that diesel fuel wouldn't burn, but I didn't take any chances, called radio and asked for a fire truck. I just knew we had to get the people out or we would lose them all. Injured cattle were everywhere. We used high powered rifles to kill the injured cattle. It was chaos.

I remember NBC had a reporter at the scene with a recording device that I could broadcast live, so the story went nationwide from the scene.

After the accident I drove back to where the truck driver started from and retraced his route to get a timeline. From the information we collected we determined that driver fatigue was the cause of the accident.

As a district commander, and later a zone commander, I made it a policy to go to the scene of all fatalities. I have been at 200 fatal accidents in my career. This was the worst.

This accident is still remembered and talked about to this day.

A REAL SCREWUP
Bud Richardson #62

Sgt Jim Hart and I were the two photo officers for southern Arizona with a dark room at the Tucson office. We used a 4x5 Press Camera.

One call-out for pictures was a Greyhound bus and a double-decker cattle hauler, an 18-wheeler. The vehicles were in a construction zone east of Tucson on US80. The impact was so great that some of the cattle ended up in the bus.

Hart and I and all the officers and reserve officers were called out because it was a real mess with debris all over the place. As time went on, Hart and I ran out of film but a reserve officer said that he would take our film packs to our office in Tucson and reload them for us. He did this, and we finished up our work.

The next day I spent the day in the dark room developing our film, and what I found was a big surprise. All of the film was blank! I called the reserve and asked what happened, and he said he reloaded the film packs as he thought he was supposed to do. Upon further questioning, I learned that he had turned on the light in the dark room so he could see what he was doing.

Fortunately, a local photographer from Tucson was at the scene, and he shared his pictures with us.

THE MISSING PASSENGER
Rick Ulrich #182

I recall one accident that Ralph McClellan was assigned. It was during the Christmas holiday period. I don't remember the year, probably 1966 or '67. I was still working in radio.

I took this call from the cafe at Sutton's Summit, which was located about 10 miles west of Miami. The waitress there was reporting a bad accident on the Pinto Creek Bridge, which is about two miles east of Sutton's Summit. It was a one-car accident, but the bridge was mostly blocked.

Ralph McClellan was the only officer working that night in the whole area. When Ralph got to the scene, he inquired if there was a Gila County deputy available that could help with traffic control. It was a cold night, and there had been a snow storm earlier. The bridge was icy, and people were driving way too fast.

The Gila County SO said that their car for the area was busy with their own traffic. Ralph said that this accident could go 963, so I advised Sgt. Snedigar of the situation. He said he would get dressed and come out.

I was the second person in the radio room that night, and we weren't really busy. I decided to go to the scene and give Ralph a hand with traffic control; I could wave a flashlight and lay out fusees.

I got to the scene and advised I would assist with traffic control. Ralph said to work the east side of the scene because that side had the least amount of visibility due to a curve in the road. Jim Snedigar arrived on the scene and started taking photos of the vehicle involved, which was a 1957 Ford station wagon.

The driver had been taken to Gila General Hospital by ambulance before I got to the scene. Traffic was pretty light, which was in our favor.

The original report from Sutton's Summit said that they were pretty sure that the vehicle involved had just left their restaurant, and there were two guys in the car. They were both highly intoxicated, and the waitress was concerned for their safety. There was some question whether this was the same car because there was only one occupant in this vehicle. The driver had been thrown out of the car onto the pavement as the car had spun.

The car had struck the bridge railing and broke through it, pushing a piece about 4 feet into space, leaving a large gap. Looking at the vehicle, it had those rear fins that were popular in that time period. The right rear fin was apparently what struck the bridge rail. The fin had blood and bits of flesh on it. Ralph said the driver didn't appear to have an injury from being struck by that fin.

Sergeant Snedigar and I were discussing that maybe there was a second person in the car and that was who was hit by the fin, but where was that person? Could that person have been pushed through the guard rail by the car? One of the guard rail posts had been pushed away, leaving a gap in the cement where the post had been.

From evidence Sgt. Snedigar retrieved, he said, "Yep, there was a second person in this accident."

I asked how he knew that. He said he found evidence on the tail fin of the car that could not have come from the driver.

So, apparently the passenger was ejected and apparently had been thrown off the bridge. From that point on the bridge, the drop to the ground must have been 100 feet or more. The wrecker had arrived and picked up the car, and the roadway was clear. Now we had to climb down into Pinto Creek for a body recovery.

Another mortuary ambulance had been called to the scene. There were five of us to make the trek down the steep walls into Pinto Creek: myself, Sgt. Snedigar, Ralph McClellan, and two guys from the mortuary.

As we got below the bridge, we had to look up where the bridge railing was sticking out and try to estimate where a body would land if it was thrown off the bridge. Luckily, the water was still below the area we needed to search.

After some time searching, one of the mortuary guys hollered out that he had found the body. You can imagine the shape the body was in. The mortuary people put the remains in a body bag, and we headed up the hill. It wasn't an easy climb out.

I left the scene and went back to the Claypool office. Sgt. Snedigar and Ralph went to Miles Mortuary in Miami to take photos of the body, or at least what was left of it. A more gruesome sight I had never seen.

We learned later that the two men in the car were from Chandler. They worked together, and they had decided to go do some pre-holiday celebrating. How they ended up going towards Globe and where they got tanked up, no one will ever know the answer to those questions. They both left behind wives and children. I can only imagine how many sad stories there are out there like this.

COW RESCUE
Dennis McNulty #1959

In September of 1981, I was assigned to Winslow, and Bob Varner was my first FTO. Bob always worked the midnight shift.

One night during our first week together, we were E/B on I-40 and took the first exit for Joseph City to make a turn to go back W/B. At the bottom of each ramp is a cattle guard to keep livestock off the interstate. As Bob starts to turn onto the ramp, he slams on the brakes. There in our headlights is a yearling cow, belly down, with all its legs in the cattle guard.

I ask how we were going to get the cow unstuck. Bob said he had never seen anything like this and had no idea. He got on the radio to Flagstaff OPCOM and asked the dispatcher to call the state Livestock Inspector in Winslow to come out to the scene.

The Livestock Inspector, a grizzled old cowboy, arrived and stood there for a moment. He muttered, "Damn cows," and then walked over, grabbed the cow's tail, and proceeded to yanking on it for all he was worth. The cow was bellowing for all it was worth, but that old cowboy actually pulled that cow up and out of the cattle guard by its tail. He then kicked it in the butt and sent it on its way.
Turning back to the two astonished patrolmen, he said, "If that's all, I'm going back to bed." We bid him thanks and a good night.

COW ENDS LIGHT-DUTY ASSIGNMENT
Dick Shafer #55

I was a sergeant stationed in Gila Bend in 1962 when Patrolman Tom Leslie wrecked his patrol car and injured his ankle. It was a bad enough injury that he was placed on light duty.

I assigned him to work in the office doing paperwork until his ankle healed. He hobbled around gingerly, not putting much weight on the ankle. The light duty went on for quite a while.

One day I had to go to Casa Grande and asked Tom if he wanted to come along. He got in the patrol car with me, and we headed east to Casa Grande. About eight miles east of Gila Bend, we came across cattle on the highway. Tom got out and together, with Tom on foot and me driving the patrol car, we herded the cattle through the right-of-way fence.

The highway was now clear of cattle except for one old, cantankerous cow. Tom tried to herd her through the fence, and the cow stopped, turned around toward Tom, and began pawing the dirt. The cow then charged, and Tom took off, with the cow in close pursuit.

Tom almost made it to the patrol car when the cow lowered her horns and came within about a half inch of Tom's back pocket. He was running like an Olympics star. He rounded the patrol car and jumped in.

From that moment on, I placed Tom back on patrol. I figured if he could move like that, he didn't need any more light duty!

THE SECOND TIME IS A CHARM
Colin Peabody 481

That reminds me of a story about Tom from 1966. I was wanting to get on the highway patrol, and I happened across Tom as he was gassing up his patrol car at Chuck Shrader's Chevron in Sierra Vista. A lot of us car guys hung out there as well, so we got to know the patrolmen and when they worked and....when they didn't.

This particular day, I was telling Tom I wanted to apply for the patrol. He dug an application out of his car and told me to fill it out and send it in. I did that, and a couple of weeks later, I got a refusal from the patrol in the mail. I saw Tom a couple days later at the gas station and told him they turned me down. He said in that drawl of his, "Aw hell, here's another one. Send it in and they'll take it now!"

I did like Tom told me, sent the new one in, and, not too long after, got my notice to go to the Tucson office to take the written. I progressed through the process and wound up in AHP Class 10 on January 8, 1968.

During the 2020 COVID-19 pandemic, I found my personnel file, and what did I find? Both of my applications, one with the turn down and the one they accepted with my photo and my December 1967 letter notifying me that I was to be appointed to the patrol and to show up for class on January 8, 1968!

Tom, I'm glad you outran that cow and came back home to Cochise County and helped this scrawny, old kid to have a great career! I am forever grateful to you and Cal Vance (there's a story there too) for watching over me.

COYOTE CONTROL
John Kennedy #119

When I was working in Show Low, they were having a bad time with the coyotes around Snowflake. The coyotes were killing their sheep. They called a meeting to get people's ideas how to address the problem.

A lady got up and said she thought they should humanely trap the coyotes and have a veterinarian castrate the males and then turn them loose. This in turn reduces the coyote numbers.

An old rancher, I think it was one of the Flakes, got up and said, "Ma'am, I think we need a dentist instead of a doctor. Those coyotes ain't scr—-ing our sheep to death; they're eating 'em."

TWO SHEEP, INDIAN STYLE
Harley Thompson #6

Back in 1965-66 it was requested by the Navajo Police Department that the Arizona Highway Patrol send someone to their organization to put on a Supervisory Training school for some of their supervisory personnel, Sergeants and above. I drew that assignment, and after conversing with their Chief as to needs and other significant material they had in mind, I put together a five-day training program and made arrangements.

I drove up to Window Rock, checked in the hotel, called the Indian Police headquarters, advised them I was in town, and requested instructions on the best way to get to their training facilities. I was advised that an officer would pick me up each morning at 0730 hours and take me to their facility.

Promptly at 0730, my ride arrived, and the officer introduced himself. "Officer Begay" he said, and he said he would be at the hotel every morning at the same time and would also take me back to the hotel.

Their Training Academy was first class. There were dorm-like rooms, a large classroom, an overhead projector, a chalkboard and a lectern. They also had a complete kitchen, where they served three meals each day and coffee and doughnuts during the breaks.

A Major Tsosie introduced me to the class, which numbered about 15 supervisory personnel, and he told me if I needed anything to let him know.

I gave them a short background on my own service with the Arizona Highway Patrol, urged them to ask questions or ask me to repeat anything they did not understand, and told them that class periods would be 50 minutes with 10-minute breaks.

For the next few days all went very well. They did ask lots of questions. They liked my jokes a lot and told some of their own during breaks.

Lunch was served each day at about 1215 hours, and the food was quite good. It was on Thursday that I began to notice a peculiar smell drifting in from the kitchen area. I couldn't put my finger on it, and when I asked, I was told we were having mutton stew for lunch. (Now, I don't like mutton, lamb, goat, or anything resembling the animal, and still don't). I was told that this was always special for them.

When lunch time arrived, I bravely went into the serving along with the others, had my tray loaded with the menu of the day, went to a table, and ate everything. Except the stew! When asked why I didn't eat the stew, I had to honestly confess my dislike for mutton.

Nothing was said and all went well until Friday afternoon, at which time Sergeant Goldtooth got up in class and read to me the letter he had dictated the evening before. The letter said in essence that they really did enjoy my classes, thought that I was an excellent instructor. Because of that, they had planned on giving me two sheep to take back to Phoenix as a token of their esteem. However, since they found out I did not like mutton, they withdrew their offer, Indian-style.

I have always regretted the fact that I mentioned my dislike for mutton. If I had just kept my mouth shut, I could have taken the sheep and brought them back with me and then, on Monday morning, taken them into Superintendent Hathaway's office and presented them to him as a gift of the Navajo Police Department.

I have always wondered what his reaction might have been. (I still think I did the right thing, but I`d still like to have known).

TWELVE DAYS BC (BEFORE CELLS & COMPUTERS)
Harley Thompson #6

This was one of the "normal" things that happened back in the early days.

I was patrolling east on US66 out of Holbrook one day when a westbound vehicle zipped by me like a scared jackrabbit at a high rate of speed. I let him go a bit until I topped a slight rise, then I pulled a fast bootleg 180, those were thrilling on an old 23-foot road,   and I was on him like a duck on a june bug.

After a few miles, I was able to get into a position that allowed me to pace the violator for a bit, until I was able to ascertain his speed. I don`t remember exactly what it was, but it was enough for a good citation.

When the violator pulled off the roadway and I eased in behind, I noticed two things: the vehicle was a brand-new Buick with New York license tags.

I got the driver out of the vehicle, and we got off the road a bit. I asked for his driver's license and registration. He produced his license but did not have a registration, stating that he must have left it at home. At this point, I began to have some suspicions, which became well founded when I looked around inside the vehicle. He had no luggage. He had about four or five days' growth of beard, his clothes were dirty, and all kinds of food wrappers were on the floorboards, all which said, "Hey, Harley, you`ve got a Dyer Act here." (Federal violation-interstate transportation of a stolen vehicle)

After cuffing the violator, I called for a wrecker to haul the vehicle into Holbrook. I waited until it arrived then took the violator into the county jail and had him booked on suspicion of car theft and violation of the Dyer Act.

You have to remember now that this was in 1950. The only agency available to law enforcement at that time for ascertaining whether a vehicle was stolen from another state was the NATB (National Automobile Theft Bureau), and the closest office was in Phoenix.

I truly thought I had a good reason for this arrest as all the necessary ingredients were there: new vehicle, no registration, no luggage, food wrappers all over the floorboards, unkempt-looking guy, although he had plenty of money in his billfold.

I gathered all the info off the Buick: license number, engine number, even the secret number off the top of the transmission housing, make, model, etc., and sent it to the Phoenix office of the NATB and waited and waited and waited, twelve days. (They must have used army heliograph and return by Pony Express). Finally, word came back, lo and behold, that dude owned the vehicle, free and clear. Well, crap, there went my good collar.

So, nothing to do but quickly inform the gentleman that you're free to go and hope for the best. I went to the Navajo County jail, had the jailer release the prisoner, informed him that he was right, he did own the vehicle. Sorry, but that's the way it is.

I gave him a copy of the info from NATB and told him that when he got to California, which was his destination, to hole up for a while and have someone in New York send him his registration—would be his Keep-Out-of-Jail ticket.

Well, that's the way it was back then, "BC."

FIRST 24 HOURS
Colin Peabody #481

I was on OJT (on-the-job training) out of the academy and had been stationed in Winslow. Bob Varner had a 1966 Chevrolet that had a bad transmission. It would downshift into low at 70 plus mph and nearly throw you through the windshield. Bob and I did my first afternoon shift in it, and the next morning, we took it to Holbrook and got a 1965 Plymouth swing car.

When we got back to Winslow, we were assigned to a fatal just west of Sunshine Overpass on Rt. 66. An elderly couple were in a 1967 Chevy Caprice, and the old man who was driving had a heart attack and died behind the wheel. The car narrowly missed a Greyhound Bus and hit a rock embankment, landing upside down. The engine and transmission were thrown from the car and were lying in the middle of US66.

The wife was pinned in the front seat by her seat belt. I was the skinniest guy there, and they had me squeeze into the car to see if I could get her loose. Unfortunately, her weight wouldn't allow me to release the seat belt. She asked how her husband was doing, and I told her he was okay. He was actually DRT (Dead Right There).
We got a bunch of truck drivers and turned the car over on its wheels to get her out, something we would never do today at the risk of injuring her more. Helluva first 24 hours!

GETTIN' EVEN!
Frank Glenn #468

This all happened back in the days when the armory was located in the basement of the training building. The culprits in this particular escapade, at least the two that started it, the instigators of it, were Sgt. Ed Teague and Officer Charlie Crawford.

Some of the upper echelon decided we needed to have an alarm on the armory. Why this was necessary was never made clear. Well, of course, now we need a code for the alarm that all of us could remember. The numbers 296 were decided on. Why, you may ask? Well, this was a gun powder, and we figured we could all remember that number.

Well, I came wheeling in early one morning about 0730, my usual time of arrival. I parked that big, white dog I used to drive and sauntered on down to the armory. I whipped out my trusty set of keys, unlocked the door, and punched the code into the alarm. That dadgum thing just kept beeping.

As I recall, we had 30 seconds before it lit off and called whoever it was going to call. The police, the fire department or whoever. I had no idea who was going to get called.

I very carefully re-entered the number, making sure I pushed the right buttons, and it still just kept on beeping. AHA! I looked above the alarm panel and saw a little note that read, "Frank, we changed the alarm code. It's easy as." Well, being under pressure of this dadgum thing fixing to go off, I couldn't think of anything.

Because the alarm ran through the telephone lines in the armory, that line was dead as a doornail, so I went out to the phone which was by the stairwell and I called security.

When security answered, I asked him, "Okay, what's the damn code for the alarm?"

Well, his unsatisfactory answer was, "I don't think anybody has changed the alarm code." He then finally fessed up and said the code was 1-2-3.

Well, at this point I kinda felt like a dummy not being able to get the drift of what the note said. With almost 30 seconds of reflection upon this episode, I thought to myself, *okay, that's the way they're going to play.*

I went to the little storage area underneath the stairwell, grabbed a box of .223 blanks, then went back to the armory and got a blank adapter and an M-16 out of the closet. I then filled the magazine completely full with 20 rounds of blanks and got out a pair of earmuffs. I then locked the door, turned out the lights, and re-armed the system.

Well, it wasn't long before Ed and Charlie came to the door. There was about a two-inch crack at the bottom of that door, and I was able to see their shadows. Still being able to hear a little bit better than I can now, I heard them asking each other, "Where is Frank?"

The armory lights are out, and the alarm system is still on. It is at this point that Ed was disarming the alarm that my finger somehow found its way into the trigger guard, and I laid down all 20 rounds on full auto. Boy, those guys about jumped out of their skin. Revenge is sweet!

GETTIN' EVEN - SORTA!!
Harley Thompson #6

It was in Holbrook, about February 1951, when one of the local car dealers came into the sheriff's office one day and was complaining about the fact that they weren't getting as many wrecker calls as they had been receiving in the past.

I tried to explain that we were not having as many wrecks as we had been having in the past and that they should remember that there were FIVE wreckers in this dinky little town, that they all wanted their share of the calls, and that everyone was called on a rotation basis. I further explained that, in every case, we always asked the owner of the vehicles, when possible, if they had a preference, and if they did, we did our best to comply.

The business owner and his son were a couple of very opinionated hemorrhoids with ears who only heard what they wanted to hear. They never listened to the facts. They go stomping out with idle threats and "we'll see about this" statements.

About a month later, I had a minor 961 around milepost 348 at Houck involving a brand new 1951 Cadillac convertible. The Cadillac had minor damage, but it caught fire. We pushed it off the road and let it burn. This vehicle burned so hotly that the only thing left was a very hot, smoldering hulk. There was not a piece of rubber or fabric left, just smoking metal that halfway resembled a car. Totally totaled!

The owner requested a wrecker to tow the remains into a dealer's place of business who sold these vehicles. In fact, I strongly suggested to the owner that he should do this and he agreed.

I called the sheriff's office and relayed the request, telling the radio operator to be absolutely sure that they were told that the vehicle they would be towing was a brand new 1951 Cadillac that had received minor damage in the collision. (I could just envision them licking their lips over picking up this little jewel.)

Now, Houck was just about 64 miles east of Holbrook.

Two days later, on my day off and dressed in dirty Levi's, old boots, and a straw cowboy hat, I wandered into this place of business and asked the guy in the parts department if they had a petition there to have Patrolman Thompson transferred out of town. He said, "We sure do!"

I said, "I'd like to sign it."

He eagerly got it out, and I put my signature on it in VERY large letters and gave it back. He looked at it sort of dumbfounded. I turned around and left, never to hear any more about any petitions. I was a happy camper, sorta!!!

As a note, I must have cost this dealer a small fortune in dealer plates. If in violation, I took them away. I did this even when I was in Winslow. I used to cut them up with shearers and send them back to MVD. Ticked them off too! But then, the law is the law!

THE ORIGINAL STING
Jim Knapp #1393

I remember a mission I flew with Greg Girard a bunch of years ago. You might call it "another sort of sting operation."

On the morning of July 9, 1975, Greg and I responded from Falcon Field, Mesa, in Ranger 30 to a reported 962 near Congress. As retired Air Rescue Pilot W.W. "Duke" Moore used to say, "There we were, just chuki-puckin' along" at about 110 mph toward Congress. (By the way, Duke is the only helicopter pilot I ever heard claiming to be "as pure as the wind driven snow.") Anyway, I digress.

As Greg and I approached the scene, we observed what appeared to be a flatbed on its side with a large number of beehives scattered on the ground adjacent to the truck. While on short approach to the LZ (Greg never, ever liked us pilots to use the phrase "final" approach), we watched thousands (slight exaggeration) of really ticked off bees attacking the thousands of moving parts on Ranger 30. It requires thousands of moving parts to "beat the air into submission."

During the approach to the landing sequence and while I was attempting to ignore the thousands of bees, the former Marine Vietnam vet, "Road Bull Turned Paramedic," sitting in my copilot's seat turned his head toward me and calmly stated, "By the way, Jim, I'm allergic to bee stings." Wow, I wondered if I, as a newbie EMT, would then have two patients to care for in the midst of thousands of bees?

Thankfully, there were no serious injuries on the ground or any medical emergencies on board the Ranger, just a pilot that still remembers a "near cardiac vapor lock" during an approach 45 years ago.

THE JUDGES
Chick Lawwill #35

When I first got to Yuma in 1952, it was the policy of the patrol to go around and introduce yourself to all of the judges in your area. It was also policy to have them ride with you and watch you work.

Judge Bill Nabours rode with me several times, and we became friends. Later, he was appointed Superior Court Judge in Yuma.

One night while I was working, I saw his car go by in the opposite direction, so I turned around and pulled in behind him. I hit him with my red light and siren, and of course, the first thing he said as I got to his car was, "What did I do wrong?"

"Nothing," I said. "I just always wanted to pull over a superior court judge."

This story got a lot of laughs at his retirement party.

Judge Haines was the Justice of the Peace in Tacna, where he owned and operated a bar. The policy in those days was to take all California violators before the judge immediately because, if not, they would cross the line into California and thumb their nose at you.

It was embarrassing to us to take a violator into his bar with drunks sitting around drinking and listening to the jukebox. The judge would always ask the violator if he was going to fight the ticket. If he said no, the judge would ask him if he wanted a beer while he waited for his receipt. If he wanted to contest it, we took the violator back behind the bar into the judge's trailer where court would be held.

The judge liked to gamble and frequented the Owl Club in Winterhaven, California. He got drunk one night and was arrested by the California Highway Patrol. Needless to say, we got a new JP in Tacna.

Judge Ersel Byrd asked to ride with me one night. The driver of the first car I pulled over came flying out of the car going on and on giving me a hard time. The judge was taking this all in, and when he had heard enough, he got out of the car. He told the fellow in so many words that he was the judge that he would be going in front of. The judge told the man that he was looking forward to the hearing.

In the court room, the judge left the bench and came down and stood right in front of the man. It was terrible, and I really felt sorry for the fellow. After that, the judge instructed me to circle my badge number on the citation if the guy gave me a hard time.

JUDGES I HAVE KNOWN
John Kennedy #119

When I worked in Holbrook, we took some people straight to the judge. When we got a speeder going really fast and out of state, we wouldn't arrest them but had them follow us to the JP (Justice of the Peace).

There was a JP in Joseph City. I think his name was Newt Kay. He had a garage on the east end of town. Several times when I took people in there, he would be underneath a car working on it. I would holler at him, and he would roll out from underneath the car, covered with grease, and we would have court.

There was a JP in Sanders. His name was McDonald, and he had a trading post there. I don't remember anything leading up to the following or afterwards.

The judge had a small office in the trading post, barely big enough for his desk and two people besides him. I had a subject that I had arrested for DWI in the office, and I didn't have him cuffed. I had a bottle of whiskey, my evidence, on the judge's desk. The violator and I got into a fight; I don't remember why. When I got him subdued on the floor, I looked up, and the judge was taking a swig out of my evidence bottle.

There was a JP that had a little office building between Show Low and Pinetop. If you had a violator who really gave you a bad time, you made a little mark on the ticket, and when he came in to see the judge, he would really give him a bad time.

When I moved to Cordes, we had a little old lady, Marion Burleson, who was the JP. She was about 5'2". We held court in her living room in Humboldt. As far as she was concerned, if one of her boys (patrolmen) said something, it was just like God said it.

I had a violator who asked for a trial. The violator, his wife, and his attorney showed up on the appointed date and time. We all sat down in the living room, and Marion said for me to tell what happened in regards to the ticket. When I was finished, she turned to the couple and their attorney and said, "I find you guilty."

The attorney said, "We didn't get to present our side."

Marion said, "Oh, I'm sorry. Go ahead."

The attorney was furious, and he and the couple stormed out.

SAVING THE JUDGE
Harley Thompson #6

Back in late 1946 or '47, I don't recall exactly, I was stationed in Williams, and we had a Justice of the Peace who was also the local town magistrate. He was always a favorite with the local officers. Well, our judge, we'll call him Nipper because he was known to imbibe a little barleycorn on a regular basis.

One cold night, old Nipper drove down to the local watering hole, the Sultana Bar, in his brand-new Plymouth sedan for an evening of fun and frivolity. One of the local PD officers and I saw him enter the old Sultana, bright eyed and bushy tailed.

The PD officer said, "He'll be coming out around midnight in a well-oiled condition. He gets all upset if we offer to drive him home because he doesn't want to leave that new Plymouth out on the street all night. What can we do so that we don't have to arrest him?"

"I've got a plan," I said. "Why don't we just jack up the right rear a little bit off the pavement, and when he tries to back out, he won't be able to go anywhere and you can take him home."

The PD officer agreed that it would probably work and that no one would be embarrassed. So, around midnight, we performed our little task and got the right rear wheel about half an inch off the pavement.

Sure enough, at closing time, here comes old Nipper, weaving around a bit as he gets into his nice new vehicle and tries to back away from the curb. The engine roars and gears clash back and forth as Nipper shifts and all to no avail as the rear wheel just spins around. The PD officer and I were standing out of sight, cracking up.

Finally, old Nipper gets out of the car and wobbled around to the back of the car looking at everything and seeing nothing. Back in the car, he gets more engine roaring and gears clashing, but again, to no avail. The local officer walked over and offered to drive Nipper home, and he accepted, along with instructions to have the local wrecker service tow the brand-spanking new Plymouth into the garage.

We took care of that and brought the garage owner into our confidence and suggested that he give him an extremely overly large bill for needed repairs. The garage owner went along, and after about three days, Old Nipper was really upset. We let him stew a bit more, and then the garage owner tells him that he really couldn't find anything wrong at all and told him that the bill was just a joke.
We never did, however, tell old Nipper what actually transpired. We had a little fun and saved old Nipper.

WHAT'S THE FINE?
John Kerr #120

From Dec 1959 to Oct 1967, I was assigned to Wenden, AZ, right after a short cadet school.

When I had to take someone to Judge Hegly in Quartzsite, he would ask me to go to the back room, and he instructed the driver to stay put. Then in a loud booming voice: "What should I fine the son of a *****?" and I knew the violator heard him.

I loudly said, "It's your case. I did my part."
His old house was built back in the 1800s, and the walls were very thin!

JUST A WARNING
Dennis McNulty #1959

I started my career with DPS (Department of Public Safety) in 1976 at Phoenix OPCOM (Operational Command), which back then was in the wing of the compound off the two-story main (then) HQ building. Rich Basso was the day shift radio sergeant, and John was assigned to work with us out in teletype where we fielded phone calls from everyone.

For some obscure reason, all warnings and repair orders were sent to OPCOM prior to going to the records section. We sorted them by date and then sent them on.

Being new, I didn't yet know much about Title 28, but one warning written by an officer up on the Navajo reservation was for 28-692A, DWI. I knew what that was, and I showed it to John who started to laugh. He took it to Sgt. Basso who went ballistic as he knew who the officer was (name lost to the mists of time).

Phone calls were made, and ass was chewed. John told me if I ever became a patrolman, don't do anything that dumb but, if I did, not to use my badge number.

JUDGE HAGLEY
Greg Eavenson #680

Western justice that you hear about and see in movies/ TV became real for me when I met Quartzsite JP George Hagely in 1970. He was in his 80's, hard of hearing, chewed on cigars, slept nude on his front porch in the summer, and used his living room as the court.

When he held a trial, he would call me into his bedroom during the defendant's testimony and in a loud voice ask me what kind of car the defendant was driving. If I told him it was a new/newer car, he would say, "Well, he should be able to pay $300," (max for misdemeanor) and then return to court and tell the defendant to continue his testimony. I was embarrassed at first but grew to accept it as normal.

One graveyard shift, I wrote a California guy a speeding ticket, and he demanded to see the judge. I advised that he really didn't want to wake him up at 0230, but the guy got increasingly upset so I had him follow me to Judge Hagely's.

After at least 3 minutes of beating on his door, Hagely finally yelled, "Who the hell is it?"

When I told him of the speeder's demands, he yelled, "Have him come back at 9:00 when court is in session."

The speeder began to scream that he knew his rights and demanded to see him. Hagely yelled back, "Let me get my pants on."

After a couple minutes, Hagely opened the door, looked at me, and said, "Bring the guilty bastard in here." The speeder paid a $300 fine for a 10-over ticket.

I WANT TO SEE THE JUDGE
Tim Hughes #793

Back in 1971 or early 1972, Judge Bill Davis in Salome was indicted and removed from office. John McCaw, a local farmer and a really good and decent person, replaced him as the Salome JP.

Judge McCaw was unfamiliar with the office, and wanting to learn as much as he could, he asked if he could go as a Civilian Observer with me to see what a DPS officer did during a routine shift.

It was evening, and we were working west of Salome in the flats of US60 when we stopped a speeder. The driver was from California and acted totally the part of a Californian stopped in Arizona for speed.

I told him why I stopped him and that I was going to cite him for speed, which caused him to launch into a fit. He demanded my name, badge number, etc. and demanded to know who the judge was. I gave him the information and told him that it was also on his copy of the citation. This further infuriated him and he demanded to see the judge and indicated that the judge was probably some hick who ran a kangaroo court.

He kept insisting he wanted to see the judge, and I finally asked did he really want to see the judge. He, in no uncertain terms, said yes, so I leaned over to the passenger door and knocked on the window. Judge McCaw rolled down the window, and I told him, "Judge, this guy wants to talk to you."

Needless to say, this was probably the quietest Californian you have ever met. He also pled guilty and paid the fine. This was definitely a highlight moment in my career.

DUI ON A HORSE
John Kennedy #119

In 1961 I was stationed in Show Low. In the wintertime there was absolutely no traffic on US60 after supper time. I used to go over to McNary when the movie let out just to see some traffic. Summer was just the opposite, traffic day and night.

One summer I got a call of a 962 south of Show Low on 60 at the trading post at Carrizo. The traffic was backed up for a couple of miles. When I finally got there, there was an Indian male lying on the center line. The ambulance was there, and we loaded him and sent him off. By the way, he was stiff as a board.

After getting the traffic moving, I went into the trading post and asked if anyone knew what happened. A witness said the subject came out of the trading post, obviously intoxicated, got on his horse, and, for the benefit of a couple young girls who were standing there, reached up and spurred the horse in the shoulder. The horse bucked him off on the center line.

About this time, John Consoni and Bobby Broan arrived on the scene. Consoni was a patrolman and Broan was an inspector at the time. After telling them what happened, they said, "Well, you're going to cite him for DWI, aren't you? He was a traffic unit." So, I cited him into Whiteriver Indian Court.

Sometime later, I got a subpoena for the subject's trial. On the appointed day, I went to Whiteriver and went into the court room. By the way, there were stacks and stacks of firewood all around the courthouse.

They brought the defendant into the court room, and presently, the judge entered. He was a pretty short guy. He got up behind the bench, smacked the bench with his mallet, and declared court to be in session. He said, "So, how do you plead?"

The defendant got to his feet and started to say, "I.. " The judge hit the bench again and said, "I find you guilty, 60 days on the woodpile." Trial over!

THE CITIZEN
Colin Peabody #481

When I first went to Winslow right out of the academy, Officer Bob Varner was introducing me to various folks around town. Being a new resident of Navajo County, I needed to register to vote, and our local JP, Judge Hastings, was one who could do that. In the process, he asked me where I was born, and I told him I was born in Shrewsbury, England. He looked up and said, "You aren't a citizen. You can't vote!"

"Yes sir, I am a citizen."

"No, you aren't!"

I finally said, "Judge, you have to be a citizen to be an Arizona Highway Patrolman."

That should have been the end to it, but he made me get my birth certificate, my documents of American citizen born abroad, and my certificate attesting to that fact from the US District Court in Tucson to prove to this judge that I was a US citizen before he would finally let me register to vote.

One of the few times I ever saw Bob Varner speechless.

JUDGE MCCALL
Greg Eavenson #680

In the early 70s, in the vicinity of Salome (that area changed districts several times back then), Justice Davis had been removed from office for keeping two sets of books, and John McCall was appointed to the vacancy. McCall was a local farmer who kept farmer hours (early to rise, early to bed).

Kerry Nelson and I were working 1800 to 0200 and met with McCall. He told us he wanted to be called whenever we booked a DWI who wanted to post bond. This was new to us since JPs Davis, Hagely, and Fuqua didn't care to be bothered.

Around 2200 hours, I bagged one and took him to Salome S. O. After completing the booking paperwork, I called McCall. He showed up all chipper like and took the cash bond. I finished my arrest report a little after 2300 and heard Kerry Nelson call for a hook for a DWI arrest. I met Kerry and waited for the wrecker. Kerry called McCall around 2330.

About 0030, I sacked another DWI who wanted to post bond. McCall arrived a little after 0100 looking pretty ragged, took the bond, and asked if it was normal to have three DWIs in one night. He left the jail muttering to himself.

As I was finishing up my report a little after 0200, Kerry walked in with another DWI and called the judge around 0230. McCall arrived with only one side of his bib overalls hooked, hair a mess, eyes bloodshot, and not in a pleasant mood. After taking the bond, he announced to us that he had changed his mind and would no longer take bonds after court hours. Judge McCall remained the JP long after I transferred but was always a friend of patrolmen.

JUSTICE ON WHEELS
Bud Richardson #62

It was common for an officer to have a doctor, judge, or DA as a ride along, which brings to mind a story about Judge Allen of Nogales.

He was riding with an officer north of Nogales when they got in a pursuit of a high-speed violator. When they got the guy stopped, Judge Allen was very upset about the chances an officer had to take, and he decided to hold court on the fender of the highway patrol vehicle.

The violator was charged with reckless driving. Judge Allen instructed the officer to place the violator under arrest and sentenced the violator to jail. He was taken to Santa Cruz County Jail that night to start his sentence.

THE CORONER
Bill Chewning #41

There was a time when, if an officer arrived at the scene of an accident and found that there was a deceased victim, the local coroner, which was the nearest justice of the peace, had to be called to the scene to pronounce the victim dead before the body could be moved. Well, back in the day, some of the JPs all too often partook of the grape. When this happened, it was up to an officer to drive them to the scene.

Officer Bill Raftery was called to the scene of a fatality on I-10 outside Benson. Arriving on the scene and finding that there was indeed a deceased victim, Raftery told the dispatcher to call out the coroner. The dispatcher called back and advised Raftery that the judge would have to be transported and that I would be taking the judge to the scene. Raftery knew immediately why the coroner was being driven to the scene.

Upon arriving, the judge got out of the patrol car and walked unsteadily through the accident scene. He spotted Officer Raftery kneeling by the body and walked over, knelt down, grabbed a wrist and said, "No pulse, he's dead".

Upon which Officer Raftery replied, "Judge, that's MY wrist".

The judge nodded, stood up, and walked to the patrol car telling me, "Take me home. I'm done here."

I GUESS I WILL PAY
Don Uhles #2092

I was assigned to Houck, AZ, Fort Courage, which I'm told recently burned down. In 1978 I stopped a commercial truck which was westbound, just east of the Sanders port of entry for speeding. As I walked up to the cab, I noted several equipment issues. After a short conversation; made much longer by the truck driver making multiple trips to retrieve all the items I asked him to bring with him at the beginning of our encounter, I told him that I was going to cite him for his speed to which he threw down his book with his DOT prorates on the ground and said, "I'm not paying that ticket."

I went on to tell him I was also citing him for a late logbook to which he again threw down his logbook on the ground and said, "I'm not paying that ticket."

Next, I told him about the various work orders I was issuing, told him to update his drivers log, and that I was going to be right back. I went to my car and ran a "27, 28, & 29" and did all the paperwork; remember "**USE BALLPOINT PEN. PRESS HARD!**"

I re-approached the driver who said, "How can I pay these tickets?"

I said, "I'm gonna make that easy." As we were in eyesight of the port of entry, I told him I was going to allow him to park his truck at the POE, and I was going to introduce him to Judge Porter. I arrested him, and we went to the Rio Puerco Justice Courthouse.

I introduce the trucker to this grandma-looking judge. She asked him a question, and with no respect, he made an off-color response. Well, I'm here to tell you that I saw a side of Judge Porter that I never saw before! She leaned across her desk, and I thought she was gonna eat him alive. He KNEW she was gonna eat him alive!

At the end of their very one-sided conversation, he pled guilty and paid his (max) fines in cash. I drove him back to the POE where he looked at me and said, "I kinda f'ed up".

I said, "The next time an Arizona Highway Patrolman stops you, be courteous, take the ticket, and go on your way; if you tell him you're not gonna pay the ticket, I guarantee you'll pay that ticket!"

On a side note: For those of you who never had the opportunity to meet Lavine Porter, you missed out. Judge Porter looked like any typical grandma. She loved the Native American people, who made up the majority of her cases, but lord help you if you came back to her court on a second offense! Her highway patrolmen were her boys. We still didn't have any female officers out there at that time, but she would have likely loved them even more!

Lavine Porter came to the Sanders area in the 60s with her husband who was an engineer and worked for Standard Oil. Their first phone number was Navajo 2; the store at Navajo, AZ, having Navajo 1.

We remained in contact with Lavine for decades after she left Sanders to live with her granddaughter near Albuquerque, NM. When she passed, she was buried next to her husband at the cemetery at McCarroll Road and I-40. In my mind she was a judge by which all judges should be judged by. A wonderful lady!

A FUN DAY IN WEST MESA JP COURT
Bob Osborn #1159

Around 1977 I was parking my patrol car in the parking lot of the West Mesa JP Court, when I noticed that the defendant also had arrived and was pulling into the parking lot in his car. Nothing unusual about that other than the fact we were going to court for a violation of driving on a suspended driver's license.

I went into the court building and called dispatch to find out if the defendant's driver's license was still suspended. It was.

In court the defendant was represented by an assigned public defender. The trial began, and the verdict was guilty.

As soon as the judge banged the gavel ending the trial, I stood up, along with the defendant and his public defender. I walked over to the defendant, told him to turn around, cuffed him, and told him that he was under arrest for driving on a suspended license. The public defender went off like a bottle rocket while the judge was laughing ad having a good time.

I walked the defendant across the street to the Mesa jail and booked him for the second time.

WILY OLD JUDGE
Harley Thompson #6

Somewhere back in the very early 50s, there was a justice of the peace who held court in the Meteor City area. I'll call him "Ole Wheezy" because he was either a lunger or he suffered from some bronchial condition. When he talked, it was a bit of a combination of wheezy expulsion of words and an equally gaspy intake of breath back and forth, very slowly.

Now, the majority of the time, he chose to run around his place of business without the benefit of a shirt. Combined with a very sunken chest, it did not lend itself to a judicial atmosphere. Nevertheless, this was his court.

On this particular occasion, I do not recall the name of the patrolman who had cited a violator into Ole Wheezy's court, but he had him for reckless driving, extremely high rate of speed. Some of those areas out there, at a time on US66 with its narrow road in some locations, made it a good call.

The patrolman informed the judge of the circumstances, and Ole Wheezy fined him $50. The violator smiled and said, "Okay, Judge, I've got that right here in my hip pocket."

Ole Wheezy gasps and wheezes and says, "And 30 days in the county jail. You got that in your hip pocket too?"

At this point the perp goes ballistic and has to be restrained by the patrolman who then carts him off to Flagstaff for his 30 days in the local facility.

AND ANOTHER 30
Larry Burns #1974

It was back in 1982, or early 1983. I know this isn't a very old story, but it always made me feel good.

I caught a DUI north on I-17 heading into the Verde Valley. Nothing exceptional about the guy until I placed him in my patrol car. Once he was secured in the back seat and after his car was towed, we headed into Prescott for booking. It was about a 45-minute drive from where we were.

As soon as we were on our way to the jail, he started talking. He began by creatively talking about my ancestry and continued to the various ways he was going to kill me.

He was continuous. Normally, I would just ignore it, but this guy was over the top. Once he started in on how he was then going to kill my family, I started writing everything that he said on my notepad. (No recorders then.) Of course, he included a long rant about what he was going to do to me if he got the handcuffs off.

Once we got to the Yavapai jail, he complained that he needed to use the bathroom. I removed his cuffs and was ready for him to explode when I released him, but he went completely meek and polite. When he was finished and I re-cuffed him, he lit right back up again.

I included all of this in my report. and was at the Justice Court the next day when he was to appear before Judge "Jack" Findlay in Cottonwood. (Judge Findlay was also a retired law enforcement officer.) I provided all of the information to Judge Findlay. Judge Findlay was not happy with what he read.

When he asked the defendant how he pled, he replied guilty. When Judge Findlay asked him if he really said these things to "His Officer," he said that he had. Judge Findlay sentenced him to 30 days in the county jail. Before he could hit his gavel, the guy spouted off, "I can do that standing on my head!"

Not to be phased, as he struck his gavel, Judge Findlay said, "And another 30 days to put you back on your feet!"

HERE COME DA JUDGE, HERE COME DA JUDGE
Colin Peabody #481

Winslow sits right on the county line separating Navajo County from Coconino, and patrolmen stationed in Winslow worked in both counties.

Justice of the Peace Goldie Newsom at Meteor City had recently passed away, and we had to cite into Judge John Brierly in Flagstaff until we got a new JP appointed. After a month or so, the Board of Supervisors appointed Ben F. Dreher at Two Guns to be our new Justice of the Peace.

Two Guns, at the time, was a wooden series of buildings housing a curio shop, coffee shop, and upstairs in the main building was a couple of rooms where Judge Dreher would hold court, and he had his business office up there. A few yards away from the main building was a motel unit of about six or eight rooms that had old cars sitting out in front to make you think people would actually stay there. Whenever we had to take a violator to see Judge Dreher, we took them upstairs, and we often had to turn in citations to him as well, upstairs in his office where he kept a very large, gray safe. It was a fairly common opinion among our officers that Judge Dreher wasn't a big fan of law enforcement, but we knew he made a few bucks serving as JP. Judge Dreher was about six feet tall, a bit stocky, and wore thick, coke-bottle-lens glasses.

Sometime around 1970, Judge Dreher was seen in Winslow in the company of a local widow who drove a new red-and-white Cadillac convertible, the only one in town. One night, I am coming back into town from the west, and I see this Cadillac going very slowly coming towards me. It was weaving across the centerline, so I pulled a U-turn and got in behind the Caddy . It turned into the street going into the Desert View neighborhood, and I turned on the lights.

The car stopped right in the middle of the street. As I walked up, the window rolled down and the smell of alcohol was strong! I looked at the driver, and he looked at me through those coke-bottle lenses and asked me with slurred speech, "Whaddya want?"

"Good evening, Mr. Dreher. I stopped you because you are driving very slowly and weaving across the center line, and now it appears that you have been drinking."

"I'm jus' taking this lady home," was his reply.

I had him step out of the vehicle, which he did. I stepped back to my car and called Ron Delong, who was also working that night, to meet me. Once he got there, we put the judge through the paces, which he failed miserably. What to do??

We decided to have Ron drive the Cadillac to the woman's house a few blocks away, and we put the judge in my car and took him to Winslow PD and gave him a Breathalyzer test, which he also failed miserably. In spite of our inner desire to put the judge in the tank at Winslow PD, we called the city magistrate, and he told us to cite Ben into the city court and then turn him loose. We did that and even drove him to the woman's house. Courteous, vigilance, and all that.

Things were never the same with Judge Dreher after that. Who knew?

Later, in 1971, we got a call about midnight that there was a fire out at Two Guns. Once again, Ron Delong and I were both working, so we responded.

When we got out there, the main complex was burning brightly in the night, and the wooden fence between the main building and the motel units was also on fire. Winslow Fire Department would not respond, and neither would Flagstaff. So we could only watch the fire burn. No one was there but Ron and I. No judge!

The thought occurred to us that there was a slight possibility that there were people staying in the motel that needed to be rescued, so we did a security check on each of the rooms to make sure no one was there, like maybe some of his help stayed in the rooms, but they were empty. Coconino County sent a deputy out, and we watched the fire pretty much burn itself out. He remained out there with us.

Once it was daylight and we could move around the site, we found what appeared to be evidence of burned fuses back behind the wooden wall between the complex and the motel. When we were able to look at the main complex, the thing that jumped right out at us was a very large, slightly burned, gray safe, sitting with the door open on the ground floor of what was the main building. The safe was empty. Either much of the trinkets he had for sale may have been burned up or simply weren't there once the fire got started. We never saw Judge Dreher after that. Strange circumstances!

Not too long after that, we began citing into Judge Joseph Garcia in Flagstaff.

KILLER CACTUS
Ralph Shartzer #220

One night during my assignment to Gila Bend (1963-1969), I was patrolling on State Route 84 east of town. Traffic was very light, and following orders to conserve fuel, I was parked broadside about 20 miles east of town, backed up to a gate in the right-of-way fence.

Recent training had stressed the issue of becoming 'routine' – complacent in our approach to violators. I was mulling over my violator approach methods as I was monitoring traffic from my strategic location. Out of the corner of my eye, in the driver's side rearview mirror, I saw a person with an arm raised to strike me!!

I remember thinking, "You're dead but shoot him anyway." I felt the hot rush of adrenalin as I drew and pointed my weapon out the window but... there was no one there. My heart was beating a jillionmiles per hour, but I couldn't see anyone. I shined my spotlight all around the left side of my vehicle! No one!!

When I shined the light directly behind me, I spotted the killer saguaro cactus with his arm raised, but no weapon. Being an Arizona Highway Patrolman, I wasn't frightened, but five minutes later, I was 15 miles down the road at a rest area restroom checking that there were no stains on my uniform pants.

KICK ASS
Bill Chewning #41

We were stationed in Thatcher, a small town close to Safford, in the early 60s. My area was Graham and Greenlee counties in the Eastern District.

Like many in the area, we had horses. I had a grey quarter mare named Becky and a white (almost appy) mule with one black spot on his rump. We called him Mr. Ed.

Early one morning in the corral behind the house, I was using a hook pick, cleaning out his left rear frog. Usually Mr. Ed was easygoing and gentle, but I must have hit a sore spot because all at once I found myself sliding down the corral fence. My young son was sitting on the gate watching, and I swear, both he and Mr. Ed were enjoying it.

In those days, I had a bit of a temper. so I said, "Golly Gee" or "Gee Whiz," or something like that and proceeded to kick Mr. Ed in the hind end. Of course, he retaliated. He brayed and kicked back. HARD! After a few exchanges with Mr. Ed, I found myself on the floor of the corral in amongst horse and mule biscuits. On trying to get up, I found that my right foot was swelling up and getting pretty darned painful.

A trip to the doctor found me to have a broken bone in my foot. I called radio in Globe and told dispatcher Ben Shumway that I'd be off for a day or so and told him what had happened.

Shortly, I received a phone call from Colonel Bob Cochran in Phoenix. He, as always, was very polite and soft spoken. "Bill, what happened?"

I said, "Colonel, I'd just as soon not tell you."

The reply from the Phoenix end was, "I believe you should, Bill."

So, I said, "I broke my foot kicking my own ass!" All I heard was a muffled laugh. Guess the top brass had a sense of humor after all.

HOPPING MAD
Gamble Dick - #1743

In the early 80s, I was fortunate enough to be the District Commander of District 3 in Holbrook. Amazing troops and staff.

One afternoon, Donna (the incredible glue that held the place together) called from the front saying, "Lieutenant, you better get out here!"

Through the front window, I could see an 18-wheeler and a cloud of dust. The driver, who looked hoppin' mad, was almost to the office. He threw open the door to the lobby and began yelling something about a complaint, and I got some of the words like "jail," "nightstick," "Trooper" with two first names (ah, Ron, Bruce, this should be good) and "I want to see the man in charge."

I introduced myself and handed him a complaint form and explained to him that, if he would write down what happened and sign it, Internal Affairs would investigate thoroughly. I told him we take allegations of this kind, whatever they were—he was still a little incoherent—very seriously. If his allegations were founded, the trooper would be disciplined. However, if the allegations were unfounded, he could be sued by the trooper for defamation of character.

That set him off on another tirade that ended with, "I ain't signing nothing, and you wouldn't be so tough if you didn't have that badge and gun."

I turned toward Donna as I unpinned my badge and told her to call an ambulance while I unhooked my gun belt. She said, "Why?" and I said, "Because one of us is going to need it." I turned back to the counter and hoppin' mad was gone. He was half-way to his truck.

THE BRIBE
Chick Lawwill #35

One night I was called out to investigate a bad accident about 45 miles east of Yuma on US80. When I arrived on scene, all I could see were bodies of both dead and badly injured people. There were three children involved, and to say the least, I was devastated. This accident turned out to be the worst accident I investigated during my early years on the patrol.

Lt. Vern Fugatt assisted me in the many hours of investigation at the scene and at the hospital. The driver was Jerry Lee. His wife and daughter along with four others were killed and five others injured. I found three driver's licenses made out to Lee with aliases. Jerry Lee was connected to the Chinese Tong in Tucson.

I was called to set up a meeting and Lt. Fugatt said for me not to be alone with this group. I was to call him when they showed up at my home. When three men arrived, Faye went across the street to her sisters' house and called Lt. Fugatt, who arrived right away.

One fellow was an attorney, one was second in command of the Tong in Tucson, and the third man was the president and CEO of the Chinese Bank in San Francisco. They arrived in a chauffeur-driven Cadillac limousine that was owned by the president of the Chinese bank. This was the day of the inquest in Welton.

When the time came that we had to leave for Welton, the bank president wanted to ride with me in my patrol car. Lt. Fugatt took his vehicle, and the rest went in the Cadillac. The bank president told me all I had to do was submit an investigation at the inquest in Jerry Lee's favor. I missed my chance to live an "easier" life!

The coroner in Wellton was Judge Tex Witten who reviewed all of the evidence and heard from all of the witnesses. It was determined that Jerry Lee was responsible for this terrible accident. I filed negligent homicide against Lee, but the county attorney reduced the charges. No Comment! Shortly after, Jerry Lee remarried.

JERRY LEE
Colin Peabody #481

In reminiscing about stories, the name Jerry Lee rang a bell with me. The accident occurred in 1953. A Google search showed Jerry Lee operated a couple of small stores catering to the Chinese population in Tucson, but he also owned Jerry's Ming House restaurant on Broadway in Tucson. This restaurant was one of the best places to get Chinese food back then. My family ate there often in the 1950s.

The Google search verified that Mr. Lee had lost his wife and family in a devastating accident in 1953. The restaurant closed in the 1970s with no mention of the Tong organization after that time period in Tucson.

BUBBA
Harley Thompson #6

Bubba first came to my attention when I was district commander in Tucson back in the mid-50s. Bubba was employed by the highway department, and his job was to wash cars and do oil changes. During one car wash, Bubba was having a hard time getting the summer bugs off the car's windshield, so he came up with the bright idea to use sandpaper to remove the bugs. The result, a foggy windshield that needed to be replaced.

Back then, the Tucson office was a converted Quonset Hut from Fort Huachuca. Space was limited, and we had no place to store evidence or confiscated liquor, so patrolmen had to stash these items in the trunks of their patrol cars. It didn't take old Bubba, who was known to take a few or more drinks on a regular basis, long to discover this. Bubba was a happy camper.

The patrolmen started to complain about tampered evidence and asked me what we could do about it. I knew just the proper deterrent!

I went to a friend of mine who was a pharmacist and asked him to get me a small bottle of Croton Oil. Now, for those of you who don't know what Croton Oil will do when taken internally, just let me say that Montezuma's revenge or diarrhea was kid's stuff! We doctored a couple of bottles of evidence, and the stage was set. I sent in a couple of units for service and waited for old Bubba to do his thing.

A couple of days later, I asked the shop foreman where Bubba was, and he told me that Bubba was sick. I asked him what was wrong and he replied, "Captain, he's got the sh_ts."

"No kidding," I said. "Let me tell you what happened." I explained the problem in some detail and suggested that he tell old Bubba to leave our evidence alone in the future.

The outcome of all of this? We never had another problem and old Bubba joined AA.

COME WITH ME
B.C. Irwin #708 (Old badge system)

Back in the early 60s, Patrolman Bob Essig had stopped a female driver for DWI north of Wickenburg on US93. In the process of arresting the woman, she became combative. Not wanting to have to wrestle a woman, Bob called for a backup.

I was working out of Wickenburg and got the call. Before I got to Bob's location, Bob called on the radio and said that he had the woman handcuffed but requested me to continue so he would have help in getting the woman in the patrol car.

As I arrived on scene, I saw that things were not quite under control. Seems after Bob handcuffed the woman with her hands behind her back, he was walking her back to his patrol car when she extended her arms back just far enough to grab Bob in a very sensitive area. I watched as the woman, with a death grip on Bob's crotch, led him down bar ditch with Bob on his tip toes hollering, "Ow! Ow! Ow!" with every step. After a few minutes of watching this hilarious scene, I rescued Bob, and they got the woman into the patrol car.

HEROES
Paul Palmer #342

Where have all of our heroes gone? I think I found a couple. No, not the current "heroes" that we are so desperately trying to come up with. People we deem heroes just because they survived a tragic accident or came home safely from a war. We even call sports figures heroes just because we don't take the time or energy to find a real one.

I was recently given some historical Highway Patrol information from retired DPS Captain Frank Hutchinson. Included in this information are copies of articles entitled "Know Your Patrolmen" which appeared in the Tucson Daily Citizen newspaper in 1953. Want a hero? How about these two officers. Here is a portion of those articles:

RAY DAHM

A 90-mile-an-hour chase down a winding mountain highway and the hour-long gun battle that followed, provided the highlight in Patrolman Raymond Dahm's six years with the Highway Patrol.

Dahm was stationed in Springerville at the time, March three years ago. A sheriff's deputy friend phoned him with a tip that a sedan with out of state plates had driven out of town at a high rate of speed. Dahm knew the car. He had noticed it pass a few minutes before.

He picked up the deputy, and they soon overtook the speeders. The officers pulled ahead and stopped and signaled for the other car to do the same. Instead, the driver jammed his foot to the floorboard and whizzed by the patrolmen's parked vehicle. The chase was on – 90 miles an hour they sped along the twisting road.

Then one of the three youths in the car ahead pushed a rifle out the rear window and bounced a slug off Dahm's hood that splattered the windshield in the officer's face.

As Dahm slowed down, the other car hit a dip, went out of control, skidded off the highway and overturned. Seeing the occupants crawl out of the wreck, the officers drove out of rifle range and radioed for help.

Deputies and patrolmen battled the trio for over an hour. Bullets whined as the men fired from behind rocks and bushes.

Finally, one of the youths was hit and fell dead. The other two surrendered.

"The boys were a gang that was wanted in Nebraska for kidnapping, jailbreak, and armed robbery," Dahm relates. "The leader – the one that was killed – was the oldest. He was only 21."

In 1942 Dahm was drafted into the air corps and was stationed at St. Johns for glider training. He went overseas as an aerial engineer on a B-17 and won the Distinguished

Flying Cross in action over Florence, Italy. The first in a string of 100-pound fragmentation bombs the plane carried had fallen through the bomb bay door and was hanging by its tailfins, blocking the others.

Dahm then straddled the bomb bay, "with nothing but scenery 18,000 feet below," and pried the bomb loose. He then released the rest of the bombs with a screwdriver.

BILL RAFTERY

It's been more than two years since Bill Raferty hung up his spurs, gave up breaking broncs, and took up breaking motorists who ignore the law on Pima County highways.

A thrice-decorated veteran of service with the Army Rangers who picked up four Purple Hearts in World War II campaigns from Africa to Germany. Raferty now drives a cruiser for the state highway patrol.

Raised on a Montana ranch and joining the army's horse cavalry when he was 16, Patrolman Raferty now lives a quiet life compared to his first 29 years. Prior to joining the patrol, he bought and broke wild horses in Tucson and Phoenix.

The army awarded him the Silver Star for an exploit in Normandy about which he will only say, "I was just messing around where I shouldn't have been." Also on his service record is the Bronze Star with an oak leaf cluster denoting a second award.

Raferty was a master sergeant leading a platoon of rangers; the U.S. equivalent of British commandos, when he got the machine gun wound that almost lost him his left arm in the Hurtgen Forest, December 12, 1944.

Army medics were set to amputate, but Bill wouldn't give his consent. So they sent him back to the states where several months of surgery restored the forearm to partial usefulness.

One war souvenir he'll always carry the rest of his

life is a German bullet which penetrated his left arm and imbedded itself just behind his heart. Military surgeons decided it would be too risky to attempt to remove the slug.

Outside of a few 100-mile-an-hour chases that "had my heart in my throat," Bill says he's had few harrowing experiences in his career as a law enforcement officer.

Two fellow officers. Two heroes. But that was 50 years ago when we had real heroes you might say. Think again. Quit looking so hard for a hero.

To me, a hero is a single parent holding down one or two jobs, sacrificing what they may truly want in life so that they can provide for their children and raise those children to become solid, upstanding citizens. Or an officer, in the middle of the night and over an hour away from his nearest backup, approaching a vehicle with suspicious occupants. Quit looking so hard; that hero might just be sitting next to you.

OLD-TIME WESTERN JUSTICE
Harley Thompson #6

There was a flavor to western justice that hung on for many years in some respects, even though times slowly changed into the modern scheme of things as the years progressed.

Early one morning (circa 1952), I checked 10-8 and asked for any traffic and was promptly informed that Patrolman Raftery was broken down at Mountain View approximately 19 miles east of Tucson. I advised the dispatcher to inform Patrolman Raftery that I was en route to his location. Unknown to anyone at this time, things were taking place near Willcox, that would bring old western justice back to life.

I picked up Patrolman Raftery, and we headed back to Tucson. We hadn't gone but a few miles when the dispatcher called and informed me that Patrolman T.K. Wootan had just called in to report that he had been shot by a violator he had stopped a few miles west of Willcox. The dispatcher advised that Patrolman Wooten had advised radio that he was en route to Willcox to a local doctor's office for emergency treatment. The dispatcher further advised me of the description, color, make, model, and license plate number of the violator. He further stated that the violator had taken off eastbound at a high rate of speed.

I pulled a hard "bootleg" 180 and advised the dispatcher I was en route to Willcox and to do the following in the order in which I give it to him and, in each case, advise everyone that these men were armed and should be considered very dangerous and not to take any unnecessary chances or action without sufficient backup.

"Call the sheriff's office in Safford and tell them to put up a roadblock south of Safford, give them all pertinent information. Call Captain Bradford of the New Mexico State Police in Lordsburg and ask him to put up a roadblock at the state line where the highway crosses from Bowie. Then call the sheriff of Cochise County, inform him, and ask for a roadblock just north of Douglas. Also ask them to have a unit check out the side roads near Elfrida, Gleason, and McNeal. Then call Benson Police Department and ask them to be on the lookout in case of a double back by the violator. Then call Phoenix, inform the superintendent, and also inform Captain Emral Ruth, our district commander. Inform them of the action taken and tell them that I am en route Willcox and will be in charge until relieved by the captain." I then advised the dispatcher to call Sergeant Holly in Bisbee and have him double up all his patrolmen, two to a unit and alert all other patrolmen stationed in Bowie and Benson to be ready to double up with additional officers that will be sent out of Tucson. I also advised the dispatcher to call two more dispatchers and have them assist in the radio room and office with phone traffic.

In order to put this story in proper perspective time-wise, this all occurred on a Monday morning.

At this point, about 3 hours had elapsed since the initial shooting, and no one had seen hide nor hair of the bad guys. Our collective thinking was that they had turned north at the junction east of Willcox and headed north toward Safford to US666, presently US191.

I had already contacted Patrolman Wooten at his doctor's office and had received a full account of the events leading up to his being shot. Wooten had stopped the violator for speeding and was in the process of issuing the driver a citation. The driver was unable to produce a registration for the vehicle, and Wooten was on the way back to his patrol car to call for a 10-28 and 29 (check registration and wanted) when the driver stepped out and fired once at Patrolman Wooten striking him in the arm, jumped back into his vehicle, and took off at high rate of speed eastbound back toward Willcox. Wooten called in the information and then proceeded to the doctor's office for medical attention.

It was determined that the wound was serious but not life-threatening as the bullet had passed through the fleshy part of his arm without striking a bone. The doctor gave him first aid, a shot to prevent infection, and recommended he go to Tucson Medical Center for x-rays and treatment. I assigned Patrolman Raftery to take Wooten back to Tucson, and Wooten's family would follow.

Captain Raymond had sent several of his units down to assist in the search, and I asked him to send a unit off US666 to check out the roads to Bonita, Klondyke, Turkey Flat, and Fort Grant. Another unit was assigned to check out Portal and Paradise. They also checked out the road to Dos

Cabezas south of Willcox. The superintendent spent his flying time all over the back country and mountains until it got dark and then he returned to Tucson and said he would be back the following day.

In the meantime, Captain Ruth showed up in the area with several units from Tucson and made assignments for two men in a car to assist in covering the highways. Captain Ruth seemed to be a bit "put out" with me because I didn't wait for him to show up before making all the assignments and calls to establish roadblocks around the entire perimeter. I explained to the captain that, in my considered opinion, that time was of the essence and that it was absolutely necessary to take immediate action. In doing so, the perimeters were surrounded. I also reminded him that he had previously instructed me to always act with decisiveness, keeping in mind the safety and welfare of our people. After explaining my reasoning, he admitted that what I did was the correct action, and he seemed to be placated by that.

The captain had also detailed several patrolmen to the area, all doubled up, and since I had sent Raftery back to Tucson with Wooten, he assigned Patrolman Harold Clark to ride with me and sent us to work the areas of Bowie and San Simon. Monday passed on with everyone taking turns driving and sleeping in their respective vehicles.

We got our first break about noon on Tuesday when the superintendent spotted a vehicle off Highway US666 about 15 miles north of the junction of US70. The vehicle reportedly was partially covered with tree branches and broken limbs. This was later confirmed by the Graham County sheriff deputies. The call went out for trackers and the dogs to be sent from the state penitentiary in Florence. The deputies confirmed that it was the vehicle used by the two men being sought.

By the time the dogs and their handlers arrived, it was already getting dark, and it was decided they would wait until Wednesday morning before they put the bloodhounds on their trail. Trackers were unable to find any definite footprints indicating the probable direction of travel of the two offenders being sought.

In the meantime, we were concentrating on the probability of the perps trying to catch a train either east or westbound. I told the captain that I did not think this would be possible since the freight train always "highballed it" and stopped for nothing and the passenger train stopped only if they were to pick up passengers. This was confirmed by a check with railroad authorities in Tucson.

On Wednesday the dogs worked tirelessly routing out rabbits, a couple of coyotes, one skunk, and generally ran around baying and tugging at their leashes, all to no avail. Their handlers tried everything, but nothing seemed to work in their favor. It seemed that the bad guys had simply vanished.

Another day and night gone. Everyone's nerves were frayed. Everyone needed a shave, a bath and clean clothes. We were red-eyed, smelly, and bad tempered by Thursday morning. I found myself driving Patrolman Clark with windows open hoping for better smells and a good day.

The dogs went at it again early Thursday, greatly enthused, probably remembering yesterday's fat little rabbits and coyotes, but to no avail. Sometime around noon, a report came in that two Graham County deputies had arrested two men wandering around just south of the Roger Lake campground. They said the two were dirty, very dehydrated, and hungry, having not had anything to eat or drink for about three and a half days. It was confirmed that the two men arrested were, in fact, the men we had all been looking for,

They were taken to the sheriff's office in Safford. Later that same day, two deputies from Cochise County drove up to Safford and took custody of the two men and transported them back to Bisbee. We sent a local wrecker to the location of the abandoned vehicle and had it towed to Bisbee.

On Friday morning the county attorney, with all the necessary prepared documents, had the two suspected felons brought into the courtroom of the local Superior Court sitting judge. The charges filed against the two men were read and given to the judge. The judge asked them if they understood the nature of the charges filed, and they stated they did. He asked them if they wanted legal counsel, and they said they did not. He then asked them if they wanted a trial by a jury of their peers, and they stated they did not. The judge then asked them how they pled to all charges, and they said they were guilty as charged. He then sentenced them to, I think, 35 years in the state penitentiary in Florence. Later that same day, two Cochise County deputies transported them to Florence and turned them over to the warden.

Quick justice! Sorta like the old "Judge Roy Bean" type, i.e. the guy looks guilty so let's hang him.
Now, that was "old-time western justice". As my friend, retired Lieutenant Bill Chewning would say, "That's the way it was heading west."

THE WOOTANS
Ron Cox #1101

Harley Thompson wrote a story about the shooting of Patrolman T K Wootan Jr. east of Tucson in 1952 and the manhunt that followed. Wootan's father, T K Wootan Sr., was a posse member who was shot and killed in a shootout with the Power brothers in the Galiuro Mountains south of Klondyke, Arizona, in 1918.

Four lawmen left Safford to arrest the Power brothers for draft evasion. Leaving their horses, they approached the power cabin and a shootout began. Sheriff McBride, Deputy Kempton, and Deputy Wootan were shot and killed. Deputy Hanes was the only lawman to survive.

The Power brother's father was shot and killed during the shootout. The brothers, Tom and John, along with friend and former army scout Tom Sisson were in the cabin and survived; however, both Power brothers lost their left eye injured in the shootout.

The brothers and Tom Sisson left the mountain on horseback, and the largest manhunt in Arizona history up to that point began. The manhunt covered some of the same area where the hunt for the suspects involved in the shooting of Patrolman Wootan occurred many years later.

The Power brothers and Tom Sisson were arrested and sent to prison to serve a life sentence. Tom Sisson died in prison, and the Power brothers were pardoned after serving 42 years behind bars.

This is a fascinating story with ties to our department. In 1941 A G Walker became the warden at the state prison in Florence. The Power brothers became concerned about retribution from Warden Walker due to the fact that Walker was related to T K Wootan Sr. Walker was also, at one time, superintendent of the Arizona Highway Patrol.

There is a picture that shows Wootan Sr.'s brother and Patrolman Wootan meeting and shaking hands with the Power brothers upon their release from prison. Not many people know the department's ties in the famous shootout that occurred in the desolate Galiuro Mountains so many years ago.

POWER BROTHERS
John Kennedy #119

Just a note referencing the Power brothers. My father-in-law, Bud Brown, was fascinated with the Powers brothers. He knew them when they were still in prison. One of them made my father-in-law and my mother-in-law pairs of really nice spurs. I think this was while they were still in prison.

About 30 years ago, my son, Lonnie, and his son, Ross, took my father-in-law and some of his friends and packed into the Powers cabin. It was pretty neat, the bullets embedded in the walls and stuff. That's a wilderness area now, so no roads or vehicles allowed.

One of the brothers worked for my father-in-law after they got out of prison.

BENSON SHOOTING - THE SHOT GLASS
Harley Thompson #6

In 1954 an individual who had been previously drinking went into a bar in Benson and ordered a double shot and a beer chaser (better known as a Boiler Maker) and, during the next hour or so, had a couple more. He then began to talk loud and became obnoxious and insulting to several other patrons who finally got up and left.

This seemed to really set him off, and he started cursing and ordered another drink, at which time the bartender politely told him that he had already had more than enough to drink and refused to serve him again. Apparently, this was the straw that broke the camel's back because he then drew a gun and took a shot at the bartender. Fortunately, he missed and the bartender ducked under the bar, then ran out the back door, and called the Benson Police Department.

The police department dispatched an officer by the name of Woodard to the scene.(Woodard's brother, Bill, later joined the highway patrol and retired from DPS as a captain).Officer Woodard went into the bar and called out to the individual to throw down his gun and surrender. He was promptly rewarded with a gunshot to his arm.

By this time, several officers were responding. Among them was Patrolman Ray Smith of the highway patrol. Patrolman Smith very cautiously entered the bar, letting his eyes become accustomed to the dim light. He told the shooter to lay his gun down, put his hands behind his head, and kneel down on the floor. The shooter told him in no uncertain terms what he could do with his proposal. Balancing officer safety against the threat to others is like dancing on the blade of a knife. You must be extremely careful.

Patrolman Smith advised him that he could not hope to get away as they had the place surrounded. He said they didn't want to hurt him in any way or to kill him. Just give up. At this point the shooter took a shot toward Patrolman Smith.

Smith called out to him and said, "Do you see that shot glass on the bar?"

The shooter replied, "Yeah, so what?"

Patrolman Smith quickly took aim on the small glass with his .357 Magnum and touched off a round, breaking the glass. (Ray Smith was a very good shot and, at one time, was a member of the patrol's shooting team). Now, either the shooter had a serious learning curve or he had a grown-man-dumb-as-sh@$-syndrome, because he raised up and leveled his gun at Patrolman Smith. Smith promptly shot him square between the eyes.

Patrolman Bill Chewning took Lieutenant Holly and the county attorney over to the scene from Bisbee to investigate. We sent our own photographer to make a record of the scene. This was ruled as a justified shooting, and Patrolman Smith was completely exonerated from any blame.

The taking of a human life, whether justified or not, is not something many of us contemplate; however, when it does, it becomes necessary to be mentally prepared and, hopefully, measure up and take the necessary action.

MY STOLEN CAR
Craig Williamson #518

Gila Bend was the crucible where I learned to be a sergeant. I had a great crew to teach me. One of those officers was Dave Holmes, #2186. Dave was a former USMC Force Recon and about as squared away as a supervisor could hope for. The rest of the cast included my wife, Mary; our infant son, Robert; and Jim Brockway, #1233, also squared away. We lived in a slump block house on North Logan, in town. We had moved out of the Gila Bend compound to build some equity in a home.

One day, I was riding with Dave Holmes west of Gila Bend. We were parked in the median clocking speeders with the radar gun when a black vinyl/yellow Chevy went by at 70. Fair game in the 55 days. Dave proceeded out of the median and started to close the distance to the Malibu. Lights on, but the Chevy began to accelerate away. This went on for a couple of miles, and obviously, the driver was not pulling over.

Dave called in to Phoenix Radio that we were in pursuit. Dave was trying to close the distance to read the

Chevy's license plate but couldn't quite make it out. So, I told him, "It's SND640. Dave, it's my car!" Sure enough, we were pursuing my stolen vehicle down I-8 at 110 mph.

The next obvious question was, where were my wife and son? My previous assignment had been working for Larry Capp, #596, in Narcotics. I didn't expect any Christmas cards from the dealers we sent to ASP (Arizona State Prison), but I didn't think they would kidnap my wife and son.

Jim Brockway was sent to my house to investigate. Meanwhile, the Chevy driver, realizing he couldn't outrun us, pulled over and stopped. I approached the driver and asked him whose car he was driving and where he was going. He told us it was his car and he was going to Yuma. He turned white as a sheet when I told him it was my car, and asked where the woman and child were.

We wrestled him into custody, cuffed him, and opened the trunk. No wife and son in the car. Meanwhile, back at the house, Brockway, not knowing what to expect, entered the house to search it, pistol drawn, only to find Mary giving Robert a bath. He asked Mary where our car was. Imagine my wife's surprise to see there was no car in the driveway! Mary was washing the car when she heard Robert crying after his nap, and she decided to give him a bath. She left the car in the driveway and went inside to check on Robert. The miscreant walking down the street spied a car with the keys in it and off he went.

So, the Malibu didn't get traded for dope in San Luis, wife and son were okay, and the phlegm wad that stole it was booked into the Gila Bend jail. Just another day in Gila Bend. Fond memories...

COWBOYS AND INDIANS
Harley Thompson #6

Nebraska - March 4, 1951 - Houston Chronicle:
Clifford Battershaw went to the Douglas County jail and pulled a gun, helping his brother, Dewey, and fellow inmate, Victor Sweet, escape. The men took two hostages and left the jail on a streetcar. They were later cornered by lawmen in Arizona, who killed Dewey and wounded Clifford and Sweet.

Oswego, N.Y. - March 16, 1951 - Oswego Palladium Times:
Jail Breaker Slain By Police In Wild West Style Chase, Gun Fight

Schenectady N.Y. Gazette - March 17, 1951:
Young Desperadoes Still "Hate Cops" After Gunfight

St Johns, Arizona, March 14 - Two sullen young survivors of a gun battle with a sheriff's posse snarled, "We hate coppers," in their jail cells today.

Rifle and six-shooter bullets killed their companion and blasted them out of a tree-covered ridge near here yesterday.

A deputy sheriff killed Dewey Battershaw, 21-year-old Omaha, Nebraska, jail breaker as he was drawing a bead with a .22 caliber rifle on a state highway patrolman.

The crime spree that brought the young trio to the end of the trail in the eastern Arizona mountains began with the arrest of Dewey Battershaw and Sweet in Omaha for a service station robbery.

Clifford Battershaw, armed with a gun, entered the Douglas County jail and liberated his brother and Sweet on March 4th. They took a deputy sheriff and an attorney with them as hostages. They added the drivers of two commandeered cars to their hostages and later released all four.

A car speeding through this little Apache County town yesterday afternoon put highway patrolman, Ray Dahm, and undersheriff, Emmett Wilhelm, on the Nebraska trio's trail. A bullet from the speeding car smashed the pursuing patrol car's windshield. Then the fugitive car swerved off the road and overturned three times.

This was how the newspapers reported the shootout. I will tell you what I remember about the pursuit and shooting.

After Patrolman Dahm had chased the fleeing vehicle out of St. Johns for some distance, it became apparent that he may be in for a long chase. It was then that he called the Apache County Sheriff's office and asked them to have a roadblock set up on the highway coming into Holbrook south of the Painted Desert. That highway is now called SR180.

Patrolman Billy Sorrells and I took the call just as we were leaving the duplex where we lived. Billy and I both ran into our homes and gathered up our hunting rifles and a supply of ammunition. We were still looking for a good place for the roadblock when we received another call stating that the fugitives had overturned their car and had taken to the hills. Billy and I continued on until we arrived at the location of the accident, and Patrolman Dahm briefed us on what had since taken place.

He stated that Sheriff Crosby was bringing a couple of horses for himself and Undersheriff Wilhelm. Shortly thereafter, Sheriff Crosby arrived with the horses and another deputy. The sheriff said that he and Wilhelm would try and go around the fugitives and asked Dahm, Sorrells, the deputy, and me to try and pin them down in one location, and they would come up behind them. Patrolman Dahm told us that one of the fugitives was apparently injured pretty badly in the accident as the other two were holding him up and kinda dragging him along and that their progress would probably be pretty slow.

With that plan in mind, the four of us spread out in a line about twenty yards apart and started out through the countryside. It was late afternoon, the wind was blowing, and we were walking directly into the setting sun. Conditions were not too good, and visibility was difficult.

The four of us walked about a quarter of a mile or so when it became apparent we were being fired upon. We could hear the ricochet of bullets hitting the rocks around us. Sorrells and I saw the fugitives at about the same time, so we found a pretty good rest for our rifles on a tree limb, and even though we were looking into the sun, with the wind stinging our eyes, we cranked off a couple of rounds at them and could see them run in behind an outcropping and drop out of sight.

I became aware of someone behind me, and sure enough, there was the deputy that Sheriff Crosby brought with him. (I shall call him Old Yaller) I told him to move back over where he was before, and we started on down through this little valley. Pretty soon, they started shooting at us again, and we could once again hear the bullets ricochet off the rocks. Here comes "Old Yaller" again and gets right behind me. I told him this time to get the hell back where he was supposed to be. I told him as long as he could hear the bullets hitting the rocks, he had nothing to worry about. I said, "You don't hear the one that hits you."

Sorrells and I laid a couple more shots down where the bad guys were, and once again, they found cover. We were getting pretty close now, and they started shooting again. This time, "Old Yaller" gets behind Ray Dahm, and Ray told him to get back where he was supposed to be. I heard "Old Yaller" tell Dahm, "Maybe I should go back and get some more help."

Ray told him, "There isn't going to be any more help. This is all there will be. Get your butt back in line."

In the meantime, the sheriff and undersheriff had ridden around to a location where they could see the fugitives laying behind some rocks. They both dismounted and came up behind their location. Emmett Wilhelm drew his revolver and called for them to throw down the rifle and surrender. Dewey Battershaw turned around and pointed the rifle at Wilhelm at which time Wilhelm shot him in the chest. He collapsed right where he was, and the other two raised their hands and gave up. (Contrary to the newspaper account, Battershaw was not pointing the rifle at a highway patrolman, but rather, he pointed it at Wilhelm).

Battershaw did not die right away. It was sometime later when he was on a gurney the medics had brought out. He looked up at us and said, "Cowboys and Indians," and with that last expression, he died.

The sheriff asked us where "Old Yaller" was, and Billy Sorrells said, "When Emmett fired that last shot, I saw him headin' back towards the highway just about as fast as he could." Patrolman Dahm told the sheriff what had happened several times when we were being fired upon. The sheriff just shook his head and said, "I hope to hell that cowardly S.O.B. never stops running."

Emmett Wilhelm later went to work for the Arizona Highway Patrol and retired some years later with the rank of sergeant.

THE STOLEN HANDCUFFS
Frank Glenn #468

I'm not sure if you remember, but there used to be a little Mexican takeout joint just south of Van Buren and 15th

Avenue, I believe. When Charlie McNeese and I were in the armory we used to go down there nearly every day for lunch.

Well, it seems one day we drove up into that little parking lot, and there was an unmarked DPS car sitting there with the windows rolled down, and it was obviously unlocked. I could see a set of handcuffs hanging off the spotlight, as we all used to do, so I walked over to the car and got the handcuffs and put them in my back pocket. I had no idea who the car belonged to, but it was obvious that it should have been locked up.

Charlie and I walked into the takeout joint, and who should be standing there but Officer Marty Dangle and Officer Chuck Wright. While Charlie got their attention, I managed to sneak around behind Marty, and if you remember, those old gederal-man holsters that we used to have left the trigger guard of our revolver exposed. I managed to silently unlock the handcuffs, and while Charlie had Marty's attention, I ran the handcuffs through the trigger guard of Marty's revolver and locked it.

Marty calmly looked down and remarked, "I guess I have a new set of handcuffs."

I said, "I don't know who they belong to. I got them off the spotlight of that unmarked patrol car out front."

Well, at this point, Chuck began to severely berate Marty over having left the car unlocked. Chuck said, "Sure, we don't need to lock the car. Nobody is going to steal anything out of it!"

Well, they walked back to the car with the handcuffs dangling off Marty's trigger guard. Now mind you, both of these guys are in uniform, and Marty asked Chuck to borrow his handcuff key. Of course, Chuck being the prankster that he was, had one but would not loan it to Marty. Chuck said, "I don't have my handcuff key today." Chuck did tell me later that he did have a key but he said, "I'll be damned if I'm going to loan it to him."

At this time, I think Marty and Chuck could have been doing background checks, and if you remember, for a while they were stationed up in the old driver's license building across the street from the compound. So, there goes Marty walking through the downstairs of the building on his way upstairs with the handcuffs dangling down from his six-shooter.

At this time, the armory was located in the basement of the training building where the ladies showers are now located. When I got ready to leave the armory about 5:00 that evening, I walked out through the door to see Chuck is out there lifting weights, and on one of the desks in the gym was a gun belt with the gun in its holster. I gave Chuck a questioning look, and he just gave the old reserve salute and said, "I don't think he is ever going to learn."

So, I hustled back into the armory, grabbed a screwdriver, and proceeded to strip Marty's gun apart. Shortly after this, Marty came out, and much to his surprise, he could see that his gun was all in pieces. I just turned to the both of them and said, "OK, I'll see you guys tomorrow."

I then casually walked out the door. I just walked up the stairs and turned around, coming back in the building from the other entrance. I came back downstairs, and there is Marty, still staring at his gun. Being the nice guy that I am, I reassembled it for him and told him I didn't think you are supposed to leave guns unguarded. He was still speechless.

THE DAY I MACED MY SERGEANT
Colin Peabody #481

It was a fairly quiet, very cold New Year's Eve in 1968, and I was east of Winslow just minding my own business looking for one eyes, vehicles with one headlight burning. I was the only patrolman on duty in the Winslow area that evening, and I was enjoying the tranquility of the moment. I was finishing my first year as an Arizona highway patrolman and had recently been issued a new 1968 Plymouth Fury patrol car with a big engine capable of speeds well in excess of what the speedometer showed.

My quiet evening was about to become disturbed with a call from Paul Palmer in Holbrook Radio advising me that the Winslow Police Department was in pursuit of a pickup truck eastbound out of Winslow, and they were requesting our help in getting it stopped.

I intercepted the pursuit as it went by the Minnetonka Trading Post at the intersection of US66 and SR87, heading up to the Rez. Winslow had two patrol units, both driving 1968 Fords with small V-8 engines. I pulled a well-executed and precise highway patrol U-turn and, with all of the 440 cubic inches and 375 ponies of mighty Mopar available to me, quickly caught up and joined the pursuit.

Just after entering the eastbound lanes of I-40, we were able to box the pickup truck in, with me alongside the pickup and a Winslow unit in front and one Winslow unit in back of the truck. The truck was a brand new, blue-and-white 1969 Chevy short bed and was complete with bragging rights. The emblems on the side of the fender said that the truck was equipped with the newly optional and deadly 396-cubic inch engine. Having been a car guy for my entire 24 plus years, I knew fully well what 396 cubic inches of Chevrolet rat motor was all about and that the 440 cubic inches of Mopar under the hood of my new steed would be hard-pressed to compete with that monster motor.

We got the truck stopped, and as I exited my vehicle, a Winslow sergeant ran up to the driver's door of the truck. I could see two occupants, both Indian females. The sergeant opened the door and began to pull the driver out, when she threw it into reverse and backed over the sergeant, knocking him down with the door. There was just enough room for her to squeeze that pickup between my vehicle and the Winslow unit ahead of her. The sergeant suffered a broken leg and was quickly attended to by his fellow officers while I took up the pursuit.

I notified Holbrook Radio of the occurrence, and Palmer dispatched my sergeant, Bob Harvey, who was enjoying the solitude of the evening with his lovely wife, Barbara, and their family, complacent in the fact that he had an experienced but rookie officer patrolling the area.

Now, Sergeant Harvey, at the time, was a 15-plus-year veteran of the highway patrol and was well known for being able to drive at maximum speed, whatever it was, at a distance of mere inches from the highway delineators and had never struck one that anyone ever knew about. He also had the reputation of being able to spot, at a distance and at warp speed, a crescent wrench lying alongside the road, getting his patrol car stopped in record distance in a cloud of smoke, grab the wrench, toss it in the trunk where he kept enough found tools to open his own Harbor Freight store, and get back to his patrolling, all in less than 15 seconds. This activity I can attest to, having been present several times when this actually happened. I was a quick study, as I was soon able to replicate this feat. I was a bit more choosey, as I only kept Craftsman tools that had a lifetime guarantee. The only problem was getting new tires from fleet that didn't have flat spots on them from the quick stops. We kept telling them US66 was a rough highway and hard on tires. But, getting back to the story...

The driver of the pickup was doing her very best to keep ahead of my mighty Mopar, weaving from lane to lane on the interstate, speeding up to over 120 mph and then back down to 85 or 90. I was doing everything I could do to stay with her, trying to pass on the right, thinking I could block her from the front, trying to pass her on the left, all while trying to keep my new Plymouth from getting hit.

The passenger was hanging out of the passenger window and began throwing objects at my patrol car. I backed off a bit as the objects bounced off of the pavement. What she was discarding were new, tall, full cans of Budweiser, and she was tossing lots of them. A real waste of beer, but that's another story.

One of the cans bounced off the asphalt and hit the windshield of my new patrol car, cracking it. That clinched it for me! She was going to pay for that! Damaged vehicle report to follow. The AHP had reports for everything.

Now, folks have told me that alcohol won't freeze, but they have never been in the Little Colorado River Valley on New Year's Eve. Beer will freeze on the windshield of a Plymouth at 100 plus mph when it is just above zero degrees Fahrenheit outside. Windshield wipers will do no good in cleaning off frozen beer, trust me.

While all of this was happening, I am trying to see out of a small spot on the windshield that is not covered in frozen beer. Turning on the defroster to the hilt, dodging the barrage of beer cans, working the spotlight, talking to Palmer, and trying to keep up with this female pseudo-NASCAR driver at speeds anywhere from 80 to 125 mph. Palmer dispatched Patrolman Tom Greenwade who was working east of Holbrook to assist.

The defroster wasn't working fast enough, and now I am forced to hang my head out of the window trying to see where I am going. Tears are flooding down my cheeks from my eyes due to the extreme speed and cold, and I am still dodging flying beer cans. This is what we now call multitasking. Back then it was called "While on routine patrol."

Now, as previous tales of Tom Greenwade have been told by Paul Palmer in this publication, you know he was and is a big guy, soft spoken, with a slow drawl, and wasn't easily excited. But the information that good Budweiser was being discarded on our highway was too much for him to dismiss, and he headed west to intercept us. Sergeant Harvey was coming up from the rear at a high rate of speed but was still quite a ways back, even for him.

The Chevy and the Plymouth passed Hibbard Road interchange and headed down the straight stretch for Jackrabbit Road (Yes, there is actually an interchange for the Old Jackrabbit Trading Post.) weaving back and forth, with the pickup leaving the high-speed lane into the median several times, leaving me to think that this pursuit was about over. Wrong! That driver could never have driven off the road and recovered that well had she been sober. She did a heck of a job! Dale Earnhardt and Danica Patrick would have been proud.

As we left the interstate just east of Jackrabbit, we entered two-lane US66 through Joseph City. Cars coming in our direction were swerving all over the two-lane to get out of the way. Our speed was still anywhere from 55 to 85 mph in this area. My communications with Tom were ongoing, and Sergeant Harvey was adding his input as well as driving inches from the delineators, searching for crescent wrenches.

Tom met us as we entered Joseph City and pulled a quick U-turn, accelerating up behind me, and as we left Joe City, he attempted to get past me and then the pickup truck. We got back on I-40 with Tom still trying to get past the truck. Sergeant Harvey had now caught up with us, but only because he hadn't found any crescent wrenches or pliers along the way.

We quickly formulated a plan. Nowadays the plan would have to be submitted to a committee in triplicate and then passed on to Legal for an opinion as to whether the plan was feasible and to make sure we wouldn't be sued and then, if okayed, on to the special operations unit to be carried out by them and all available air power. But back then, we **were** the highway patrol and that **was** our highway and we **were** going to take it back from these offenders of truth, justice, and the American way. Besides, we didn't have an SOU, and helicopters had never been seen in northern Arizona before.

Anyway, our plan was to try to get Tom ahead of the truck. I would be on the passenger side, and Sergeant Harvey would take up the rear. We would then try to force the truck into the median where the soft, sandy soil and snow would bring it to a stop, whereupon three highway patrolmen would leap out of their Plymouths and capture these no-gooders. That was the plan. Now they call it intervention/boxing, but we did it first! Stop sticks? What are they?

Tom made several attempts to get past the truck, which was still being driven with expertise, weaving from lane to lane, the passenger leaning out of the window yelling obscenities in Navajo. Tom was finally able to squeeze past the truck on the left by partially driving in the median and then back up on the pavement. Believe me, he did a heck of a job in his cool, calm manner. His account of the pass was characterized by his statement in his report, "The driver tried to ram me, but the pass was complete". Talk about an understatement!

With Tom now in the lead, Sergeant Harvey directed us to slow our speed down and begin forcing the truck into the median. This effort took us almost to Holbrook, where we were finally able to get the truck into the median and stopped. I bailed out of my car, and as I did so, I pulled my newly issued and as-yet-unused canister of chemical mace from its new, shiny holster.

As I pulled the passenger door open, I began spraying mace everywhere and then pulled the passenger out, who was by then screaming louder due to the mace. I could hear her screams over the sound of that big Chevy rat motor being revved up to the red line due to the driver's right foot being implanted to the firewall. There was much noise, and I believe I may have heard, but couldn't possibly swear to it, obscenities being directed at these two females in violation of the Arizona Highway Patrol's Courteous Vigilance motto.

We got both females subdued and handcuffed, and as I walked around to the driver's side of the pickup, I saw Sergeant Harvey with a handful of snow pressing it against his face, tears running down his cheeks. My first thought was the driver had thrown Budweiser in my sergeant's eyes and that she was really going to pay for that! My second thought was Sergeant Harvey was so glad we weren't killed he was crying for joy. When Sergeant Harvey recovered sufficiently, he asked if anyone had used their mace, to which my third thought was, "Oh shucky darn," (this being a family publication and all), and I fessed up to using my mace. One does not lie to one's sergeant!

This usage of the mace canister prompted yet another full report in addition to the DWI arrest report detailing the hows and whys of the usage and why I had used the near-lethal weapon at my disposal, because I must have been in fear of my life to do so. This was almost as forbidden as breaking the yellow paper seal on our issued shotguns. Yes, we had seals on our shotguns and with it was the threat of instant termination or days off if you broke the seal at any place other than the range. The fact that if you removed the shotgun from its scabbard for required cleaning and replaced it on more than one occasion the seal would be torn never entered into the discussion. But again, I digress.

Once we had the situation under control, we transported and booked the unruly ladies into the Navajo County jail in Holbrook. The driver kicked the toilet and broke her leg, but that was a Navajo County problem then.

Sergeant Harvey counseled Tom and me about violating the Courteous Vigilance motto and gently reprimanded me for missing my target with the mace and hitting him. I wasn't fired or otherwise disciplined for macing my sergeant and even today, nearly 40 years later, I hold the distinction of being the only Arizona highway patrolman to mace his sergeant and live to tell about it.

God help me if I had done that to "Iron Pants" Ernie Johnson or Dick Sandheger, who both scared the bejesus out of me in the academy. All I have to say is it's a darn good thing they issued mace when they did or I might have shot my sergeant, and Barbara would have never forgiven me!

DAREDEVIL DUKE
Greg Girard #1151

Duke Moore landed a DPS helicopter up at the 7000' level for a two-semi head-on collision. Duke and I were told by a highway patrolman that semis were not allowed on that route. I said, "Do you want us to go back to Falcon Field?" I was kidding, but it would have been a good option.

Both semi drivers were huge men (redundant?) We loaded both, but Duke couldn't lift off with the under-powered equipment. We off-loaded one patient. Even with "Tiny" absent, we still couldn't lift off. Duke told me to off-load anything I didn't need. So, I kicked Duke out and... I'm kidding.

I off-loaded a lot of gear, and Duke said that he was going to ground-taxi the bird over to the edge and throw it over the side. I said, "Sure, why not." Duke had the habit of putting his harness on and going. If the aircraft wanted to come along, it was fine.

He did and I was introduced to an "E-ticket" ride. The aircraft fell several thousand feet into the canyon, until it reached translational (Dumb computer didn't recognize that it was spelled correctly; look it up) lift. We made it and dropped the patient off at the Clifton hospital.

We went back up to meet with the ADOT truck to pick up the other patient and equipment. By that time, an ambulance brought the other patient in.

SOMEONE LIED TO ME
Don Uhles #2092

After eight years with the department. I finally achieved my dream job as an officer/paramedic in the DPS Air Rescue Unit.

Now as the old-time DPS medics were grooming me for my new job, they explained that I was gonna fly into these hospitals in a million-dollar helicopter, a man in uniform who saves lives but also carries a badge and gun – a man of authority! The nurses are just gonna throw themselves at you!

Well, mid-afternoon Ellery Cramer and I get a call to fly out to Rattlesnake Cove at Bartlett Lake for an unknown medical emergency. Back then, there were no services at Bartlett Lake or cell phones, so it took quite some time for someone to get out and request us.

We arrived on the scene to find three drunks taking turns giving "drunk CPR" to a fourth drunk. I take over and start one-rescuer Advance Cardiac Life Support treatment (ACLS). Oh, did I mention that it's about 10,000 degrees along the shoreline? I do some chest compressions, bag (breath for him with an Ambu bag), more compressions, intubate and bag him, more compressions, start an IV, more compressions; well, you get the picture. I go through my standing patient care orders. We load him and fly him to Scottsdale Osborn Hospital. I continued the care I mentioned above on the flight there.

When we finally arrived at the hospital, I'm soaked in sweat, I have sand in every crack and crevice on my body, and I smell like a drunk threw up on me cuz a drunk threw up on me. I'm standing alone in a corner of the trauma room all by myself. No one wants to be anywhere near me because I'm dirty and I smell so bad. As I'm standing there, feeling miserable, I'm thinking to myself, this is not the way Pete Perkins and Greg Girard described this job to me.

Someone LIED to me!!!

1936 FATALITY
Norm Jones #957

This is the text of an article in the *Graham County Guardian–Gila Valley Farmer* on Friday, April 17, 1936. The accident in the article occurred April 6, 1936.

TWO ARE KILLED IN AUTO COLLISION ON HIGHWAY 70
Second Auto Accident in Two Weeks Claims Lives of Mrs. Emily Payne and Roy Hall – Four Taken to Hospital

Twice within two weeks, death traveled along U.S. Highway 70 in the darkness of night, leaving in his path the lifeless forms of a man and a woman lying on the cold pavement, victims of a collision that meted them instant death and sent four others to the hospital, two critically injured and two suffering from minor injuries.

Mrs. Emily Payne, aged 40, of Virden, N.M., the mother of 12 children, and Roy Hall, aged 35, of Oklahoma City, OK, were killed almost instantly in a head-on crash between two automobiles on a slight curve on the highway about 30 miles east of Safford last Thursday night about 10:30.

The injured were Ezra C. Payne, husband of the woman who was killed; his two daughters, Adelma, aged 15, and Vetta, aged 16; and a man who at that time gave his name as Marion Moore but later was identified as Frank McWilliams, believed to be from Texas.

Payne sustained two punctured lungs, a broken arm and hand, a crushed leg, nine broken ribs, serious cuts about the face and head, and a badly injured foot. His condition was critical, and for several days his life hung in a balance but reports today are that he has safely passed the crisis and has a favorable chance to recover.

His daughter, Vetta, received a fractured jaw and ribs and remained in the hospital only a few days. Adelma was only slightly hurt and, after receiving treatment, went to the home of her uncle, President H.L. Payne. Moore's or McWilliams' injuries consisted of broken ribs and chest injuries. Reports are that he is recovering.

Mr. and Mrs. Payne and their daughters were returning to their home in Virden after a day's visit with relatives in Safford.

Mrs. Payne was riding in the front seat of the car, which was eastbound, and was catapulted into a wash at the bottom of a 25-foot rocky embankment. It is said that when help reached her shortly after the accident, she was still alive but died a few seconds after she was taken to the highway. Death is said to have been due to a deep cut on the left temple.

Hall, who was driving the westbound car, died of a broken neck the attending physician stated. His lifeless body was lying over the steering wheel.

The crash occurred about a quarter of a mile west of the Ash Peak service station where the impact of the collision was heard. Shortly afterwards, assistance reached them, and Payne was brought to Safford by the Greyhound stage. The others were brought here by tourists who came upon the scene.

Highway Patrolman Seth Dodge of Safford and Patrolman C.E. Ellsworth of Duncan were notified. They went at once to the scene and made an investigation. Ramon Michelena, justice of the peace and ex-officio coroner, was summoned, and a coroner's jury went to the scene, where, with the assistance of County Attorney Ben Blake, Dr. W.E. Platt, and Court Reporter Daunt Merrill, they held an inquest over the bodies of Mrs. Payne and Hall. The body of Hall was removed from here by the Rawson Mortuary and that of Mrs. Payne was taken to her home in Virden by relatives.

After making the investigation at the scene of the accident, Moore, or McWilliams, was questioned at the hospital the next day and is reported to have stated that Hall picked him up at Las Vegas, N.M.; and that after he got into the car and up to the time of the accident, Hall had drunk a half pint and almost a pint of whiskey and that he had cautioned him he was drinking too much and that he was driving too fast and on the wrong side of the road.

The verdict of the coroner's jury was that Mrs. Payne and Roy Hall met death in an auto collision which was the direct result of "driving while intoxicated on the part of Roy Hall" and that he was "driving at an excessive rate of speed and on the wrong side of the road."

Members of the coroner's jury were Lou Heinz, foreman; W.E. Williams; Alfredo Madrid' Champ Palmer' J.O. Archer' and Abb Gillespie.

As an aftermath of the accident, it is learned from county officials that a federal warrant charging McWilliams with violation of the Dyer Act awaits him upon his release from the hospital. The man who first gave his name as Moore was identified as Frank McWilliams by N.W. Tipps, sales manager for an El Paso motor company, who told officers the man had applied to his company for employment early Thursday morning and that a few hours later the man and the Texas car involved in the accident had disappeared.

Hall was the son of Mr. and Mrs. J.Y. Hall of Marana, Arizona, and came here Saturday to make arrangements for funeral services, which were held Sunday afternoon at the grave in Union Cemetery, with Rev. Edward Lester, pastor of the Baptist church, officiating.

Note: Ezra and Emily Payne are the grandparents of Norman Jones

THE DEER AND THE VOLKSWAGEN
Rick Ulrich #182

Retired Sergeant Rick Ulrich, badge 182, tells this story about Patrolman Ben Shumway.

Ben Shumway was working the midnight shift in the Miami radio room. It was three or four in the morning, and most, if not all, of the units had gone 10-7. So, it was really quiet.

Ben said this Volkswagen pulled into the parking lot and stopped by the patrol office door. This kid in his late teens or early 20s burst through the front door, and his eyes were as big as saucers. The kid said he was coming from Superior to Miami, and he had hit a deer. Ben asked where this had occurred, and by the description the young man gave, Ben surmised that it occurred near Sutton's Summit.

Ben asked if the deer was still at the scene or did it run off? The kid said he thought the deer was dead, so he picked it up and put it in the back seat of the Volkswagen rather than leave it on the highway. The kid said, as he drove to Miami, he heard a noise in the back seat and realized that the deer was not dead but very much alive and was now fully conscious and apparently trying to figure how to get out of the car. Ben said no wonder the kid's eyes were as big as saucers. Can you imagine, he continued, driving with the live deer in the back seat kicking and trying to get out? Ben said, if it had been him, he would have stopped the VW and gotten away from the deer for his own safety.

I can hear Ben telling that story and grinning and chuckling. I heard him repeat that story at least a half dozen times. I wish I could remember his exact words. It would probably sound a lot funnier. I wish Ben was still alive, and he could tell you in person. Sure miss ole Ben.

SHORT CREEK
Chick Lawwill #35

In 1953 there was a group of highway patrolmen who went to Short Creek, referred to as The Short Creek Raid on the polygamists living there. It is now known as Colorado City, located right on the border of Arizona and Utah in a very remote section of Arizona. Depending on the location, to investigate an accident, a patrolman had to go through Nevada or Utah to reach the accident scene. This was a very isolated area.

The governor at the time, Howard Pyle, was confronted with the occupancy of the polygamists living on our Arizona border. People had played politics, and the governor knew his actions would ruin him politically. But he went ahead, being a good Christian.

Each patrolman was asked if he had any problems participating in the raid, since there were several Mormon boys on the patrol at the time and some had relatives in Short Creek. One of these patrolmen was Lt. Vern Fugatt who headed one group in the raid.

Lt. Fugatt and I left Yuma and went to Phoenix and picked up Patrolman Lane from Tucson and another patrolman, and we headed to Williams. We received our briefing at the Williams High School auditorium. Half of the group went from Williams up to Short Creek, staying within state boundaries, going from Williams north to Kaibab to re-group. The patrol cars were spaced out about 5 minutes apart. Locations were mapped out along the way for re-fueling, etc. My group was headed up by Captain Ruth. The other group of patrolman headed up by Lt. Fugatt drove over to Kingman then up to Henderson, Nevada, and St George, Utah, going through southern Utah and coming out at Short Creek.

We had an informant inside the group, a deputy sheriff, and Captain Bob Cochran had managed to hide in an attic and was the point man giving instructions. We were told the people had only one firearm, an old rifle. Little did we know that one fellow in the compound was a ham radio operator and was picking up all of our radio conversations. He could receive but not send any transmissions. At a certain designated time, with two patrolmen to a car, we were all told to turn on our red lights and sirens and go in.

There were 2-3 men up on the tower with a rifle. Shots were fired, but no one was injured. Dynamite was thrown at the bridge another group of patrolmen had to cross to enter Short Creek. It was told that Lt. Fugatt remarked that it looked like there would be an opening for a lieutenant after dynamite was thrown at the bridge he was crossing, however, there was no damage to the bridge.

We had warrants for every man, woman, and child thanks to the inside informant. We were each given maps and assigned to certain areas to search and arrest people. The stench and smell was overwhelming with 3-4 families (15-16 people) living in a one room shack, if they were fortunate. Others were living in cars, buses, and other junk. In all honesty, there were few nice buildings. The houses had dirt floors, no plumbing and outhouses. There was only one light bulb, and that was in the main store, a 20 x 20 building. They had their own school and teachers. They paid no taxes and barely existed. A wire fence separated Arizona and Utah or you would not know what state you were in.

The raid was planned for a weekend as most of the males that worked in the sawmill or other outside jobs would then be home with their families. Thanks to the ham radio operator, most of the males took off across the state line, leaving the wives and children behind. It was a real mess, and we went out of our way not to scare the children anymore than possible.

All of the girls that were born into the group when 4-6 years of age were designated to be wives of certain older males. When they were of age to conceive., they were given to the individual. We found out that those who were unable to conceive were ostracized, and the people had nothing to do with them.

The families, 2-3 wives and children belonging to one man were gathered in a group and put on a Greyhound bus and taken to Phoenix and Tucson. We were able to arrest some males, and they were transported to Kingman to be incarcerated and arraigned at a later date.

Short Creek was a community to itself. All of the monies that they collected and worked for in the mines and sawmill went to one individual. He lived in Utah, and once a month, he would come down to dole out so much food for each family. That had to last them until their next allotment. If they ran short, they did have a barrel of beans in the store that they could get a cup of to carry them over until the next visit. All of the money and all of the power belonged to this one individual. They lived and existed by this one individual who ran the whole show.

Jim Phillips and I were teamed up to transport one of the main people, Jessup, back with us with two of his sons in their 20s. Jessup was 91 years old, the oldest of the group arrested. He also had a one-year-old son. We had to bring Jessup and his two sons back to Kingman to be arraigned. We had to go the long way, as we could not take prisoners out of state. The old man was stove up with arthritis, and we had to stop every so many miles for him to exercise.

None of the three we were transporting had eaten in quite some time, so Jim and I stopped in Williams to get them hamburgers at a cafe. Jim and I bought the food. The rest of the males were taken to Kingman and arraigned. Jessup passed away a short time later.

The patrol got a national reputation from the Short Creek raid, and we were referred to as Nazi Storm Troopers because of the way the raid was conducted. We took a lot of heat over the raid, but we also received some good publicity.

SHORT CREEK RAID
Harley Thompson #6

One of my all-time favorite stories occurred in September 1953. At 0400 hours on the day of the Short Creek raid, roughly 35-40 highway patrol vehicles were lined up for gas at the state yard in Cedar Point on US89. A passing motorist slowed down and asked what was going on. Patrolman Carl Back, without missing a beat calmly said, "Shift change." The open-mouthed motorist drove off down the road shaking his head.

CARNIE BROTHERHOOD
Paul Palmer #342

Russ Dunham was always a pleasure to work with, and I was pleased to learn that my state fair supervisor would be Russ. We were on the graveyard shift, and one night we got a report of a carnie who was injured. Russ told me to go over and check it out.

When I got there, a carnie, reeking of alcohol, was laying on the ground passed out. He was surrounded by other carnies. His breathing was normal, and his unconscious state was due to his drinking and not his injuries. He had some cuts and bruises on his face, and I was told that he had been in a fight.

I called for an ambulance, and since this guy had not seen a shower or bathtub in weeks and since I did not have any rubber gloves, I asked if any of the carnies knew first aid. Seems they all had first aid training, and one carnie proudly told me that carnies were just like police officers. They were trained and they took care of their own. I told them I understood and suggested they take care of their friend until the paramedics arrived.

Ever try to keep from laughing when four carnies are trying to keep count while other carnies preform CPR? "One, two, three, four."

"No, that was five!"

"Give him some breaths of air!"

"No, he needs more pounding".

"One, two, three."

"No, that was two!"

NERVOUS GEORGE
Frank Glenn #468

You probably read the story about Security Supervisor George Snyder and the purple dye. Well, here's another George story.

George came over to the armory one day, and we were sitting there talking, and he told me a story about one of his men getting into trouble. It hadn't been more than two or three weeks later until another one of his people got into trouble. Now, George's boss at that time was Gordon Selby, and if you remember Gordon, he was not one to be trifled with. I think over those two incidents George lost the seat of two pair of uniform pants courtesy of Gordon Selby.

At the time, our work in the armory was either feast of famine, so I was sitting there one day with absolutely nothing to do, and I got to thinking about George's troubles and another bright idea flashed into my mind. At the time, George's office was over there in some little cubbyhole in the photo lab. Well, I dialed his number and, without giving him a chance to speak, said in a rather forceful voice, "This is Selby! One of your men has gone and done it again. I'm on my way over there and when I get there, you had better be waiting on me!"

I gave it about 10 minutes and then strolled over to George's office to have a visit. He was acting like he was sitting on thumbtacks. We were sitting there shooting the breeze for a while, and George was getting more and more nervous as time went on. Directly, he looked at me and said, "If Selby comes in here, would you just get up and leave?"

I said, "Sure, George," and sat there biting my tongue to keep from laughing, with a little smirk on my face. George looked at me questioningly but didn't say anything. Well, after about 10 or 15 minutes, I looked at George and told him it was not Selby on the phone but me. George was so relieved that he didn't even get mad.

I had a lot of fun with George because when he first came into the armory, he told me what a prankster and jokester he was. So, I thought, *oh boy, open season.* As far as I can remember, George never tried to pull a joke on me. He was really a great guy, and I hated to see him retire and move, up to Globe, I think. His demise saddened me greatly.

Earl Rogers on right with wrecked 1920s car

Highway Patrol Station 1934

Captain Dysart Murphy 1955

Greyhound Bus cattle truck fatality east of Tucson Dec. 1959

A law enforcement officer confiscates dynamite during the 1953 raid on the polygamous community of Short Creek in July, 1953. AP

Ptlm John Gantt at Short Creek 1953

42 YEARS LATER—Tom Power (#5173) was greeted by Frank Wootan (left) when the parole board voted to release him and his brother John on parole 42 years after their imprisonment. Frank, the brother of Deputy Sheriff Kane Wootan who was killed in the shoot-out, was one of the possemen who pursued the Power brothers and Tom Sisson in the largest manhunt in Arizona history. The man in the center is T. K. ("Kane") Wootan, Jr., son of the slain deputy sheriff. *Arizona Republic photo.*

143

Ptlm T. Wootan with Power Brothers at Florence Prison

Ptlm John Gantt 1951

Ptlm George Schuck with VASCAR 1967

Florence Prison Riot 1958

Capt. Everett Bowman on bronco statue

Sgt. Jack Monschein at switchboard 1960

Dale Cain hat badge and bullet 1971

Weapons inspection by Supt. Hathaway and Curley Moore

Supt. Hathaway 1960

First Freeway Squad Phoenix 1966

Capt. Whitlow and Ptlm Harold Clark

Ptlm Bill Hangar and Dick Shafer 1954

Sgt. Ernie Johnson US 60, 1963

Arizona Peace Officer Memorial

TO OFFICERS PAST - A TRIBUTE.
TO OFFICERS PRESENT - A REMINDER
TO OFFICERS YET TO COME - A LEGACY.

AZDPS Officer Memorial

Sgt. Homer Keeton and sons Jim and Dennis, 1969

President Roosevelt and Ptlm 1937 Zane Grey Cabin

Bob LaRue and dispatchers 1943

Tom Mix Memorial Dedication 1947

Morenci 1983

LT Dick Raymond 1951

HE KICKED A BLASTING CAP
Steve Page #2095

I was working a night shift at the north end of the divided highway just north of the Saguaro Lake turnoff. I stopped a speeding pickup, and as I approached the driver's side of the truck, the driver jumped out and told me he was taking his friend/passenger to the hospital because he had hurt his foot.

I noticed the passenger had his right ankle/foot wrapped in a white towel with a lot of blood showing. I examined his foot, and it only attached to his leg by the width of my index finger. I asked him what happened, and he told me they were drinking beer down at Sycamore Creek wash and there was a campfire. Someone threw three blasting caps in the fire and one didn't ignite. So, he kicked it with his foot, and you guessed it, it ignited, causing the injury. His injuries were so severe that I had to call for a medical helicopter because he was bleeding so severely. Dumb is as dumb does.

I WAS JUST TRYING TO GET HOME
Rick Tannehill #1235

Back in the mid-seventies, I was in Flagstaff doing some engineering work on our Mt. Elden communications site. I was spending a couple nights up there that week. One evening, I had dinner with my sister-in-law, who was in college at NAU at the time. Afterward, I didn't feel tired, as it was still fairly early, so I went to the Flag 103 communications dispatch center and asked if there was anyone out I could do a ride-along with for a few hours. They set me up with an officer who had just come in for gas and whose shift was supposed to end at 10 PM. We cruised I-17 for a couple hours with no real activity, so just before 10, we started back up the hill toward Flagstaff.

Shortly after turning around, a grey Ambassador 990 blew past us going south at an extreme speed. The officer reluctantly turned around again and started pursuit. It took some doing to catch up with the guy as he was going well over 100 at the time. We finally caught up with him with the lights on, but he didn't slow down or pull over.

His Ambassador was a gray U.S. government-plated car. (As I remember, those Ambassadors had a 348 V8 with a light body that really would go) Even with his spotlight on him, he didn't pull over.

He asked me to call it in on the radio and handle all radio duties until he got this guy stopped. He approached 110 at times but did slow down to about 90 for the night construction going on I-17 at that time. We thought he might be FBI on a case, but the officer said he could at least stop to tell us what was up.

The dispatcher realized we had a problem and got an officer in Camp Verde to be ready with the stop sticks to deflate his tires. Just before we started down the hill to Camp Verde, the gray Ambassador finally pulled over and stopped. The officer approached cautiously and found an Air Force recruiting sergeant from Phoenix who was in Flag for the day, trying to get home that night to get some sleep. However, the officer smelled alcohol on him and had him do a breathalyzer and found he was about twice the legal limit. The officer asked the driver why he didn't stop. He replied, "I just thought it was some punk kids trying to harass me because I was Air Force."

Shortly after, another officer approached the scene and transported the sergeant back to the Flagstaff/Coconino jail for the night. The officer I was with returned a lot more slowly to Flag and dropped me off at the 103 about midnight.

I think he was kind of wrung-out, as I was. I would like to find out who that was to say "hi" to him again.

I'm told the next day another DPS officer who happened to be at the Coconino jail saw the sergeant's C.O. bail him out, and he was definitely not a happy camper to have to come to Flagstaff to take care of this matter.

Definitely one of the more fun times of my 30-year engineering/management career at DPS. Thanks for all the memories, guys!

JAIMIE TEYECHEA
Chick Lawwill #35

Jaimie Teyechea was my girls' idol. While growing up in Yuma, they thought he was just SO handsome. At the time, even Elvis Presley didn't stand a chance if Jaimie was around. He teased the girls and told them they could call him The Latin Lover. The name has stuck after all these years.

One evening Jaimie and I were parked side by side just east of Ligurta "swatting flies." He claimed his car was faster than mine. We both had 1949 Fords and mine had over 170,000 miles on it. I always thought his car was faster because he was a personal friend of Superintendent Hathaway and got better equipment. As we sat there talking about how fast our cars were, a speeder went by, and Jaimie thought he would impress me with one of his fast starts. He impressed me, all right. He broke the rear axle taking off. He never again mentioned how fast his car was.

I TOLD YOU I WAS SICK
Chick Lawwill #35

It was mandatory that every patrolman had to qualify with his sidearm a least once a year. One year Jaimie Teyechea and I had to drive to Wickenburg to a pistol meet. We decided that we would take my car since it was unmarked and we could make better time. Because it was so far and Highway 95 from Yuma to Quartzsite was gravel, you were limited as to how fast you could travel with all the dips and curves. It was decided that I would drive to Wickenburg, and Jaimie would drive back to Yuma.

After the pistol meet, we were on our way back to Yuma when dispatch called and advised us to stop in Salome, pick up a prisoner from a deputy, and then transport the prisoner to Yuma. As I said, Jaimie was driving, and it was getting late in the evening, and we were anxious to get home. Jaimie had to drive another 40 miles to his home in Tacna.

When we picked up the prisoner, the deputy told us that he had arrested the prisoner the night before in a bar in Salome for fighting and being drunk and disorderly. He told us that the prisoner kept telling him that his stomach hurt, but the deputy said it was because of all the drinking and fighting and not to worry and that the prisoner was just putting on with all the moaning and groaning. We took the deputy's word and headed for Yuma.

Things were going along pretty good as long as we were on the black top, but once we got on the gravel road south of Quartzsite and started hitting the bumps and curves, it was a different story. It was getting late, and we had started a 6:00 in the morning from Yuma. We were tired, dirty, and just anxious to get home. We had this prisoner that was moaning and groaning that did not help our disposition, either.

Every time Jaimie would top out and then bottom out on the dips, our heads would hit the headliner and our butts would lift then hit the seat. All the time the prisoner was acting like he was going to pass out. Jaimie would holler back at him to quiet down and quit complaining. I forgot to mention that he was handcuffed with his hands behind his back.

We finally got to the jail in Yuma and got him booked. The next morning I went to the sheriff's office to check in. The jailer asked me what in the h... we did to the prisoner last night. I told him we did nothing; we were just transporting him from Salome to Yuma. Well, it turns out the prisoner suffered a ruptured appendix at the jail. He had to be rushed to the hospital for emergency surgery.

MORE THAN JUST A TRAFFIC VIOLATION
Tom Gosch #1172

In the spring of 1973, I was just months out of the academy and patrolling I-40 east of Ash Fork. In the spirit of the philosophy that "eight a day keeps the sergeant away," I was sitting at the "fishing hole" watching the intersection of I-40 and US89. In those days, it was a "T" intersection just goofy enough to produce violations and accidents.

I watched a westbound vehicle turn left as if to take 89 south and, to this day, can't describe the unusual movements he made before ending up headed back east on I-40. Sure that I was about to bag a drunk, 1 got right on it.

He had barely cleared the intersection before I hit him with the lights.

In those days, the outside speaker for the radio was activated by the far right switch on the "tree" [a support with five toggle switches which operated the top mounts, back flashers, siren, wigwags, and outside speaker]. Dutifully, I turned on the outside speaker as I exited the car.

As was standard procedure in those days, I approached the driver's side window and asked the driver to come back with me to the right front fender of the patrol car. During this time, I observed three other black males also in the vehicle. The driver was very nervous and apologetic, wanting to just get going. About this time, an APB came out over the radio advising the Safeway store in Williams had been robbed. It gave a complete description of the suspect vehicle and stated that there were likely four black males in it. Everything matched.

The secret was out; they knew that I knew, or should have known, that they had robbed the store. Figuring that I was in deep water, I thought playing stupid might work. By this time, the other three started to get out of the car, and I was yelling for them to stay in the car, stating that I was just going to give the driver a warning. With a strong desire to have my shotgun in one hand and the radio mic in the other, I came to the conclusion that my trusty model 15 SW six-shooter would have to be called into service.

With the other occupants exiting the car, I kept the driver between them and me as I drew my revolver. Thank God that they responded well to my demands that they line up by the car. Now what to do? I couldn't reach the radio and didn't know how long this could last with me standing there with four suspects at gun point.

After an eternity, probably less than a couple minutes, I saw the local deputy, good old Lee Insco [he was a great guy and so laid back], coming by and about to pass. Waving frantically with my non-pistoled hand and probably jumping up and down just a little; I caught his attention. As he returned and came up behind me, in his relaxed country way said, "What's up, buddy?"

I'm sure that my rather excited explanation left much to be desired. As he watched the prisoners, I advised radio of what we had. They advised Williams PD, and they soon brought a witness by to positively identify them and take custody.

Quite certain that 1 had solved the crime of the century, even though it only turned out to be a snatch-and-grab from the cash register, I was quite proud of myself. Turning in my report, to the sergeant, Sgt. Carlton Jones, 95, he advised me that, if we couldn't handle it with a warning, ticket, or repair order, we probably shouldn't be doing it. Busted.

Fortunately, he transferred out. Thank God for Barney Hays.

DON'T ALWAYS THINK WHAT YOU SEE IS RIGHT
Bud Richardson #62

On a Saturday afternoon, I was sent north of Tucson to take pictures of a rollover in the ditch which was reported as a bad accident. Upon my arrival, I found a patrolman investigating the accident involving a truck in a ditch carrying Smucker's jelly. The driver had been taken to the hospital in Tucson. As it turned out, the driver died.

I took my pictures and waited for the wrecker. As the wrecker was hooking up, a man drove up and said he was from Smucker's and he had a truck en route to pick up the load. I told him that a man had already been there and took the load. I thought he was from Smucker's. Yes, you guessed it. He was not.

I advised the real Smucker's guy not to worry, that we would get his inventory back. I then went to the office in Tucson and ran the film and bingo! There was the truck, license plate and all, loading up the inventory. I got Sgt. Jim Hart to go with me to San Manuel, to the man's house that I had photographed, and sure enough, there he was washing off the jelly jars. He stated that he thought no one would want the inventory, so he picked it up. Results....one dead, one thief.

I'M NOT DEAD
Paul Palmer #342

The following, like all good sea stories starts out with, "Now this ain't no s__t!" Sgt. John Consoni told me this story when I was stationed in Holbrook. This occurred before he was promoted to sergeant. (ED. Note: Prior to 1967)

John said that he had been sent to a fatality on the bridge that crosses Carrizo Creek just south of Carrizzo on US60. He was told that the bridge was blocked and that a patrolman from the Globe district had been dispatched to cover the south end of the bridge. John and the Globe patrolman got there about the same time. It was a head-on and the bridge was totally blocked.

John walked through the accident scene and saw a man laying in the middle of the road on the north end of the accident scene. He was obviously dead, so John walked past him to check the vehicle for other accident victims. After checking the scene, John walked back to his patrol car, and when passing the body on the highway, he called back over his shoulder to the other officer. "We got one dead over here" and continued to his car.

Sometime later as they were investigating the accident, the Globe patrolman happened to walk past the deceased on John's end of the bridge. As he walked past, the "deceased" grabbed his pant leg and moaned, "Tell that big son of a b———ch I'm not dead."

The "deceased" was transported to the Show Low hospital and survived his injuries.

THE HIDDEN GUN
Dysart Murphy #906

There was a bond drive going on down in Ajo, and they wanted the governor down there, and I was assigned the job of taking him. He said he would rather that I wouldn't be in uniform. Be a bodyguard for the governor unarmed? That didn't make much sense. So, I got out of uniform and figured out a way to conceal my .38, and we started for Ajo.

Down south of Buckeye, someone had run over an old tomcat, and it was laying in the road, trying to get itself off the highway. The governor said, "Don't you think you should go back and put that cat out of its misery?" I backed up and I'm sure glad the governor wasn't looking because it took me it seemed like 15 minutes to unwrap that sidearm and dispatch the cat.

When we got to Ajo, the meeting was in the women's club. There was this sweet little old lady there, and the governor told her, "This is Assistant Superintendent Murphy of the Arizona Highway Patrol."

"Oh, forevermore," she said. "Does he have a gun?"

"He's got one somewhere," the governor said.

SAN CARLOS
Craig Williamson #518

I was trying to keep the story about my stolen car short. Here is the rest of the story...

My wife was washing the car when she heard Robert crying. The Mom radar switches on, and she went in to take care of the baby, forgetting about the car. Of course, leaving the keys in the ignition wasn't the best idea, and after it was all over, she felt badly about it. Truthfully, she never did it again.

Mary and her sister, Jean, were teaching school in Holbrook when we met. Growing up in the country, both her and her sister would leave the keys in the ashtray! On our first date, I drove her car. Keys in ashtray, first lecture. I put on my seatbelt, but Mary said she didn't need one. So, there we sat. Me refusing to start the car until she put on her seatbelt. After 20 minutes, she relented, belted up, and off we went.

Holbrook was unique. We went to the Roxy movie theater one night and saw Steve McQueen in the Great Escape. The next night we watched the same movie on TV!

I wanted to transfer to Holbrook to be nearer Mary, but I didn't have my probationary year in. Mary came down to Globe to visit. Of course, being a rookie, I had to work on a Saturday. Mary was the guest of Rick Long's future in-laws and went to a rodeo with them out at San Carlos. She met Carlos Salas, the Rice School superintendent. He offered Mary a teaching job on the spot. So, instead of me transferring to Holbrook, which wasn't going to happen, she would teach 5th Grade in San Carlos.

So, shortly thereafter, I went into the Claypool Office and asked my sergeant, Dean Sousa, #750, if I could move to San Carlos. He practically leapt out of his desk chair and told me the tribe had been requesting a resident officer for some time! So, Mary and I got married and lived in San Carlos.

Many good memories and friends. There were several Apache officers who came after me, but I was the first resident patrolman in 1970.

BALLISTIC PHONE BAGS
Dave Denlinger #2747

On a fine Monday morning, a memo intended as a joke ended up in a secretary's mailbox in the Criminal Investigations (MVD) building. As announced on official letterhead, the "Technical Communications Bureau" would be performing maintenance on the building's phone lines the following weekend. According to the memo, they would be blowing high-speed compressed air through the phone lines to blow out accumulated rocks and debris that could slow down phone calls. Because of the ballistic hazards from flying projectiles, employees needed to pick up ballistic phone bags from Supply. The memo escaped. It seems Supply didn't have the phone bags yet. The crisis escalated. The threat loomed for five days. And three floors.

THE DELINEATOR
Jeff Trapp #2608

There are a thousand things they teach you at the Police Motorcycle School, things that are important for young Highway Patrol motorcycle officers, such as I was – so many years ago. But as any of you know, there's always one thing that you have to learn about, painfully, all by yourself.

I was sent to the scene of a multiple=car crash at the intersection of I-10 and I-17, two major highways here in Phoenix. A little jockeying of cars off of the road, and we were able to put them all in the "safety zone," in the dirt – well off the highway.

As I was filling out the paperwork, something made me look over my shoulder, and I saw a woman with a look of horror on her face . . . broken down in the middle of the highway . . . cars buzzing around her. With a feeling of superhero, I ran out to her and barked out, confidently, "Don't worry, ma'am. I can help you. Put your car in neutral. Turn your key on. I'll push you. See those little things sticking up along the highway? Don't worry, they are made of rubber and I will just push your car over them."

I knew what they were really called, delineators, but what I didn't know was that, although they were made of rubber, they were also held up with big rubber bands, bungee cords, elastic mounts. As I pushed her car over the delineators, they bent over easily, and right as her car passed over, right when I was over them, right when my legs were spread apart to allow me to push that car over them, one of them sprung back up and hit the target; the target that will cause all good men to drop to their knees and pray for an immediate end of pain.

I didn't have time to drop to my knees, but I did tell her that she was safe now and not to worry. I just didn't have a superhero's deep timbre to my voice.

A WOMAN IN THE CAR
Dysart Murphy #906

Horace Moore became chief in 1941, and he didn't make us swear that we wouldn't have nothing to do with no women like Chief Rumens did. But he did say that, if he saw a woman in a patrol car, she better have cuffs on. And sometimes that would be a hardship on the families of the patrolmen.

When I was assigned to the northern district in that year, two of our kids were in high school and were staying with their grandmother in Phoenix. There were times when I came to Phoenix that Elma and Elma Jane wanted to come with me, so I complained.

Horace said to come down at night but don't let anyone see you. That was pretty hard to do. If I went by way of Williams, I'd have to stop and have coffee with Jack Powell, and if I went the other way, it was by way of Jerome. You see, there was no I-17 in those days. You either went by way of Ashfork, or you went over Mingus Mountain and Yarnell Hill to Phoenix. But there was a stop sign in Jerome, and the sidewalk on the right was a little higher than the street and that's where John Law was. He could look down into your car and tell you what kind of socks you wore. Well, that wouldn't work either.

Then, I thought there must be some way to get through this little mountain town without going by the stop sign. So, I went down there one day and checked it out, and there was a road that doubled back and goes around the east side of the town where the front of the houses were at street level and the backs of the houses were 20 feet off the ground. A route bad enough in the day time with good weather, but this was winter and there was snow on the ground. But we had chains and we made it. Old John Law in Jerome didn't have anything to talk about. I often wonder what Horace Moore would do today. We not only have women in patrol cars; they are driving them!

After Horace joined the Army and Ed Bratlin became chief, things were a little different. By that time, we had two-way radios, and that was something new because, back in '38, all we had was a receiver. When a car in the Phoenix district was needed to investigate an accident, the patrol office would call the Phoenix police, and the police would call that patrol car on their frequency, which was the only one at the time, and the instructions were to call the patrol office. That's all the information they put out. Sometimes, we would go right by an accident looking for a phone.

But by '41 they did have two-way radios. Ed's policy was that every time there was a female in the patrol car, the office was to be notified. There was this one patrolman who didn't do that, and in the next couple of days, a committee appeared at the patrol office with a young lady who said she could identify the patrolman. Well. the solution was short and sweet. Ed said, "You failed to call in. Turn in your badge."

MAKE A WISH
Paul Palmer #342

I have always been proud to be a part of the Arizona Department of Public Safety. I spent most of my life with the department. Over 40 years. There are many things to be proud of, but one that really sticks out and one that a lot of people do not know about is the department's involvement in the Make-A-Wish Foundation. More than just involvement, however, is the fact that people in our department created Make-A-Wish. Through their dreams, big hearts, and hard work, Make-A-Wish was founded.

In 1980 two battles were being waged. Seven-year-old Chris Greicius was battling the cancer that was slowly taking his life. His mother, Linda, a single mom, was fighting to provide for Chris while taking care of him, scheduling appointments with specialists, maintaining his medications, and making sure that her seriously ill son could be as happy as any seven-year-old boy. All while trying to hold on to her job as her son's needs played havoc with her work schedule.

One of Chris's heroes was U.S. Customs agent, Tommy Austin. Chris wanted to be a police officer just like his friend Tommy, and he wanted to fly helicopters. One day Tommy told Department of Public Safety officer, Ron Cox, about Chris and his fight with cancer and about Chris wanting to be a policeman. Tommy told Ron that Chris didn't have much more time to live and asked Ron if DPS could do anything for Chris.

Ron called DPS Public Information Officer Sgt Allen Schmidt, and told him about Chris. Sgt. Schmidt took the information to DPS Director Ralph Milstead who said DPS would do everything it could to make Chris's wish of being a police officer come true. This set in motion the creation of Make-A-Wish.

Everything moved fast. Ron Cox and Tommy Austin were in constant contact with Allen Schmidt, arranging a day at DPS for Chris. A day was set up for Chris to tour DPS, but Chris was admitted to Scottsdale Memorial Hospital for treatments for his cancer. The treatments left Chris sick and weak and time was running out. They felt he was too weak to be driven from Scottsdale to DPS headquarters and spend the day visiting DPS.

Sgt Schmidt got permission for the DPS helicopter to pick Chris up at the hospital and fly him to DPS. He was flown from the hospital to DPS headquarters in the DPS helicopter with the Channel 12 News helicopter piloted by Jerry Foster also flying to DPS with media representatives. DPS personnel were there to meet him when he landed.

Sgt. Jim Eaves had his patrol car and Motor Officer Frank Shankwitz had his motorcycle. Chris had his picture taken sitting on a DPS motorcycle, with paramedics Doc Holloway and Steve Lump and sitting in the Channel 12 helicopter. One of my favorite pictures is of Chris sitting on Sgt. Jim Eaves's lap behind the wheel of Jim's patrol car. Chris had a wad of bubble gum and is blowing a big bubble.

Chris then had his tour of DPS where he met Director Milstead and Colonel Dick Shafer, who was head of the Highway Patrol Bureau. Colonel Shafer gave Chris a DPS Smokey Bear hat along with one of the colonel's own personal badges. Chris became the first and only honorary DPS Officer.

Chris won the heart of every DPS employee he came into contact with that day. It is a day no one will ever forget!

Jim Eaves and Ron Cox went to Johns Uniforms and asked them to make a uniform for Chris. Knowing that Chris did not have much more time to live, the people at Johns stayed all night to make the uniform. The next day officers went to Chris's home where they delivered his uniform and watched as he rode his tricycle in the driveway through cones which had been set up. He passed the course and earned his motor wings.

The next day Chris's condition became so bad he was admitted to the hospital. He would never walk out. On May 3rd, 1980, Chris gave one last smile and passed away while clutching his motor wings.

Chris was to be buried in Kewanee, Illinois. It was decided that, since Chris was an honorary DPS officer, he should have a police officer's funeral. Two DPS motor officers, Scott Stahl and Frank Shankwitz, were granted approval to fly to Kewanee to provide a police escort for Chris's funeral.

As you can imagine, getting two DPS motorcycles to Illinois would be a problem. While logistics were trying to be worked out, two local men from Kewanee read about Chris in the local paper and notified DPS that they would be proud to provide our officers with their personal motorcycles for the motorcade. Chris's two fellow motor officers led his procession that sad day. Mourners wept as Chris was buried with full police officer honors.

On the flight back to Phoenix, Scott and Frank talked about how great it would be to be able to do this sort of thing for all terminally ill children. Later, Scott and Frank talked about the idea with others who also thought it would be fantastic. A meeting was held with Scott, Frank and Kitty Shankwitz, Kathy McMorris (wife of DPS Captain Jim McMorris), Alan Schmidt, and Chris's mom, Linda. They came up with the name Chris Griecius Make-A-Wish foundation, and later, with Linda's approval, dropped Chis's name, making it the Make-A-Wish Foundation. It started with a $15.00 donation, hard work, love, and dedication.

From humble beginnings and one brave little boy's dream, Make-A-Wish is now located in all 50 states and in countries around the globe. Over 330,000 wishes have been granted.

ABOVE AND BEYOND
Ron Cox #1101

When so many of us helped make Chris Grecius' wish come true back in April 1980, here's one that most folks aren't aware of.

When Chris passed away, I ran into John Desanti in the hallway at work. He was the president of FOP Lodge 32 at that time, as I recall.

I told him about Linda, Chris's mom, needing money to take Chris back to Illinois and bury him there. I asked if our Lodge could donate.

I don't recall if it was that same day or the next day, but I came into my office and on my desk was an envelope. Inside were three $500 checks. One from Lodge 32, one from MCSO Lodge, and one from PPD Lodge. All were made out to Linda. John went above and beyond, without hesitation, and never asked to be recognized for it.

In Linda's book, she mentions receiving the checks from me, and they were truly a Godsend for her.

EVERETT BOWMAN
Harley Thompson #6

In September 1946 during the Labor Day weekend, it was customary in Williams to have a local rodeo and celebration as had been the practice for years. Captain Jack Powell informed me that Patrolman Everett Bowman from Wickenburg would be coming up to help during this holiday. I was excited about the prospect of working with Bowman. I had heard of him long before I came on the highway patrol.

Everett was well known throughout the rodeo circuit. He was World's Champion Cowboy 1935-1937, had 20 champion belt buckles, five saddles, and many trophies. He was also five times national bulldogger, four times national calf roper, and once held titles in steer roping and team tying. (Additional information about Everett may be read in the 1931-1981 Arizona Highway Patrol first 50 years book.)

The first day of the celebration, right after the downtown parade, Bowman was riding with me, and we decided to go over to the rodeo grounds and make our presence known to the local cowboys. As I turned on Second Street and headed north across the railroad tracks, a local woman of rather large proportions was riding her horse in the same direction we were headed. Her horse suddenly shied off to one side rather violently and threw this woman off on her rather large rear end and took off running.

We stopped to make sure she was all right, then Bowman jumped up on the running board and shouted to me to take off after the runaway horse. When I caught up to the horse, Bowman yelled for me to get close, and when I did, he dove off the running board and grabbed the horse around the neck and brought him to a stop. He then mounted the horse and rode back to where the woman was waiting and returned her animal to her. He assisted her in getting back in the saddle, and with a word of thanks to Everett, she rode off down the road, not too much worse for the wear.

I want to go on record as saying that Everett Bowman was a great guy to work with and to be around. He was a great public relations person who talked louder than anyone I ever knew. Everett was congenial and never knew a stranger. Some of you might remember an FBI agent by the name of Vern Tuckey, whose services I always liked to use in cadet classes. This would be a contemporary comparison. Both were big men, outgoing, and fun to be around.

Everett told me about an occasion when he ran a speeder down in his airplane and gave him a ticket. He said he was working west of Wickenburg and had turned on a speeder but couldn't catch him. So, he drove to his ranch, fired up his airplane, and gave chase. When he caught up with and identified the vehicle, he flew on ahead and found a suitable landing spot, put the plane down, flagged down the erring motorist, gave him a ticket, and then flew back to his ranch.

For me, this time with Everett was most certainly a memorable occasion and one I shall always remember. Bowman was one of the good guys!!!

LOUIE COCHRAN
Chick Lawwill #35

I was given permission to take the family to Phoenix in the patrol car as long as I patrolled and worked coming and going. We were returning from a trip to Phoenix on December 22, 1958, and upon reaching the Tacna area, I called Louie Cochran on the radio to inquire how things were going. Louie answered that things were fine. I told him I would be home shortly and to call if he needed anything.

We arrived home, unpacked, and got ready to settle down when the phone rang. I was informed that there had been a fatal accident involving a patrol car in the Dateland area. It had to be Louie. At that time, we had to take a judge with us to a fatality, who also was the coroner. I picked up Judge Witten in Wellton. Louie never had a chance. He was sitting along the highway in his patrol car and was hit from behind, his car catching fire.

His sidearm was melted onto the metal floorboard. No badge and little else was visible.

THE MARINE
Jack Bell #1777

On one of our trips to Phoenix, Sergeant Maynard Schoen showed me a monument south of Interstate 8 that had been erected by the locals to honor Patrolman L.O. Cochran, who had been killed in a horrific car crash prior to Christmas in 1958. Once I knew it was there, I would always glance over to see it as I passed by in my travels.

While working in the Patrol Bureau, I had an opportunity to attend the dedication of the agency's monument to Patrolman Cochran at the highway rest area near Dateland. Lieutenant Dan Mitchell and District 4 did a very honorable job of setting the stone, coordinating the event, and including the family. Lieutenant Mitchell even petitioned the retirement board and secured a pension for the widow after forty some years. My hat was off for all of the good my old District did around Patrolman Cochran.

I believe it was a couple of years later, Betty Gallery, better known as "Highway Patrol Betty," handed me a letter that had been sent to the highway patrol from a gentleman in Texas. After reading the letter, it was shared with Colonel

Reuter, Major Coleman, and everyone in the office. It was a stunning letter and brought Patrolman Cochran back to mind.

In the letter, the author shared his regrets over the death of our patrolman he never knew. He explained that in 1958 he was a U.S. Marine stationed at Camp Pendleton, California. I don't think he used the date, but said he was onboard a bus loaded with marines heading home to Texas for Christmas leave when they had to stop outside of Yuma for a crash in the road and one of the cars was on fire.

The marines had been asleep but awakened with the stop, got off the bus, and saw the car on fire was a patrol car, and it was said the patrolman was still inside. Jumping to action, the author stated the marines began scooping dirt in their hands from the side of the road to throw at the patrol car to extinguish the fire. The efforts were too late, and they were unable to save Patrolman Cochran. As other help arrived and they were called back to the bus, the author said he found the patrolman's cap on the centerline of the highway, so he laid it on the roof of the patrol car out of respect.

I apologize for not remembering the marine's name. The purpose of his letter was to relate his experience with us nearly 45 years later, and he inquired about Patrolman Cochran's family, sharing it was a terrible thing to happen at Christmas time. We wrote him the most sincere, personalized thank you letter I can recall for sharing his story with us after all these years. We shared the story with many, but I have no idea where the letter ended up in the old files or if it was saved after we moved on.

I've always thought highly of the marines, and this story gave me an even deeper appreciation towards them. If we have an annual CDPSR meeting, I'm going to ask that we toast the United States Marines on behalf of Patrolman Cochran.

LOUIE COCHRAN MEMORIALS
Paul Palmer #342

Jack talks about the memorial to Louie Cochran on I-8 that was erected by Bud Bell and his wife who ran the wrecker out of Dateland.

They thought the sun rose and set on the Arizona Highway Patrol, and they loved their patrolmen.

To honor Louie, they made the cross and erected it alongside I-8.

After it was erected, a dedication ceremony was held at the cross with the Bell's and Lt Chic Lawwill, along with patrolmen from district 4.

What many people do not realize is the fact that this is the second cross to honor Louie.

Soon after Louie's death, Bud Bell and his wife erected a large wooden cross on the north side of old US-80 at the site of Louie's crash. The cross still stands to this day, weathered with little of the white paint still visible.

Later, the stone memorial made by retired sergeant Tom Gosch was placed at the rest area that Jack spoke of.

Louie is the only patrolman, I am aware of, that has three memorials to honor him.

CLARK GABLE
Harley Thompson #6

Here is a very interesting sidelight into a very famous movie star, Clark Gable, and a gesture he made that most assuredly endeared him in the hearts and minds of a young couple.

One of the patrolmen working for me when I was stationed in Tucson was Dave Smith. Dave was a very good officer and a hard worker. One day while working in the Marana area, he had the occasion to stop a violator driving at an excessive rate of speed. It turns out that our violator was none other than Clark Gable. Patrolman Smith cited Gable to appear in front of a local justice of the peace in the time allotted for the appearance.

Mr. Gable did appear at the appointed time, and the local judge was talking to a young couple who had asked him to perform a marriage ceremony for them, but they lacked the necessary witness until, lo and behold, Mr. Gable said he would stand in for them. Gable not only signed their marriage certificate, he also booked them into the Santa Rita Hotel for three days and nights, all expenses paid.

The judge found Mr. Gable guilty of speeding, fined him, and then suspended the fine. He also got Gable's autograph. Gable always had the reputation of being an all right guy.

THE DESSERT THIEF
Frank Glenn #468

Well, I guess it's time for a little confession here. The statute of limitations has expired on this particular episode, so I think it is safe to tell it now.

Ed Teague used to bring all kinds of nice desserts for lunch each day. One day during lunch time, we had visitors. Charlie McNeese and Jim Bob Davis showed up. Charlie, in his usual outgoing manner, exclaimed, "Oh boy! Apple Pie! I think I'm going to get me some of that." Well, Ed started faking spitting on the pie. Of course, if you know Charlie, that didn't bother him one stinking bit, and to Ed's chagrin, Charlie walked over, grabbed a fork, and got a bite of the pie.

A few days later, I was sitting around the armory doing nothing. It was about 10:00 in the morning, and I was as hungry as a bear. I wandered out into the gym and looked in the icebox to see what was available. I spied Ed's lunch sack, and I was rummaging around in there and ran across a piece of dessert. Now, I would never eat another person's lunch, but dessert? Hey, that's another matter.

At various times, this kinda became a game to me, and so, I would on occasion go out to the old icebox and grab Ed's dessert and help myself. This had been going on for a couple of weeks, and one day Ed asked me, "Have you seen Charlie lately?"

I said, "No I haven't. Why do you ask?"

Ed replied, "Oh, I was just wondering."

Well, after that, I got to thinking that someone may be laying a trap for me. You know, the old chocolate cake with Ex-Lax in it or something of that ilk. So after that, I stopped eating Ed's dessert. I suppose that when Ed reads this it will be the first time that he really finds out who was eating his dessert all those years ago.

SMALL-TOWN TOUGH GUYS
Harley Thompson #6

I love small-town Arizona. I think it is because every small town in Arizona has its characters. Some funny, some quirky, and some are just plain old mean. Over the years, I dealt with many of these "town characters."

Some of the characters think they own the town, and they just think they are mean when all they are is just cantankerous. I hadn't been in Holbrook long before I had the occasion to greet three members of the same family for the same traffic violation within three or four minutes. I had started north out of town, and as I passed what was known as Heward Hill, a vehicle ran the stop sign at the bottom of the hill. I pulled the violator over quickly and was in the process of issuing a citation for failure to stop at the appropriate stop sign when another vehicle ran the same stop sign, immediately followed by a second vehicle which also failed to stop. I stepped out and flagged both cars to the rear of my patrol car and proceeded to finish up the first citation.

About this time, an older man got out of his vehicle and started in my direction, with fire in his eyes. He wanted to know just what the hell I thought I was doing. I asked him to go back to his vehicle and told him that I would be with him shortly. Ignoring my request, he said, "Do you know who I am?" (I knew who he was because I had dealt with him before, having taken several sets of dealer plates away from his business. I had also dealt with his son for reckless driving when I was stationed in Winslow).

I said, "No, I don't believe I have ever had the pleasure, sir." He then proceeded to let me know who he was and how important he was. I walked him back to his vehicle and asked him again to get into his car.

He then said, "That's my stop sign, and I'll run it whenever I choose." I told him that the sign was the legal property of the State of Arizona and that it did not belong to him. He continued to blow his cork and rant and rave as I issued him a citation for failing to stop and also the driver of the vehicle behind him for the same violation.

The first violator was the daughter and the second was the son with whom I had dealings with before. Three members of the same family all of whom gave me a very bad verbal tongue lashing and assured me that my bosses would hear about this terrible miscarriage of justice. It was a good day. Nice catches!

Now, those folks just thought they were mean. In the spring of 1950, when I was again stationed in Holbrook, I had the occasion to make contact with a local with an extremely bad reputation for resisting arrest and giving officers a bad time.

On one particular day, I had just come from the highway department yard after gassing up. I made it my policy to gas up whenever I could since, in an outlaying station, you never knew if you would be called out during the wee hours, nor did you know how long you would be gone.

As I approached Penrod's Bar, located on the south side of the railroad tracks in Holbrook, I saw a vehicle slowly moving with its right side wheels up on the sidewalk. The vehicle rolled to a stop near the bar entrance. I stopped right behind the vehicle and lit it up with the red light and approached the driver. As I looked into the vehicle, I immediately recognized the local bad guy, whom I shall call Old Mean Dude. He was drunker than seven hundred dollars.

Crap, I thought, *why me?* So, I said, "Hey, Old Mean Dude, what in the world are you doing up on the sidewalk?"

He smiled and said, "I told my wife that I would pick her up at the front door, and that's just what I intend to do."

"Old Mean Dude," I said, "You know that I can't let you do that. How will people get where they are going if you have the sidewalk blocked?"

"Hell," he said, "I don't know, and I don't care. I'm just here to pick up my wife." By now he is out of his vehicle and weaving around all over the place.

So, I said, "Come over here, Old Mean Dude, and sit down and let's talk this over." I led him to my patrol car and seated him in the right front seat, and I got in on the driver's side.

He looked at me and said, "Are we going to jail?"

"Yes," I said, "We're going."

"Are you going to handcuff me?" he asked.

"Hell no, Old Mean Dude. You and I are good friends, and I don't think it will be necessary." I knew this was wrong, but I had not placed him under arrest and my reasoning was that, as long as we were talking friendly and since it was only four or five blocks to the sheriff's office, it would be to our mutual benefit if we could avoid an altercation, plus remembering this guy is 6'3" and weighs about 240 pounds and he has always resisted arrest before.

When we reached the sheriff's office, I helped him out, and we went into the booking desk to take care of business. All this time, I'm joking with him, and he is being cooperative. I wrote him up for DWI and in he goes. The booking deputy and two city officers along with another deputy were standing there open-mouthed. They said nothing until the door clanged shut, and then they wanted to know how I got him there without a fight. "Simple," I said. "I just convinced him we were damned good friends!"

Later on in the spring of 1951, my partner, Billy Sorrels. and I were both promoted to Lieutenant and transferred from Holbrook. We were relieved by Patrolmen Carl Back and Don Naval. About a month later, I had to return to Holbrook for a court appearance, While I was there, one of Sheriff Ben Pearson's deputies told me an interesting story.

He said that he was in the office when one of the locals whom I had arrested several times for DWI came into the office and spoke to Patrolman Carl Back, who was sitting at a desk doing some paperwork.

The man tapped Patrolman Back on the shoulder and said, "What would you do, little man, if I got drunk and you tried to arrest me and I resisted?" Yep, you guessed it. It was Mean Old Dude.

Patrolman Back very slowly stood up, looked him up and down, then stuck his finger into Mean Old Dude's belly and said, "I'd probably shoot you just about here."

Mean Old Dude laughed and said, "Little man, you and I are going to get along just fine."

Shortly after I had been in Williams, they had a Labor Day celebration and rodeo. During this time I often assisted the city PD when asked. There was a minor 961 at the local railroad crossing, and they asked me to investigate it.

During the investigation, it was determined that one of the drivers, whom I shall call Tex, was extremely intoxicated. I told a couple of the city officers that I was going to arrest old Tex and book him into the local jail. At this point they pleaded with me to just write a ticket. He was well known to them, and they would vouch for his appearance at the appointed time. They stated that he was a long-time resident who worked as a cowboy and was a good guy. So, for the sake of good public relations with the local boys, I relented and wrote old Tex for DWI and cited him to appear in court.

A couple of days later, my captain, Jack Powell, confronted me about the situation and wanted to know why I had not put Tex in jail. I explained what had occurred with the local PD and that, for the sake of good relations, I had done what they asked. The captain then proceeded to chew on me pretty hard and explained to me why they had gone to such great lengths to make sure he was not arrested.

Now, what he told me cannot be authenticated and it may be only "BS" as far as it goes, but this is what he said. When old Tex was in the marines during WWII, he was stationed at Camp Pendleton when he went across the border into Mexico, got a little too drunk, and the local gendarmes tried to arrest him. The result was that he put four or five of them in the local hospital and came back across the border a free man. Later, while in San Francisco, he got drunked up again, and the local PD tried to put him in the Bastille, and again, old Tex put several officers in the hospital and walked away.

To put this in perspective, I should describe old Tex. He was not too tall, about 5'9" or so, and weighed about 230 pounds. He was thought of locally as a damned tough cookie, and they had trouble with him before, and they didn't want to do it again. The captain told me in no uncertain terms that if I should have the occasion to stop him for DWI that I was to put him in jail. Period!

Well, several months went by, and then one night as I came into town, I saw an old pickup fail to stop at the intersection across from the Sultana Bar. I pulled the vehicle over at the next intersection. Wouldn't you know it? It was old Tex and he was stoned!

I got him out of the truck and placed him under arrest. At this time he told me to go f--k myself, that he wasn't going anywhere with me. So, we went to "Fist City" with a passion. Fortunately for me, old Tex would swing, I'd duck and then hit him with everything I had, including a beaver-tailed sap. This, for the most part, would put old Tex down, but he'd get back up and I would have to put him down again.

I broke a finger in my left hand, and after a good long time, I found myself getting nowhere fast. So, in desperation, I pulled my gun, stuck it in his middle, and told him, "Get into the patrol car, or I'm going to shoot you."

I'll be damned if he didn't stop resisting and said, "Well, all right, if that's the way you feel about it." He then walked over and got into the right front seat, and I drove him the few blocks down to the local jail.

I got him out of the car, and we started for the front door. Then he bowed up again, and we started all over again. There were three city officers inside the building, and they saw what was happening and came out to assist. We finally got old Tex in a cell.

Now, old Tex was a mess. I had really worked him over with the sap. Both eyes were swollen nearly shut, his nose was broken, and he was peeled up pretty good. As I said before, old Tex never hit me with anything but glancing blows or he would have probably put me in the hospital too. He was just simply too drunk on this occasion to do any great harm.

The following day, several people came down to the jail just to look at old Tex. They couldn't believe he was in the pokey!

The other part of this story is that, after Tex got out of the county jail, where he served 90 days, he came back to Williams. His wife called me one night and told me that Tex had a gun and he was looking for me. So, I went downtown and parked where we normally parked at night, and pretty soon, here comes old Tex. I got out of the patrol car and stepped up on the sidewalk and started walking towards him.

When we got about 10 feet from each other, I said, "Tex, are you sure you really want to do this?"

He looked at me for a moment and then said, "No, guess not." He turned around and walked off.

Later, we had an occasion to talk to one another, and we became very good friends. Tex told me that he respected me because I had done what nobody else had been able to do. Later, Tex even rode with me once in a while.

SHE'S NO LADY
Larry Jensen #819

When I was in the Academy in 1972, in the 15th week, I was riding with Frank Healy, #359, in Globe. We were dispatched to US70 and SR77 for a 962 one-vehicle accident. When we arrived at the scene, we found a young, black couple, very nice and friendly. The male was the driver, and the female was in the back of the camper.

This was at night, and the driver was not paying attention going northbound on SR77, when he didn't see the stop sign. This was a T-intersection. He drove over US70 and went down a creek bed. I was assisting the ambulance driver and was able to get her onto a gurney and into the ambulance. The ambulance then took the injured lady to Gila General Hospital.

When we arrived at the hospital, I spoke with a nurse. When she brought their IDs out to me, they indicated that both of the IDs were males!

I advised her that "No, one was a female."

That's when Frank started laughing. He asked if I really couldn't see that the person that looked like a female was actually a male also? The nurses all had a good laugh too. That got around really quick that I could not tell that she was really a guy. That was with me for twenty years! (Hahaha)

MULE SKINNER BLUES
John Kennedy #119

When I was working out of Cordes, I got a call for a 961 south of Cordes on I-17. When I arrived at the scene, lo and behold, it was my father-in-law. He had run off the road and down an embankment in his horse truck. Neither he nor the mules he had in the truck were injured. I asked the dispatcher to call my wife and tell her to bring the horse trailer, and we took his mules to our place.

I told my father-in-law I would call someone to investigate the accident. He told me to investigate it as I was already there. I said I thought we had a conflict of interest. He insisted that I investigate it. I had been receiving some heat before that for not citing drivers in one-vehicle accidents. I felt that, if having the accident, and some with injuries, hadn't penalized them enough, I wasn't going to prove anything by citing them.

I told my father-in-law that we wrote citations in accidents like this. I thought that, with the conflict of interest, I better do what I had been told to do. So, I wrote him a citation.

He came and got his mules the next day. The next day, he showed up with a newspaper article which he showed me. Someone had run off an interchange in Phoenix, and they hadn't been cited. What could I say?

He didn't speak to me for two or three years. He finally made amends though, and everything turned out good, mostly because of my mother-in-law.

A CHICKEN S— STOP
Jim Carroll #2470

I came on Arizona DPS in 1979 and was stationed right back at home, District 9, Area 2, Benson. In 1983 I transferred into CI and really had two great assignments, the Script Squad in Tucson and the ILED Squad back in southeastern Arizona. I gained some invaluable experience while in patrol and the Miracle Valley events in Cochise County and in CI during Tent City and as a primary investigator during the Morenci Copper Strikes, learning how to read people and knowing who the really bad ones are.

In 1985 I decided to transfer back to a patrol position in D-9, Area 2, as my CI job was keeping me too busy to study for the sergeant's exam.

One early evening, I was running radar on I-10 at milepost 300 clocking eastbound traffic. I got a speeder running around 80 mph, as I recall, and pulled out of the median to chase down the violator. The car exited onto the SR90 ramp. I activated my bubblegum lights, and the car abruptly stopped off the roadway prior to the stop sign at the intersection.

While grabbing my clipboard, I observed four younger females in their 20s inside. As I approached the driver's window, I immediately got an earful from the driver about how "Chicken S___ this ticket was!" She went on and on about how "C.S." this ticket was, and I hadn't said a word.

Finally, I had an opening, and I asked the scantily dressed woman for her driver's license and registration, which she practically threw at me. I then asked her where they all were headed, and she said they were all topless dancers headed to the Sabra's Lounge in Sierra Vista to perform. I then asked her for her current address. All this time she kept saying how Chicken S——-this ticket was.

I walked back to my left front fender and prepared the paperwork and ran a 27 and 29, leaving the half-dressed woman in her car.

Upon returning to the driver, I explained the requirements of contacting the court and explained the citation: "Now, this is a citation for 80 mph in a 55 mph zone. This is not a Chicken S—— ticket. Now, this is a citation for failure to change your address on your driver's license. This is a Chicken S——- ticket." She signed both!!

A check with the local JP Court a few weeks later, she pled guilty to the speed violation and to the "C.S. ticket!"

AIN'T GOT NO LADDER
Dysart Murphy #906

Down near Gila Bend, after the new divided highway went in, the highway went through a small cut about as high as a one-story house. Bob Tsudy was on patrol and saw a man standing on top of the cut jumping up and down like he was on an ant hill. He was as naked as a jaybird. So, Bob stopped and hollered up, "What are you doing?"

The guy hollered down, "Who, me?"

And Bob told him, yes, that he was talking to him and asked him what he was doing.

"Can't you see I'm trying to get my wife's attention?" Bob asked him where his wife was. "She's down there in the house" Bob asked him what house. "This house right here I'm standing on. Can't you see, stupid?"

Bob told him that it wasn't a house; it was a pile of rocks. When the guy demanded that it was a house, Bob asked him if he had key. The man ran his hands up and down his bare legs and said, "No, ain't got no key."

Bob told the man to climb down so he could talk to him. The man told Bob he couldn't climb down. Bob asked him why, and the man responded, "Cause I ain't got no ladder, stupid."

Bob finally got the man down and figured he must have been drinking something stronger that Pepsi Cola.

SMILE FOR THE CAMERA
Allan Wright #629

A lot of us remember the riot and baton training we received in District 9 (Cochise and Santa Cruz County) along with the Tucson District.

Several of us were called out to the U of A Vietnam riots in the early 70s. The first night, we received rocks, broken glass, and bottles being thrown at us from the pack of rioters. Some of us were assigned to civilian clothes to arrest the perpetrators. It was quite the experience. Clarence Carpenter wrote his name across the face of his suspects with lipstick.

Not long after that incident, I was called to the office by Sgt. James Chilcoat, #741, at that time. We only had one day unit and I was it. Sgt. Chilcoat told me we were going to the Apache Powder factory as there were riots at the gate from union busters and union workers. "How many are going?" Just me and him.

"Do I need to get my shotgun?" "No, just get in the car." I was thinking, just me and him, rioters, how will this turn out, with the U of A fresh in my mind?

We arrived at the gates, and several union workers were threatening the truckers and union busters entering the plant. There were about 30, some carrying bats in their hands. I thought, *Oh boy, here we go.*

Sgt. Chilcoat popped his trunk, pulled out his North Western Traffic Institute camera we were issued for injury studies and started snapping pictures. The union strikers started talking among themselves and shortly disbursed. Every one of them!

So, I asked Sgt. Chilcoat if we were going to develop the film and go long form on the people that were threatening and striking the vehicles as they entered the property. "Nope," he said, "don't even have film in the camera." We returned backed to Sierra Vista. Riot over.

BUG SPLATTER SPEEDO-METER
Harley Thompson #6

Long before the days of "Courteous Vigilance" and the standard of introducing yourself to the violator, telling him what you stopped him for, and what you were going to do about it, (a standard approach taught to cadets for many years), I had a little gimmick of my own, "the Bug Splatter Speedo-Meter," which consisted of a small 6-inch plastic ruler having inches on one side and millimeters on the other. I carried this on my clipboard at all times and used it whenever I felt that the violator might just be a "hardass or perhaps grouchy".

I would approach the vehicle, ignore the violator, and go to the front of the hood or look carefully at the windshield. When I could see numerous "bug splatters," I would take out my trusty little ruler and carefully measure the length of the splatters, sometimes seeming to be astonished by the length of the splatter. Almost invariably, the violator would say, "What are you doing?" and I would smile and respond by saying, "Man oh man, you must have been going pretty fast sometime recently".

Of course, then he would then say, "How do you know?" and I would say, "Well, according to my scientific measuring device, the Bug Splatter Speedo-Meter, which indicates by the length of the bug juice residue left on the windshield or hood, you have recently been going at some excessive rates of speed."

Of course, by then I'm really smiling or about to laugh, and the violator begins to catch on to the fact that I'm jesting. This usually led to a very nice contact and made the issuance of a citation much more palatable. I only used this procedure on special occasions.

Now, let me be perfectly clear, that was then, but this is now. There is no substitute for the exercise of the use of sound judgment. We used to teach, I hope they still do, that not all situations are covered by a law or a rule, and many times it is necessary to improvise. Improvisation must always include sound initiative, based upon the evidence of the situation in all cases. Discretion is always the better part of valor.

HER LEG!!
Paul Palmer #342

The state fair was always a money-maker, and I am reminded of the week I worked the state fair on the graveyard shift with Sergeant Russ Dunham as our supervisor.

One day, after a long boring night, at just about shift change, we got a call about a car-pedestrian accident at the south gate at 19th Avenue and McDowell. Russ and I jumped in a golf cart and headed for the gate. We were the first law enforcement to arrive at the scene, so we prepared to put our first aid training to use.

The lady was lying in the road right next to the curb. She didn't look too bad, not even any visible blood. Then we saw it! Her right leg was off her body and was laying next to her with her foot next to her ear.

Russ and I looked at each other, each hoping that the other would sacrifice his belt as a tourniquet for the lady's wound. We knew that, in the confusion that would follow, the belt would be lost and never returned. As we tried to out-fumble each other removing our gun belts, the lady rolled onto her side and picked up her leg and began to reattach it.

No wonder there was no blood. It was an artificial leg!

Ever try to keep from laughing when a lady who has just been hit by a car is lying in the roadway looking up at you wondering when you are going to help her up?

THE DENTIST PATROLMAN
Bill Chewning #41

One Sunday afternoon, I was at home in Benson with my family enjoying a rare day off. I heard a car pull into the driveway and looked out and saw that it was my old buddy, Officer Bill Raftery, driving up in his patrol car.

Raftery got out of the car and approached the house holding his jaw in his hand. He explained to me that he had a toothache and couldn't find a dentist's office open since it was a Sunday and couldn't find one who would make house calls. He asked me to pull his tooth. I agreed and had Raftery sit down at the kitchen table while I went out to the toolshed to get a pair of pliers.

I came back in and began the procedure. I reached into Raftery's mouth with the greasy pair of pliers, grabbed the offending tooth, and began pulling as hard as I could. The tooth would not budge. I readjusted my grip on the tooth, and with much moaning coming from Raftery and a few *oh my goshes* coming from my wife, the tooth popped free. I packed the gaping hole with gauze from my first aid kit, wiped the sweat from Raftery's forehead, and announced the job done.

To help with the pain, I reached into the cabinet and grabbed a bottle of Old Granddad and offered the bottle to Raftery. Raftery took a big mouthful, swished it around and spit the booze out. He wiped his chin, thanked me, got in his patrol car, and drove back to Tucson.

Note: To this day, Bill Chewning swears that Raftery did not swallow.

GOVERNOR OSBORN'S TICKET
Dysart Murphy #906

When we graduated from Ellis Watts Patrol School, the governor came and gave us a little pep talk. He told us, "You write tickets, and I'll take care of the rest." I hadn't had the opportunity to write too many tickets when here comes this car out of the north entering Chandler, and when I stopped it and walked up to the car, you guessed it, it was Sidney Osborn, himself. So I did what he told us to do.

Later, Horace called me into his office and asked me, "What do you mean writing a ticket to the commander-in-chief?"

"Well, that's what he told us to do," I said.

He said, "Yes, I know it. Do you remember what you said when you walked up to the car?" I said I didn't remember.

He said, "You walked up to the car, and your jaw dropped, and you said, 'Well, I'll be dogged gone.'"

But the governor meant what he said. He was that kind of man, and there was never any ego with him.

THE HIGHWAY COMMISSIONER
Dysart Murphy #906

One time, when Rumens was chief, I stopped one of the highway commissioners at almost the same spot where I stopped the governor. He said, "You write that ticket, and I'll get your job."

I told him it wouldn't be much of a job if he could take it. But he did, and I got fired from the highway patrol.

(Note…but not for long)

THE COURTESY STOP
Jack Bell #1777

I always enjoyed working the road, and aside from accidents or an occasional call for service, as a patrolman, we were pretty much able to determine productivity and what kind workday a shift would be.

Believe it was on a Thursday in April of 1980, I was working the afternoon shift on US95, in District Four Yuma. I was out north of town near the army proving grounds when I observed a cream-colored Chrysler dropping its speed from 72 miles per hour. I chased the car down, pulled it over, and made a driver's-side approach. I did not know the car, but I sure knew the driver from many other "Courtesy" stops.

Before I could say anything, the driver started yelling, "Bell, I swear to God I wasn't speeding."

The driver was recognized as the Monsignor of Yuma. I immediately thought having a priest swearing to God over speeding is not a good sign. Knowing it was a borrowed car, I made mention the speedometer might be a bit off and wished him well.

As expected, both of our first calls were to Sergeant Hugh Hegarty, and he skillfully balanced the world for me – (Sadly, I was second place on the phone). This was one day I "waved the flag in the area" and laid low until end of shift.

A ROOKIE'S PRIDE
Doug Kleunder #363

Globe, AZ, became my new home upon graduating from the Highway Patrol Academy in December 1966. It was a culture shock for this 22-year-old, single Rookie who had spent most of his life in the big city (Phoenix).

At that time, I was a Country & Western music fan. KIKO was the only broadcast radio station in the Globe-Miami area. They played Country & Western music from 11 AM until noon on Saturdays. There were no sing-song (later known as Civil Defense) radios in our patrol cars and carrying transistor radios was strictly forbidden except during the World Series.

Housing was scarce in Globe. Fortunately, my classmate, Frank Healy, was being assigned to Superior. He literally moved out of one door of his apartment while I moved in the other. Social life was virtually nonexistent for a single, probationary rookie in this small town. It was limited to infrequent trips to Phoenix on my days off.

After completing a break-in period with Dick Lewis, I was finally on my own. Several months later, I was patrolling US60 northeast of Globe on a sunny afternoon. On the flats below Apache Pass, I met a late-model Oldsmobile headed toward Globe at a high rate of speed. I turned and paced the vehicle at over 70 mph in this 55-mph speed zone.

He pulled over when I activated the top lights. The driver was an African male, and another male was asleep in the back seat. The driver was very chatty and friendly.

I told him why I had stopped him and that I was going to issue a citation for the speed violation. When I came to the employment portion of the citation form, he said he worked for a well-known music company. I asked what he did, and he replied that he was a singer. I asked what type of music, and he replied Country & Western. I was a little skeptical, but he signed the citation and we were both on our way.

Some time later, I was in Phoenix for my days off. I met up with some friends, and we went to Mr. Lucky's to hear some Country & Western music. The show featured a new artist, none other than Country Charlie Pride, the same guy I had cited on that sunny afternoon near Globe.

He must have paid the fine as I never received a disposition code 57 (failed to appear, out of jurisdiction) from the court.

Charlie Pride's account of our encounter can be found on page 183 of his biography. It is more dramatic than my recollection.

I'VE GOT GOOD NEWS AND BAD NEWS
Colin Peabody #481

In late August 1972, I took a couple of weeks off out of town from my duty station in Winslow, and when I returned, Bob Varner #438 came by the house to say hi and see how my vacation had been.

I asked him what had been going on in my absence. "Well, I've got good news, and I've got bad news".

Expecting the worse, but being optimistic about things, I said "What's the good news?"

"The good news is we got it back!"

"Got what back?" I asked.

"Your patrol car!"

"What happened to it?"

"That's the bad news!"

"WHAT HAPPENED TO MY CAR?"

"It got stolen!"

Knowing I had parked my almost-new, dark-blue 1972 Mercury Monterey with a new experimental engine installed by Ford at the ADOT yard next to our office, I was taken by surprise.

"What do you mean it got stolen? Who stole it and where did they steal it?'

"A drunk Navajo woman stole it."

"How did a drunk woman get my patrol car? " I was now getting perturbed with Bob's responses, and he could see the veins sticking out on my neck and my face getting red.

"Well, George's car had to go to the shop (George McGuire #231), so he used your car for a couple of nights. He stopped a DUI female in a Volkswagen bug just north of US66 on SR87 heading to the Reservation. He ran her through the tests and she failed, so he cuffed her and seat-belted her in the front seat (this was before we had cages); then he went to inventory her VW. Next thing he knew, a blue blur went past him with red-and-amber lights flashing. Well, George had no option but to get in her VW and give chase. She was headed back to the reservation, not driving over about 60-65 mph, but not doing anything to slow down either."

This was my patrol car, fully capable of speeds well over what the speedometer indicated, now being driven by a drunk female, and hearing that George was chasing her in a VW, which he had probably never driven a VW before, was almost more than I could bear.

"So, George isn't gaining on her much over the next 15 miles, and when he got to Borderland Trading Post about a mile south of the Reservation line, he commandeered a Chevy pickup to give chase. The Chevy pickup had a 6-cylinder engine in it and wasn't much faster than the VW. About 10 miles north of Borderland, she turned off on a dirt road and stopped. Red-and-amber lights still going. That's where George finally got her."

"He got her out of the patrol car, cuffed her hands behind her back, seat-belted her back in the passenger-side seat, turned control of his final pursuit vehicle back over to its rightful owner, and drove back to Borderland, where he finished the inventory of the VW and called for a tow truck."

"Was my patrol car injured?"

"No, only George's pride!"

Bob took me to the state yard, where I carefully inspected my Mercury, ensuring that she had not been mistreated, and drove her back to my house.

When I tried to ask George about it, he said, "I don't want to talk about it."

And with that, the Good News, Bad News story was history in his mind! We gently reminded him of it for years after, though.

Within a month, I had a cage in my Mercury and the rest of the squad who drove Mercuries had them too.

IT'S THE THOUGHT THAT COUNTS
Don Williams #1096

George McGuire stopped a drunk driver headed north from Winslow towards the reservation. He was originally stopped for speed, but it wasn't too long before George determined the driver was DUI.

The driver told George he was on his way home to Second Mesa. When George asked him why he was speeding, the drunk pointed to the backseat, which had five or six strawberry sundaes from Dairy Queen. The drunk said he was in a hurry to get home to his kids before the ice cream melted.

Even at that speed, he would never have made the 65-mile trip in time in the middle of the summer in a car with no air conditioning. But it's the thought that counts.

A LESSON LEARNED
Kevin Willams #4588

I was just a young kid living in Winslow when I first met George McGuire. When my dad graduated from the academy and got stationed in Winslow, George McGuire was his OJT coach. Many years later, I graduated from the academy, and George McGuire was my OJT coach.

I certainly learned a lot from George. Many times he let me learn by making my own mistakes.

One day, I pulled over a cattle hauler on I-40 near Winslow. I got out of the patrol car, and after talking to the driver, I had him go with me to my patrol car where George was standing. I had to return to the cab of the truck to get some numbers off of the truck, and since traffic was heavy, I walked down the right-hand side of the truck. The shoulder of the road dropped off sharply, so I was walking pretty close to the hauler.

About midway back to my car, all of a sudden, a bull in the hauler raises his tail, and the loudest bull fart you ever heard rumbled across the high desert. Then, erupting from the bull's rear was the greenest, foulest-smelling rodeo guacamole you have ever seen. I got covered from my Smokie to my Wellingtons. I looked like the Incredible Hulk.

Dripping bull residue, I walked up to the driver, who had a big smile on his face. One word handled the situation. "DON'T," I said and pointed toward the truck. He meekly walked back to his truck and pulled away. I had to go home and shower and get a fresh uniform.

I wish George had warned me about walking too close to a cattle hauler. That is one lesson I wish George had not let me learn by myself.

FBI TOP 10
Harley Thompson #6

For most of us in law enforcement, we have perhaps a secret longing to make the BIG arrest or apprehension, i.e., a bank robber, kidnapper, murderer, very large drug bust, or some other type of crime. For the most part, this never happens as we go through our careers doing what we are trained and paid to do, and this we all do well to the best of our abilities.

The flyers we have seen in the post office, for longer than I can remember, depict the Top Ten wanted most by the Federal Bureau of Investigation and they show likenesses of criminals. The word *criminal* is more an emotional than legal term. Go to any post office, and you can view the faces on the wanted posters. Like Dick Tracy caricatures, they stare out of the black-and-white photographs often taken in late-night booking rooms, unshaved, pig-snouted, rodent-eyed, and hare-lipped, reassuring us that human evil is always recognizable and that, consequently, we will never be its victim.

But every long-time cop will tell you that the criminals who scared him the most were the ones who looked and talked just like the rest of us and committed deeds that no one ever wants to have knowledge of. What I'm saying is that there are no hard and fast stereotypes.

In the month of April 1964, retired Lieutenant William P. Chewning #41 arrested William Beverly Hughes, one of the top ten wanted by the FBI. Bill was a sergeant in charge of the eastern portion of old District Two, which included both Graham and Greenlee counties at the time of this arrest. I have tried for a very long time to have Bill write this story, but he is too modest. He said it would be like, in his words, "Tooting my own horn." The following is in his own words:

I had gone out to Fort Thomas that day and was talking to the local justice of the peace, Lyman Holyoak. While we were talking, a broadcast came over the radio, an APB, describing a vehicle pulling a small two-wheel trailer, with a man and a woman with a small baby. The broadcast stated that the driver, William B. Hughes, was wanted by federal authorities on the following charges: interstate transportation of stolen property, burglary, larceny, armed robbery, and theft of government property. The broadcast went on to say he was carrying a concealed weapon and was known to be armed and dangerous.

While I was standing there with the judge, the vehicle described in the APB came by headed west. I told the judge, "I gotta go. See you later."

I jumped in the patrol car and caught up with the suspect just west of Bylas. All the while, I'm thinking, *got to catch up slowly so as not to spook this guy*. While I was doing all this, I called both Globe and Safford for backup but received no response. So, I told myself, *I'm going to be very cautious and, at the same time, make it appear as though I'm friendly*. I took into consideration that a shootout should be avoided because of the woman and baby in the vehicle. If I let it go until we were in town, some innocent bystander might be injured. I tried to justify in my own mind the risk involved in doing this alone and knew it was dangerous, at best.

I put the light on him, pulled him over, took off my hat, and, very nonchalantly, walked up to the driver with a BIG smile on my face and told him that the right rear wheel of his trailer was loose and wobbling. I stated that I was afraid it might cause him to have an accident, and I didn't want that to happen, especially with a wife and baby in the car. I also told him that it was a long ways to the next town, so he might want to check it out.

I could see at that point that Hughes visibly relaxed and the tension left him. He got out of the car and walked around to the rear of the trailer, knelt down, and placed his hands on the wheel and said, "This wheel is not loooose!" just as I pulled my gun out of the holster, hammered it back, and told him to put his hands behind his back and assume the position.

I cuffed him and then told him to call to his wife and tell her to get out of the car, leave her purse, and walk slowly back to where we were. His wife did as she was told and picked up the baby and went over to the shade of a bush near the side of the road. I then called a 926 (wrecker). At almost the same time, the Indian Police from San Carlos showed up complete with submachine guns. I didn't need them, but I was happy to see them.

We transported Hughes to Safford and turned him over to the local FBI agent G. Wayne Mack.

Now, Bill made that sound all so simple, but I'm here to tell you that it could have gone sour at any moment and have ended in a completely different manner. The old poopie could have hit the fan!

I personally think that traffic officers are the bravest cops around as they go about their assignments each and every day. Every traffic stop, for whatever reason, could be and is potentially dangerous. You NEVER KNOW who you're stopping, what he or she may have or have not done, and your life is on the line each and every time. And they do this for twenty or more years, knowing that this is the best job they ever had.

One more thing to say about Bill Chewning. He worked for me both as a patrolman and as a sergeant on more than one occasion. If I ever had to go after the BAD GUY anywhere and could choose who I wanted to have beside me, it would be my friend, Bill. He is one COOL cat.

In April, Director J. Edgar Hoover wrote an extremely complimentary letter to Colonel G.O. Hathaway, Superintendent of the Arizona Highway Patrol, praising Sergeant William P. Chewning for apprehending William Beverly Hughes, wanted by the Federal Bureau of Investigation and commending the San Carlos Police Department for their part in the arrest.

Thanks, old #41 from old #6.

I WON'T SIGN
Willie Hall #608

I was working south of Payson and made a stop on a "Gentleman."

His first reply was, "Sonny, I have driven cars older than you."

I informed him, if that was the case, he should know what the solid line was for. Then he told me he wasn't signing the ticket. I explained it to him a couple of times and told him that, if he didn't sign the ticket, I was going to arrest him.

He said, "You mean to tell that, if I don't sign the ticket, you are going to arrest me."

I said, yes, that is what I have explained to him several times. At that point, his wife said, "Sign the damn thing."

When I told Dick Lewis #176 aka The Tall Man the story, he told me, at that point, I should have thrown my pen over the right-of-way fence and arrested him, no pen, no sign. Dick always had a solution for every situation.

THE QUICK DRAW
Chick Lawwill #35

Whenever the Highway Department paint crew came into the Yuma district to stripe center lines on the highway, it was our job to straddle the center line in front of the stripping machine with the red light on. We did this going 4-

5 miles an hour, in the heat, with no air conditioning. It was always done in the heat of the summer.

One time when painting the center line on highway 95 to the Mexican border in San Luis, one of the crew fellows kept asking me about my sidearm. He wanted to know if I was any good, and I told him I did all right, holding my own. He asked, "Can you quick draw?".

This went on and on. He had just bought a new straw, ten-gallon cowboy hat that he was so proud of owning. Finally, I told him at the next break I would shoot his new hat if he threw it up in the air. He agreed and we both agreed that the loser would buy all of the crew a coke upon reaching the port of entry.

At break time, after the paint barrel was refilled for more stripping, the two of us and the crew went off the highway into the sand. The fellow threw his new hat way up in the air. It circled and fell. I casually walked over to the hat laying there on the ground, drew my gun, and put a hole in the hat. His mouth flew open and the crew hollered.

I bet, if any of them are still alive, they are still talking about that incident. It was well worth having to clean my gun when I got home that night.

WHERE THE HELL AM I?
Frank Glenn #468

I was working the night shift up in Williams, and it was about 9:00 at night. I had a fierce headache, and a storm was looming, with a light rain beginning to start. About a mile out of town, I ran across this little VW bug sitting alongside the two lane road on the shoulder. I thought, *sure as heck, if I leave this guy sitting there without seeing what his problem is, I'm going to be called out later to investigate*

203

an accident. So, as bad as I felt, I stopped to see what the problem might be.

After turning around, I pulled in behind the VW and turned on those magic lights that indicate, HERE IS A TARGET! As I walked up to the driver's side, I knocked on the window, and the driver rolled down the window. The guy looked drunk. You know how it is after you have arrested a few of these guys, you can almost always tell.

I invited him back to have a seat in my patrol car and was filling out that form that we used to use with all those questions, and I came to the question, "Do you know where you are?"

He said, "Sure, my brother-in-law's house is just down the road a little bit." Well, I knew that there was nothing out there down the road a little bit except more pine trees.

I asked, "What was the last town you passed through?"

He named off some town that I had never heard of, so then I asked him what state this town is in, and he replied, "Oklahoma."

I asked him to read the words on my AHP shoulder patch, this being before we became DPS. I could see him mouthing the words, and then he looked at me and said, "You have to be shi__ing me!" I couldn't get him to believe me.

When I was in the process of booking him in the Williams jail, the Williams PD dispatcher came back to see what was going on. I told the drunk to ask her where he was. The dispatcher got a really funny look, and when he asked her, she replied, "Williams." I then asked the dispatcher to tell him what state Williams was in. Needless to say, the drunk still did not believe her either.

The next morning, just before I took him in to see the judge, I asked him if he still believed he was in Oklahoma.

He gave me a sheepish kinda look and said, "No, I was just kidding you."

God only knows how this drunk kept from wrecking himself or someone else on his trip from Oklahoma to Williams. I bet the people he was staying with were wondering where he was. Of course, my last contact with this fellow ended when I took him before the judge, so I had no idea if those people really existed or whether he was even coming from Oklahoma, because he had California plates on the car as I remember.

A BOY AND A SILVER BULLET
Harley Thompson #6

I first want to give credit where credit is due to retired Sgt. Greg Girard for reminding me of this story and some of the details. I remember the incident; however, the exact location escapes me, but it was someplace in the southern part of the state.

Another patrolman and I were having lunch in a booth next to a young boy and his mother. The young man kept staring at us and looking at our badges, gun belts, and other equipment. He seemed to be extremely curious. We smiled at him and winked, and he smiled and kept watching us until his mother told him to turn around and eat his dinner.

It wasn't but a few seconds later when he again turned around and was looking at us again. His mother spoke sharply to him, telling him to turn around and eat his dinner. Another minute passed, and here he was back watching the other patrolman and me again. This time the mother screamed at the boy like some old harpy and said, "If you don't turn around and finish eating your peas, I'm going to have these officers put you in jail."

The little boy whirled around and I lost it! I came up out of that booth with fire in my eyes, and I sat down next to the boy and I said, "Young man, don't you ever believe for a minute what your mother is saying because it is not the truth. A police officer is the best friend you will ever have when you are lost, sick, or hungry. If you don't know where you are, just find a police officer, and he will take good care of you. He will feed you and give you something to drink, find your parents for you, take you to the hospital, or do whatever may be needed, but he will not put you in jail and most certainly for not eating your peas. I don't like peas either."

His mother spoke up about that time and said, "Oh, I'm sorry, I didn't mean it that way".

I said, "You are sorry, and you should be. It's people like you that make their children grow up hating policemen and being afraid of them, when what you should be doing is teaching them to respect the police and tell them that the police are there to protect them and keep them from harm."

Then I turned to the little boy and said, "Young man, I'm going to give you something to remember me by." And with that, I took a silver bullet from my cartridge holder and gave it to him. I told him, "This is to remind you that I am your friend. Keep it in a safe place." With that, the other patrolman and I left.

I fully expected that very soon I would be called up on the carpet with some scathing report as a result of this incident, but it didn't happen. I always tried to keep in mind the motto of the department, "Courteous Vigilance," but in this case, I truly lost it!

Thanks for jogging my memory, Greg.

NO BRAKES!
Vern Andrews #264

I pulled over a car on I-40 east of the Petrified Forest because the driver looked guilty. I had him out of his car, and I ran a registration check and a check for stolen. As I was waiting for radio to call back with the information, the driver and I were getting along fine. We were joking around about his car, and he kept telling me he thought he could outrun me if I chased him. I got to thinking maybe I was wrong. This seemed like a pretty good guy after all.

As we were visiting, I looked down the road and saw a patrol car headed my way with his top mounts flashing. He was really covering ground fast, so I assumed that he was responding to an accident. It was Don Sipes, and as he got closer to us, all of a sudden all you could hear was brakes squalling as Don flew passed us. Don had a 1967 Chevrolet and was constantly having brake problems with his car.

I laughed as Don passed us, and then he threw the car in reverse and headed back to us. By now, the violator was laughing. Don finally got behind us, and he jumped out of his patrol car and ran up to the violator and threw him over the trunk of my patrol car and began cuffing him. The violator and I stopped laughing.

I thought Don had lost his mind. Don secured the violator and then told me the car was stolen and the driver had felony warrants. The dispatcher had told Don to change radio channels, and then she gave him the information on my violator. That's why I had no idea what in the world was going on. On the way to jail, the violator told me that he liked me more than Don.

THE WARNING
Colin Peabody #481

One morning, Vern wrote a warning to a driver from St. Louis for speeding. An hour and a half later, he was a delayed fatality at MP235 in my area. He went 63 at the hospital. He was impaled on the steering column when his Mercury ran off the highway and hit a dirt embankment at about 65 mph. I found the warning in the Mercury.

THE DAY I MADE AN APPALOOSA
Bill Chewning #41
J.R. Ham #142

In 1962 I was a sergeant stationed in Safford. Being a small country town, there were a lot of people who owned horses. Joe Layton, the undersheriff of Greenlee County, loved Appaloosa horses and was willing to pay anything for one. He found a local rancher who said his Appaloosa was recently bred, and when the colt was born, he would sell it to him.

That's all we ever heard, Appaloosa, Appaloosa, Appaloosa. Every conversation with Joe eventually somehow got back to his Appaloosa. He was like an expectant father. Finally, the colt was born, and to Joe's amazement, the horse had no spots. An Appaloosa with no spots. Go figure. He was told that eventually the colt would have spots, that sometimes it takes a while.

Every evening when Joe got off work, he would take his son over to the ranch and enter the pasture his colt was in. By lantern light, they would walk around the colt, looking for spots. Each day, his son would say, "No spots, Dad."

One afternoon, I took a large piece of cardboard and cut irregular holes in it and got myself a bucket of paint. I took back roads so I wouldn't be seen and headed to the ranch and the Appaloosa pony. With my piece of cardboard, a bucket of paint, and a brush, and with Sid, a deputy with the Greenlee County Sheriff's Office who I had enlisted to help me hold the pony, we entered the pasture. With Sid holding the pony, I held the cardboard with the holes in it next to the pony's flank and began painting spots. By the time we were finished, the pony was a real Appaloosa!

We left the ranch and. again taking back roads so we wouldn't be seen. headed back to Safford. That evening. Joe and his son headed to the ranch with their lantern to check the pony for spots. As the son held the lantern, he walked around the pony and excitedly yelled, "He's got spots. Dad. Our Appaloosa has spots."

Joe walked around the pony admiring the spots and rubbing the pony's flank. He began to feel something strange and looked down at his hands, which were now covered with still-damp paint! Now, Joe didn't take kindly to this practical joke and called the highway patrol dispatcher to find out when I was working and in what area that day. He knew it was me but couldn't prove it.

The dispatcher was no help at all. He fussed, he fumed, he ranted, but he never found out who had painted his Appaloosa. Turns out, his pony finally did get spots, but they were tiny dots covering the pony's flank looking more lie freckles than Appaloosa spots.

THE PHONE CALL
Harley Thompson #6

When my office was in the training building across the compound, we had a pretty good group of jokesters, and we tried to utilize our various talents at every opportunity. One I recall vividly. The victim was Sergeant Jerry Wenzel, who was always good for a well-executed funny since he would, more often than not, really come apart at the seams.

On this particular day, I just happened to be in the office when someone said, "Here comes the sergeant."

I reached over and picked up his phone as the sergeant came into the office and began to carry out a pseudo-conversation which went something like this. "Why, yes, sir, I'll be most happy to help you in any way I can. What seems to be the matter?" I then pretended to listen and then spoke into the phone, "Well, no, sir, I really can't comment about that kind of situation because I was not there." I pretended to listen again. "Well, no, sir, I won't be a party to that at all. It is not our policy to take that kind of action under the circumstances."

I pretended to listen for a long time, acting as if I was becoming aggravated. Loudly I said, "You don't have to be nasty about it. Well now, to hell with you, too! I really don't give a sh-- what you do. Well, $^%%# too! Why don't you just come down here you miserable (*&^%#%%W&$^%, and I'll be happy to kick your %&%^#%$&* all over the compound. You want my name? Its Wenzel, Sergeant Jerry Wenzel you ^%$^##$. ^%$^#$^$^%#^%! I hope your mother crawls out from under the porch when you get home and bites you!" With that, I slammed the phone down and looked into the terrified eyes of the good sergeant Wenzel and said to him, "This guy will be down here shortly to kick your butt. Please take care of him, Jerry."

With that, I got up and left the office. Jerry followed me down the hallway all the way to my office almost with tears in his eyes and said, "Captain, how could you do this to me? I thought we were good friends."

Finally, I told him that there had been no one on the line. I just made it up as I went along. Old Jerry was so relieved he couldn't think of anything to say. That little joke made my day.

THE ELK CALL
Paul Palmer # 342

When Lt. Dave McDowell was assigned to the training division, an ever-present item always sat on the corner of his desk. It was a brass horn, a brass elk call. From the mouthpiece, it curled around in a loop, and the bell of the horn ended up pointed back at your face.

Of course, anytime someone visited Dave, they would at some point pick up the horn and ask Dave about it. He would explain that it was an elk horn that he used, with great success he would add, whenever he got a chance to go elk hunting. Naturally, the person would put the horn to his mouth, and Dave would tell him not to blow it because it was very loud and would interrupt the students in the classroom at the end of the hall.

Dave would have to warn them several times, but the temptation would be too great. With a great breath of air, they would blow the horn only to have talcum powder that was resting in the loop of the horn hit them full in the face. They would sit there with their face covered with talc, a look of shock on their face, eyes as big as hubcaps, and with their jaw hitting the floor as Dave would roar and laugh until tears streamed down his face. I don't know how many times those of us assigned to the training division saw this, but each time it was just as hilarious as before.

One day, after getting the elk hunting spiel from Dave, Rocky, the mailman, asked if he could borrow the elk call and go scare the women in data entry, which were being temporarily housed in the training division. After getting approval from Dave, Rocky was followed down the hall by almost the entire training division staff. Rocky hid the horn under his shirt and entered the room filled with the data entry personnel. He casually walked around, saying hi to each woman, (Rocky was quite a flirt) and made his way to the back of the room.

As we peeked around the door frame, Rocky, standing in the back of the room, slid the elk call from under his shirt and placed it to his lips. You could see his chest expand as he took in a deep breath and then blasted the horn. To this day, I can still see the look on Rocky's talc-cover faced. Stunned disbelief! Of course, we all roared, and the women turned around to see what was so funny and, seeing Rocky, began to roar along with the rest of us. Rocky stood frozen to the spot, too shocked to move.

Later, an officer who we will not identify sat at Dave's desk, turning the elk call over and over in his hands looking at it. He had just witnessed Rocky's initiation with the elk call. He then asked Dave if it really worked. Dave got a funny look on his face, and then began telling how well the horn worked in calling elk. The officer smiled and then put the horn to his lips and gave a hearty blow into the horn. Of course, there was still some talc left in the horn, and the officer, just like Rocky, sat there in stunned silence, his face covered in talc. The building erupted in Dave's laughter.

We couldn't figure out what had happened. We knew there was no one in Dave's office but the officer who had returned the elk call. He wouldn't have!!?? He did!

ESCAPE PLAN?
Brad Butler #1058

It was 1984, and I worked in HPB as Major Goodman's admin sergeant, and Sgt. Jim Eaves was the admin for Major Ernie "Iron Pants" Johnson.

Jim was extremely goosey and also loved to play pranks like sending you something in an official envelope, and when you opened it, he had a paperclip set on a twisted rubber band so, when you opened it, the thing sounded like a rattlesnake going off, scaring the heck out of me and others.

Because I knew Jim was very goosey, I got the bright idea to beat him to the office, hide under his desk, and wait to grab his legs as he sat down. Jim jumped in the air, ran in place for a few minutes, and then snatched my 160-pound body from under the desk and held me in midair.

Major Johnson was watching all of this action and laughing so hard. He told me I executed the plan perfectly, except for I didn't have an escape plan.

Just one of the things that kept us alert at the old HPB.

THE MAYOR OF SAN LUIS
Chick Lawwill #35

Any time a senator or legislator requested transportation, it was the patrol's responsibility to chauffeur them around to the places they wanted to go. Colonel Hathaway asked me to attend to their needs when they were in Yuma.

A lot of the dignitaries, when they came to Yuma, the first place they wanted to go was San Luis, Mexico, to party. I was allowed to drive my patrol car over the line, and I became known laughingly as "The Mayor of San Luis."

After I had investigated three head-on traffic fatalities with 16 fatalities and 12 injured, I was given the title "The Fatality Kid."

The other titles bestowed on me are not printable.

SURPRISE, SURPRISE
Harley Thompson #6

I don't know if anyone else on the department has ever encountered this situation before because it is entirely unique.

Right after I was transferred and assigned to Tucson, we had three new cadets come down to the district for assignment. One of those new officers was assigned to Tucson. I shall call him Chicago, since that was where he was born and raised. Old Chicago, incidentally, had the foulest vocabulary I have ever heard in my life, coupled with the dees, does, and dem accent. But when he had a motorist contact, he was absolutely great, extremely polite and courteous and had many compliments from the public.

Well, right after Chicago came down to the district, I had him ride for about a week with another patrolman to acquaint him with the area, even though he had already been on the Tucson Police Department for two or three years. Finally, the day came when his coach said he was "good to go." I assigned him a patrol vehicle and told him he would work south on US89 as far as Kinsleys.

Chicago looked at me with a sort of bewildered expression and said, "Lieutenant, I don't know how to drive."

I said, "How in the hell did you survive on the Tucson PD for two or three years?"

He said, "I always rode with another officer."

Well, we took Old Chicago out and taught him to drive and finally got him a driver's license.

There are some other stories about Old Chicago we will discuss later.

OLD CHICAGO
Harley Thompson #6

I've told you about Old Chicago, the patrolman we had to teach how to drive after he was hired by the department. Here's another Old Chicago story.

Back in the early 50s. we had an in-service training school in Phoenix, and several patrol officers from the old Southern District were scheduled to attend. Among those officers was Old Chicago. Most of us from the district stayed at the Traveler's Motel out on east Van Buren. It only cost $2.00 per night, and we were certain that our expense accounts would get prompt attention since the motel was owned by our chief clerk.

The first morning, after a night on the town, Old Chicago was singing and whistling "Oh Delores, I love you." I asked him if he had been on a date, and he told me he had picked up a girl at a local bar. I decided right then and there to put a stop to this little affair before it went any further. I said, "Chicago, was this girl's name Delores?" He replied that it was, and I said, "Oh hell, Chicago, every cop in town knows about her."

"How's dat?" he asked.

I said, "Chicago, she's the Typhoid Mary of social diseases. She is infected with Systemic Gonococcus Bacterium Spirochete. It's a very dreadful disease. It results in the swelling of the tongue and gonads and results in loss of hair."

His eyes got big and he asked, "What can be done for it?"

I said, "You need to gargle every chance you get. Rest is essential. You should get two to three times the normal amount of rest and, whatever you do, do not go out for at least a week."

Well, needless to say, the rest of the training session found Old Chicago very quiet and subdued with Listerine in hand, gargling at every opportunity.

A tremendous change took place in Old Chicago. He became very quiet in his demeanor, cursed not at all, and about two months later, he resigned from the patrol and moved his family to St Louis, Missouri. He entered a seminary and became a minister of the Gospel. He later located in a small town in California and took a position in a small, non-denominational church.

Who knows how many people I may have helped save, in addition to Old Chicago.

THE TWO-WAY MIRROR
Frank Glenn #468

When I went through the academy, it was **HIGH STRESS!!** None of this mamby-pamby stuff they might have now. I mean, when Sgt. Wentzel and Sgt. Sandhegger said jump, you asked how high on the way up! Those guys didn't take any sh-- from anybody!!

When somebody got fired, usually during a class break, we would come back to one of the following situations. When we were all seated, one of the sergeants would come in the room and look around at all of us, then take the poor departing fellow's books and dump them in the wastebasket. Or they would walk over and tear up
his name tag, look around, and then walk out without saying a word. We usually didn't know what happened to the departing guys I am here to tell you that it sure got the attention of all of us!

One day, Ron Delong came to me when we were on our break and said, "Let's tear up Jim Bob's name tag." Thinking this was a good idea, we did just that, except we took his real name tag and put it in his desk, and we tore up a blank one.

Now, for those of you who didn't know Jim, he was always acting the big cut-up and was kind of a loud and boisterous fellow. Well, we came back into the room, and Jim was being loud and yakking about who knows what when all of a sudden he stopped when he saw that his name tag was torn up. He stopped in mid-sentence and was just completely silent, aghast! Sgt. Sandhegger was standing on the stage at parade rest with a smirk on his face.

Jim soon discovered the joke and was mighty relieved. I later learned the reason for Sandhegger's smirk. Unbeknownst to me, that little mirror that was up in the front of the classroom was a two-way mirror! Nobody got in trouble over this, and I bet the sergeants were laughing their butts off.

THE AWOL
Paul Palmer #342

In 1963 I was a Navy hospital corpsman stationed at the Marine Corps base, 29 Palms, California. I know what you're thinking. Born and raised in the middle of the desert in Gila Bend, I join the Navy to see the world, and I get stationed in the middle of the desert in 29 Palms, California. Believe me, tears were shed. But I digress.

I had gone home on a weekend pass, and when it was time to head back to the base, I rechecked the bus schedule and realized I had misread the schedule. My bus had already come and gone.

I was headed for the highway to start hitchhiking when Lt. Chick Lawwill #35, Yuma district commander, came driving up to visit with my father. We told him of my plight, and he said, no problem, he would give me a ride to Yuma. I figured he would drop me off, and I would start hitching from there. But Chick had other ideas.

We had a great visit on the way to Yuma, and when we got there, instead of dropping me off on the highway, we went to the USMC air station. We drove up to the provost marshal's office and went it. Seems the provost marshal is an old friend of Chick's. He told him of my situation, and the marine picked up the phone and made a call. When he hung up, he advised us that there was a flight leaving Yuma in the morning at 0900 and I was scheduled to be on board. That would get me to the base a few hours before the time I would be listed as AWOL.

Chick and the marine visited for a bit; then Chick shook my hand, said good luck, and then he was gone. A Marine lance corporal arrived and talked to the provost marshal. He then took me to the barracks and told me he would pick me up later for chow. True to his word, he picked me up, and together, we ate our evening meal. He told me he would see me at 0700, and we would go to chow and then he would take me to the flight line. My head was still spinning trying to process all that had taken place.

At 0700 the lance corporal showed up, and we had breakfast and then drove to the flight line. He took me in the office and then departed. The marine at the counter looked at me kinda funny and said all was set, that I would be flying to 29 Palms with two lieutenant colonels. As I waited, he kept looking at me, trying to figure out how this lowly E-3 sailor had the pull to get a flight with two lieutenant colonels.

The time finally arrived, and I was taken to the plane. It was a twin-engine craft, and as I got on board, I realized that I was the only passenger. The pilots got on with their lieutenant colonel insignia shining brightly on their uniforms, said hello, then began their pre-flight check. Every once in a while, they would look back at me, trying to figure out who the heck I was. This would be my first plane ride. I hoped I wouldn't get airsick and puke.

We took off, and it wasn't long before we were landing at 29 Palms. I hadn't puked. and I wasn't AWOL. The pilots still looked at me strangely as I got off the plane.

I bet for years they talked about their passenger and wondered who the heck he was to be afforded this privilege. Did Chick have some pull or what?

CAPTAIN BUTTERMILK
Dysart Murphy #906

I have heard some people refer to me as a legend. Not so.

There was a small cafe on the west side of Aguila called Burro Joes. They had pretty good hamburgers, but I didn't particularly care for their coffee, so I always took buttermilk. One day, I pulled up to the cafe, and as I was getting out of my car, I heard someone holler, "Here comes ole Captain Buttermilk." So, I guess that's the legend.

CHINO VS INSPECTOR MURPHY
Harley Thompson #6

In the early 50s, when I was assigned to the old Southern District with headquarters in Tucson, I had a young patrolman working for me by the name of William D. Raftery. Now, Bill was a WWII veteran who served with the Army Rangers in the European Theater. I want to also add that Bill had received every military decoration except the Congressional Medal of Honor, and some of them more than once. He also had a French decoration and others. He won the Purple Heart three times and still carried a slug from a German Burp gun near his spine.

Well, Bill had this scruffy-looking dog which was half Australian Heeler and half coyote. He called him Chino. Old Chino rode in the backseat of the patrol car most of the time, and I never did say anything to Bill about it because, when I was stationed in Winslow, I had a German Shepherd with me and my partner up there had a Doberman with him. So, I felt a rather kindred spirit there.

Well, Inspector Dysart Murphy came down to Tucson one time and rode with Bill for a while. He, of course, noticed old Chino and ordered Bill not to carry him around anymore. Bill, of course, complied for a while and time went on.

Several months later, Inspector Murphy came down again and rode with Patrolman Raftery. As they went down the highway, old Chino raised up out of the back seat and proceeded to lick old Murphy behind the ear. Raftery whirled around and said, "Chino, you son of a bitch, where did you come from?"

Needless to say, poor old Bill got a real reaming, Murphy got a clean ear, and Chino got grounded.

B.C. IRWIN
Paul Palmer #342

B.C Irwin was one of the funniest guys I ever met. We worked together in communications. B.C was an old-timer. He had been on the patrol, then quit and ran a service station. He missed the patrol and gave up the station and hired back on the patrol. Our families spent a lot of time together. But beware if Don Barcello showed up. Things could get wild. Ask Don sometime about the hot peppers from Village Inn.

Smoking used to be allowed in the radio room, and Patrolman B.C. Irwin really took advantage of it. One evening when things were quiet, I happened to look through the small window in the radio room door and saw B.C. standing in the doorway between the radio room and the equipment room just next door. There was no smoking in the equipment room, and here was B.C., standing under a NO SMOKING sign, smoking and tapping his pen against a clear, car-sized battery that was on the radio equipment rack and watching the bubbles rise to the top. His mind was a million miles away.

Not one to let a moment like this go, I quietly opened the radio room door and silently walked over to the doorway where B.C. stood smoking and tapping that old battery, and I slammed my hand against the door and yelled. B.C. jumped three feet vertically and hollered loud enough for the units to hear him without keying the mic. He later told me he thought the battery exploded. I sure am glad he had a sense of humor!

B.C. was funny as heck, and you never knew what he would do. One day, he was dispatching and Col. Milldebrandt was in the radio room for one reason or another. A patrolman called in with a pretty ridiculous question on some matter or another. Milldebrandt snidely remarked, "Tell him to get his head out of his butt and use his common sense".

Without a second's delay, B.C. swiveled around in his chair and, in a manner that Milldebrandt could see, pressed the mute button, saying, "Per C57, get your head out of your butt and use your common sense." Milldebrandt thought B.C. had actually keyed the mic and broadcast his comments. The colonel's face drained of all color, then changed to bright red as B.C. began laughing and telling him what he had just done. That old mute button had its purposes after all.

Rank meant nothing to B.C. One evening, Sgt. Forgia checked out 10-10 with his men at the Range Coffee Shop in Glendale. Upon seeing the cafe was packed, Sgt. Forgia and his men returned to their cars, intending to find another 10-10 spot. Forgia advised B.C. to cancel the 10-10 to which B.C. replied, "Can't, I already wrote it down." Sgt. Forgia later said he was taken aback so much by B.C.'s transmission that he didn't know whether to drive off or sit in the parking lot until his 10-10 time was up.

MY SUSPENSION
Bud Richardson - #62

While on patrol duty west of Tucson in the early 60s, I was driving an Oldsmobile, and Ray Dahm was driving a green Ford with a highway patrol sticker on the right front door.

The officer that used that car would take it out when activity was down. We would drive in the right lane under the speed limit, and when a speeder passed us, we could get hot on his tail. When we pulled up on his left and he saw our right front door, his jaw would drop, and we had a citation.

Anyway, this story is about Ray Dahm chasing a car west from Tucson on SR84, and the suspect had just pulled a robbery with a gun. I got behind Dahm, and when we got to Cortero, the crook pulled a U-turn and headed back to Tucson. I advised Ray to pull over as he was going to burn the Ford up, and I was sure I could catch him in my Oldsmobile. We were far out in the desert, and it was obvious that the crook was not going to stop. So, I pulled out my .38 and fired two shots at his car. He went off the right side of the road and hit a highway sign and then went into a ditch.

We hooked him up, and he complained that I had shot out his right front tire and this caused him to wreck. I sure did not know that I was that good a shot to hit his right front tire when I was behind him on his left rear. Now's the goofy part. Captain Harley Thompson had been called out and was told an officer had fired his weapon.

The Captain, Dahm, and I met at the Spanish Trail, our coffee stop in Tucson. We explained the whole story to Captain Thompson. He asked for the spent shells, which I gave to him. After he examined them, he said, "Well, I hate to do this, but you just got a two-day suspension. One for each round." I protested but to no avail. The captain said, "It is because you missed him."

End of story. I did not pull my weapon again for the rest of my career.

THE NUDE DRIVER
Steve Page #2095

I was working stationary radar about three miles south of the Saguaro Lake turnoff (Bush Highway) one warm December day. I stopped a Toyota pickup with a male driver and two female passengers. When I approached the truck, I noticed the driver bending down towards the steering wheel and reaching down towards the floorboard.

I made contact with the young man, probably in his early 20s, along with two female passengers. The driver was naked from the waist down, the middle female passenger was completely naked, and the second female passenger was completely dressed. Needless to say, I was somewhat shocked, even for a "Beeline Hwy" stop.

I told the driver to get dressed and step out and meet me on the right side of our vehicles. He sheepishly told me that he probably owed me an explanation. I agreed, so he told me that the truck was his, the naked girl in the center was his girlfriend, and that they liked to drive naked from where they lived in Strawberry.

After a moment, I asked him who the lady was that was fully dressed. He said that it was a sister, and they were coming down to Phoenix to go Christmas shopping. I had no words to reply. I told him to slow down and go on his way. Just another day on the old Beeline Hwy.

THE YOUNG DRIVER
Anthony Dees #2052

In early 1956, at the ripe old age of nine, I witnessed a man die on our farm. We called him Blackey. My father called the police, and then he told me to take the Buick and go to Highway 8 and the Y at Gin Road to wait for the officer to show him how to get to our farm. I had started driving at seven on the farm and had even pulled two cotton trailers at a time to the gin three miles away, so he had confidence in me.

The officer showed up in his brand new 1956 Ford. He questioned me about my age and then told me to lead the way. After he had completed his investigation, he told my dad to follow us, and he told me to get in his patrol car. He told me that the highway patrol had the job of investigating deaths on and off the highways. When we got to Highway 8, he told my dad that I drove very well, but he needed to send someone else the next time.

The ride and talk with him is when I decided I was going to be an Arizona Highway Patrol officer. It took me a while to make the leap and join in 1977. I have always regretted not trying to find that officer that was stationed in Casa Grande and came out to our farm that day but thought he was probably retired. Looking back, he could have been around, and I should have looked for him.

My 24 years with DPS was the best and proudest part of my life. I thank everyone that I worked with over those years for being there for me when I needed them.

THE OPEN MIC
Paul Palmer #342

Patrolman Alex Carrillo had to go down to Phoenix to get a new car, and knowing I was going to be on a day off that day and would do anything to get out of Holbrook, he asked me if I wanted to go. Let's see, go to Phoenix or sit in Holbrook and watch the wind blow. Think I'll go to Phoenix.

We had a great trip down. We got his new car and saw some folks who were walking around actually not having to lean into the wind. After lunch, we stopped back by the patrol office, got some supplies, and headed out the gate back to Holbrook. We were no sooner off the compound when we began discussing some of the brass in Phoenix. We badmouthed and complained about these people as we made our way back north.

When we hit Sunflower, still discussing the brass, Alex poked me in the shoulder. I looked over, and he had this sick look on his pale face. He pointed to the radio. The red transmit light was on! Everything we had said since leaving the compound had gone over the air.

For the next 30 miles the only sound in the car was Alex nervously tapping the steering wheel and me popping my knuckles as we waited for those dreaded words from the dispatcher. "Unit, identify yourself!" Nothing. Finally, Alex reached for the mic and called Holbrook. Nothing. He called Phoenix. Nothing. Flagstaff. Nothing.

We began laughing and talking about how lucky we were that the radio in the new car wasn't working. Had it been, Alex probably would never have made lieutenant and I'd still be in Holbrook.

WHAT'S THE CODE?
Rick Ulrich #182

I was fairly new to the AHP, working in communications. It was a Friday night, and we were working with a three-person crew. I was working teletype, Jack "Snoopy" Schwarz was working CW, and I don't recall who was working radio.

Some might be questioning what was this CW thing? Before NLETS, the National Law Enforcement Teletype System, the states used radio telegraph and Morse code to send interstate messages by radio. It sounds a little crazy, but that was what was available, and each state had at least one station to relay messages for that state. Teletype was available through the phone company, but the landline charges were the same as a telephone call, so the cost was prohibitive. Arizona had two stations, one in Phoenix, KOB34, and one in Flagstaff, KPF46. There were four or five radio telegraphers at each station. When NLETS came online, the radio telegraphers became obsolete.

I took this phone call from a lady, and she asked me if we had anyone on duty that could understand Morse code. Well, that was a really odd request. I told her we did, but he was buried in work and wasn't immediately available. Jack was working from the back room, which meant that conditions weren't great for sending Morse code and he was having to make adjustments to the radio receiver and transmitter.

The lady asked me if I would take her name and number and have him call her. I said I would but that it was really an odd request and could she tell me what she needed so I could relay that to him before he called her back. She said she was lying in bed trying to go to sleep, and she said that she could hear the sound of Morse code. Upon further investigation, she determined that the Morse code was coming from her bed springs. She was wondering if someone could understand what the Morse code was saying and then maybe she could get to sleep.

Well, now I am wondering if she is pulling my leg or do I have a real nut case. I talked to her a bit more, and she ensures me that she is serious and this isn't a joke. Okay, I agree to pass the information on to the radio telegraph operator. Snoopy takes a break, and I tell him about the phone call. He looks at me like I am nuts and asks, "What is this person's name?" I tell him, and he gets this silly grin on his face. He says she used to work here; she is a nut case.

Jack says she is just trying to get someone to come to her house so they can lie on the bed and listen to the Morse code together. I don't think Jack called her back. Jack asked me if there was a full moon out. I went and checked, sure enough there was a full moon.

I WAS NOT ARMED
Jim Eaves. #227

This is a story that that I have not shared with very many people over the years. Only now do I feel comfortable talking about it.

On April 26, 1967, my wife, Fran; son, John; and myself were returning to Apache Junction from visiting my mother and Father and celebrating my son's fourth birthday in Phoenix. I had been on the patrol for just over two years.

It was around 10 PM when I had to take the exit ramp at 40th Street. I-10 was under construction and was closed to traffic. As we approached the stop sign at the top of the off ramp, I saw a southbound vehicle pass in front of us at an extremely high rate of speed. There were cars stopped at the traffic light at Broadway. The high-speed driver skidded for a long distance but still rear ended one of the stopped cars.

As I pulled up, the speeding driver was out of his car screaming at the driver he had just rear-ended. As I pulled alongside, I told them I had called the police and they were on their way. (I hadn't called anyone yet. No cell phones in those days). The suspect jumped in his damaged car and attempted to do a bootleg turnaround, but he backed into an irrigation ditch that paralleled 40th Street. The suspect jumped out of his car and disappeared into the darkness.

There was a pay phone nearby, and I did call the police. A Phoenix officer (Kenton Smith) arrived a short time later, and I explained what I had witnessed. Smith requested that I fill out a witness statement.

Using the hood of the suspect's car as a desk since it was under streetlight, I began filling out the statement. Suddenly the suspect appeared out the darkness, opened the door of his car, retrieved a handgun from under his seat, and began walking southbound across Broadway. I ran to Smith, telling him that was the other driver and to watch him, he has a gun in his waistband. (Note: I had not told anyone that I was an off-duty highway patrolman).

As Smith approached the suspect, yelling at him to stop, the suspect did stop and turned, putting his handgun in Officer Smith's stomach. The suspect refused to follow Smith's instructions to drop the weapon. I was unarmed, standing less than 10 feet behind the suspect. The only thing I could think to do was grab the suspect from behind. As I moved in, Smith ordered me back. As I was backing away, both Smith and the suspect began shooting.

To this day, I can't get the sound of the bullets hitting Smith out of my mind. Smith immediately emptied his service revolver and was limping back to his patrol car. The suspect was sitting on the pavement, leaning back on his left arm, and was methodically still firing at Officer Smith as he limped to his car. What I did can only be described as a reflex. I ran as fast as I could and kicked the suspect behind his right ear. The suspect was now unconscious, and I began looking for his gun, which was not found until later.

While looking for the gun, I heard a man shout, "Get your hands up!" There was a truck driver about 20 feet away holding a (big) gun on me. Now I want everyone to know that I'm an off-duty cop. I yelled back at the truck driver that I was a police officer and to put his gun away. I must've been convincing, since the truck driver complied.

I ran to the officer's car. Smith was lying on his back in the front seat with blood everywhere. I picked up the mic and called a 999 998 at 40th and Broadway (officer has been shot, roll an ambulance). Smith had most of the fingers shot away on one hand and was bleeding heavily from his upper right leg. I removed my belt and was attempting to get a tourniquet on his leg when I was suddenly airborne, landing flat on my back on the pavement with a foot on my chest and another gun two inches from my nose. I did my best to explain to this big Phoenix PD detective that I was on his side, and he let me up after showing him my ID.

Officer Smith survived, but I lost contact with him. The suspect was pronounced dead when he arrived at the hospital. The suspect had just been released from the Atascadero Institution for the Criminally Insane in California. My wife, Fran, told me later that our car was parked down range from Officer Smith when the shooting started, and the bullets were ricocheting very close to our car. She pushed our 4-year-old son to the floor and laid on top of him until the shooting stopped.

It seemed like everyone there had a gun except for me. At the inquest, I was asked under oath, Why did you kick the suspect in the head? My response was, "The only reason I kicked this man was because I didn't have a gun. If I'd had a gun, I would not have kicked him. I would have shot him between the eyes." There were no further questions.

DUMB IDEAS AND OTHER STUPID THINGS
Harley Thompson #6

During my tour of duty with the Arizona Highway Patrol, I observed and was party to many well-intentioned ideas, programs, and other operations that went awry. Probably the worst of these was the ill-fated and hated POINT SYSTEM. (I want to point out and make perfectly clear that, in all cases, the authors of these programs were, in their mind, making an endeavor to initiate a program or procedure that was truly intended to make operational features of our department better and more effective and efficient.)

The idea behind the Point System was to increase activity, make more traffic stops, and be seen by the motoring public, thus being a true deterrent to violators. Officers were given points for citations, warnings, repair orders, and other activities. The value of the points varied with the type of activity and was used to help evaluate the performance of the officer. (More points, better evaluations.)

This in itself was totally unfair. Officers in remote areas could never hope to have the kind of activity of those in more congested areas. This system also required officers to stop a vehicle at least once every ten or fifteen minutes, if for no other reason than to check for driver's licenses or registrations. In some locations, you were lucky to see a vehicle once every half hour, particularly at night.

It wasn't long before this system was discontinued!

CODE 500 was another innovation designed to keep officers on the road during their entire shift. Officers were required to take their code 7 in their assigned areas and were to eat in their vehicles. This in itself caused some concern because uniforms got dirty from time to time because of what they ate or spilled. This system did not allow the individual any time to relax and rest a bit.

Again, it was doomed from the start. Imagine just having started your lunch with all the goodies spread out and you get a call to a 963, multiple fatalities, etc. and you are the only officer and you gotta go! This is most certainly not a desirable situation. This program did not last too long.

DUAL YELLOW STRIPES ON LEFT BUMPERS was a District 2 program. This was my own ill-fated idea. The idea was to put two yellow fluorescent stripes on the left front bumper of all my District 2 vehicles. By doing so, I would be able to easily identify my units at night whenever I met them on the highway. I remember the resistance of most of the guys. They told me that every person in their areas would pick up on this in short order, and it would be a deterrent to the officer at night. I insisted, however, and they all complied, with me helping with the installation.

The next time through the areas at night, I had trouble picking out the yellow stickers. Reason being, without exception, the officers simply put a dab or two of mud over the two yellow stripes. Result: I could see the error of my dumb idea and told all the guys to take 'em off. You guys are right!

In any event, we all went right on trying to do our best with the desire to improve the department as best we could with the knowledge that we achieve results through trial and error many, many times.

I THOUGHT IT WAS A METAL FLASK
Paul Palmer #342

I was assigned to attend a week-long video training school being held in San Jose, California. This meant I was going to have to fly. The thought brought terror into my heart. I would rather have walked.

As the time for the school got closer, I became more nervous. The day arrived and Gary Josephson of the video unit drove me to the airport. When we arrived, he handed me a flask filled with whiskey that was in a leather pouch. He said if I got to feeling tense or nervous, just take a drink. As nervous as I was, I was tempted to drink the entire thing right there. But I needed to be somewhat sober when I arrived in San Jose. I thanked Gary and put the flask in my back pocket.

The flight went fairly well with just a few moments of stark terror when the plane hit an air pocket. About ten minutes out of San Jose, all of a sudden, my butt became wet. The flask had broken! I thought it was a metal flask. The alcohol began to burn my butt, and I sat there with my rear on fire, wondering what to do. Then an idea hit me.

I looked for a barf bag in the pouch of the seat in front of me. No bag! I motioned for the stewardess and asked for a barf bag. She brought one and couldn't get back down the aisle and away from me fast enough. I got the flask out of my back pocket and put it in the barf bag and then began to wonder. What do you do with a full barf bag?

I sat there holding the bag as we made our final approach and landed. I will never forget the looks I received as I got off the plane with wet pants, reeking of alcohol, and carrying a barf bag. To top it off, I had to buy Gary a new flask.

A BOOT TO THE REAR DIDN'T CUT IT WITH CAL
Colin Peabody #481

During the months prior to my being appointed to the AHP, I continued to see both Cal Vance, Tom Leslie, and Gary Phelps, who was recently assigned to the area. Cal suggested that I take night courses from Cochise College up on the Fort that were attended by several local officers and patrolmen from Benson, which I did.

Once in the academy, the staff brought in additional instructors, of which Cal was one, who was present for the firearms training portion of the academy. We would go down to the Phoenix PD range at their academy. We were instructed by a large sergeant, who showed us trick shooting and some proper shooting procedures.

I wasn't doing particularly well with my target shooting, which did not sit well with the sergeant. His large, size-15 boot made contact with the seats of several cadets, mine included, along with the threat we probably wouldn't be around at the end of firearms training. On Friday afternoon, Cal caught me and asked if I was going back home this weekend. I was, so Cal said to meet him at the Sierra Vista City dump at 8 am Sunday morning, and when we got done, I would know how to shoot and could pass the qualification shoots.

We met for four hours. Cal told me he didn't go for kicking people in the ass during firearms training, so we kept my extra training to ourselves. I had enough time to go home, have lunch, gather my clothes, and head back to Phoenix.

I passed Firearms and the academy. Cal was staying in a small apartment near the Capitol and let my wife and I stay in there for graduation weekend. What a guy! He did, however, mark the level in his whiskey bottle!

SIGNAL 101
Dysart Murphy #906

Chief Brastelein had to take the governor to Tucson for a Board of Regents meeting, and I was now it. Those were the days when almost every train going west was a troop train and men in uniform had the pole position. Public feelings ran high, and it wasn't very popular to inconvenience someone who was in the service. Many were crossing the United States for the last time as they headed for the West Coast and then on to the islands.

Well, it was late afternoon, and a young lady came into the office and said she needed help. She wanted to know if the patrol could help her. She had a problem. Her boyfriend was coming through on a troop train, and they would have a short stopover in Tucson, and she had no way of getting down there to see him. I was familiar with those stories when someone got a ticket. "My old clunker wouldn't go that fast," or "that stop sign wasn't there yesterday."

But this was something new, and I have to admit I didn't have an answer for it. While we were doing everything we could to help the servicemen, still, we weren't operating as a taxi service. Maybe she was just a good talker or maybe she wasn't. Maybe she was telling the truth. I could just imagine the headlines in the Arizona Republic "Highway Patrol refuses to help lady in trouble causing her to miss her last meeting with her boyfriend who was in the service." We didn't need that kind of publicity.

Patrolman Giner was the only patrolman around, and he was busy filling out his daily report. I said "Fred. come with me. We're going to Tucson"

Within minutes we were gassed up and headed to Tucson. Then it struck me. I was taking a lady passenger to Tucson and I hadn't notified the office. Sure, I could call on the radio, but what would I say that wouldn't offend the lady? She didn't have handcuffs on and we weren't taking her to jail.

So, I identified my unit and said, "Signal 101.

The dispatcher said, "Would you repeat your message please?"

"Signal 101."

"Sorry, but we don't have a 101 on our log."

I said, "Write it down, and I'll tell you about it later." We got the lady to Tucson, and I called in on the radio and I said, "Signal 102."

"We don't have a signal 102," the dispatcher said. Write it down I told her, and I'll tell you about it later.

And that is how 101 and 102 came into being.

HARLEY AND JON
Paul Palmer #342

Recently, I had the chance to drive up to Camp Verde and meet with Retired Captain Harley Thompson, badge #6, and Retired Lieutenant Bill Chewning, badge #41, to look at old photos. (Bill was the first District 12 district commander when the district was established in 1973.) I needed help in identifying some officers in some old photos, and who better to help with that than 6 and 41? Those guys are sharper than tacks and have memories that are unbelievable. I have learned more about the department from these two guys than I thought was possible. I don't know how many times I said, "I didn't know that," about things I thought I was certain about.

We met at the Camp Verde patrol office and were welcomed by Sergeant Moran and several officers who were doing paperwork. But there was no paper. I guess they were doing computer work. As we set up the laptop to begin looking at the photos, we visited with Officer Jonathan Dexter, badge #7277. Ole 6 and 41 kept looking at that badge number and then at each other, both wondering how in the world they got that huge number on a badge.

As we talked about the old days and today's department, I started to take notes. Here is what I found out.

Jon came on the department in 2009 and earns $64,000 a year. (Jon is a lateral transfer, so his wage is higher than the normal entry-level officer) He works eight-hour shifts assigned by his sergeant and gets overtime pay or comp time.

Harley came on the highway patrol in 1946 and was paid $2,400 a year. He worked six days a week, and they were usually 12-14-hour days. He made up his own schedule and never heard of overtime or comp time. Harley retired after 28 years with the department and has been retired for 35 years.

Jon is stationed in Camp Verde, and his area covers approximately 100 miles. There are six officers and one sergeant assigned to his area, and 202 officers are assigned to the Northern Zone with 877 officers for the entire state.

Harley's first duty station was Williams, and his area covered approximately 150 miles. He was the only officer in the area. There were 13 officers in the Northern Zone and 47 officers on the patrol.

Jon drives a 2005 Ford with a top speed of 128 mph. He has air conditioning and an AM/FM radio.

Harley was assigned a 1941 Ford with a top speed of

92 mph. The car was black and had no air conditioner. Mileage was not a factor in turning in a vehicle It was the number of engines the car had gone through. Harley's Ford went through three engines.

Jon has an 80-channel radio, and the car has six antennas.

Harley had a one-channel radio (which worked sometimes) with a nine-foot whip antenna.

Jon's Ford is equipped with a fire suppression system.

Harley's Ford had a nonfunctioning, handheld fire extinguisher.

Jon has a car camera and radar.

Harley asks, "Radar?". To Harley, radar was a new invention used when he was in the Navy to spot ships over the horizon. But you couldn't clock their speed. The only camera was a large Speed Graphic still camera which the sergeant carried.

Jon has a three-tone electronic siren with an air horn and a p.a. system.

Harley had a siren that would finally wind down and stop groaning just about the time he finished writing a person a ticket. The siren button was located on the floorboard between the brake and clutch pedals. It was later placed over next to the headlight dimmer switch on the floorboard. This sometimes caused embarrassment when all you meant to do was dim the headlights and you activated your siren. Not good at 2:00 in the morning when pulling into a residential area. At night, if you used your siren, the headlights would dim or go completely out.

Jon's car has an anti-theft device.

Harley had a set of keys.

Jon contacts the dispatcher to get him any assistance he needs at an accident scene. If by chance he can't get the dispatcher because of radio problems, he will use his cell phone.

Harley would stop a passing motorist and give him a piece of paper with the phone number to the wrecker or ambulance and ask the person to make the call when they got to the next town.

Jon has air rescue and trained paramedics to assist him with the injured at accidents.

Harley had a first aid kit.

Jon sometimes has trouble with the fire department blocking the highway or driving through the accident scene, destroying evidence.

Harley never saw a fire truck outside the city limits. They were not allowed to leave town because of insurance issues.

Jon carries a department-issued, .40-caliber semi-automatic weapon that holds 13 rounds. He has two magazines on his belt with 12 rounds in each magazine. He also has an M4 rifle and an 870 shotgun.

Harley carried his personal .38 caliber wheel gun. (Officers had to provide their own weapons) It held six rounds, and he had an extra six rounds on his belt.

Jon has a taser, mace, expandable baton, and wooden night stick.

Harley had a sap slapper and a pair of leather gloves with lead foil stitched into the knuckles and palm of the gloves.

Jon carries two pair of handcuffs on his belt and has two extra pair in his car. He also has 20 flex cuffs.

Harley had one pair of handcuffs and 3 pigging strings.

Wow! Have times changed or what? One thing, however, has stayed constant. Arizona highway patrolmen are some of the best people in the world. Whether 1946 or 2009, the officers are still friendly and helpful.

When we arrived at the Camp Verde office, Sgt. Moran and his men welcomed us and made us feel that we still belonged to the department. Stories were told, lies were swapped, old secrets revealed, and laughter filled the office. What a great time! I can't thank these District 12 men enough for making us feel that we still belong and that we are appreciated. I'm sure ole 6 and 41 feel the same.

BUSTED
Greg Eavenson #680

I really enjoyed reading about Harley Thompson and Bill Chewning. I didn't know Lt. Chewning very well, but Harley taught us "ethics" in the academy. Carl Svob #375 related that, while walking across the compound one day, he met Harley and said, "Hello, Harley. How the hell are ya?"

Harley responded, "Damnit, Carl, why don't you address me by my rank?"

Carl responded, "Hell, Harley, I don't know from one day to the next what your rank is going to be."

Note: Harley Thompson holds the department record for the number of times an officer was busted and then promoted again.

IMPERSONATOR
Scott Lane

Regarding John "Bones" Matthews, one day back in the '90s, I saw him in uniform after he had worked an overnight construction detail. I commented to him that I would have to arrest him for the then misdemeanor of

Impersonation of a Highway Patrolman. I had to run for my life out of the shop at the Tucson 103!

THE TUMBLEWEED
Ernest F. Tofani #4040

I was stationed in Nogales, and my second Field Training Officer was Gordon Hopke, badge #403. One of many stories I can tell about Gordon while I was being trained was in March of 1988.

While northbound on I-19 at M.P. 28, I stopped a black Ford Fairmont station wagon for unsafe lane usage. The driver, a middle-aged man, appeared annoyed to have been stopped. I directed him to the right rear side of his car and began writing him a warning. I tried to talk to him; however, he wanted to stay annoyed.

While I was writing him the warning, a gust of wind stirred up and a very large tumbleweed flew over my and Gordon Hopke's back, striking the violator in his face. There was a large vertical scratch from the tumbleweed on the violator's face, trickling blood from it. I asked the violator if he was okay, and in a very terse tone, he said he was. I explained the warning and finished writing it. The violator signed it, got back in his car, and drove away.

Gordon kept a very serious face on himself as he returned to the patrol car. Gordon and I got back in the patrol car. Gordon covered his mouth while he began laughing. Gordon said, "It could only happen to you, and you'll probably get a complaint it from it" (the tumbleweed).

MY FOURTH WRECK
Dysart Murphy #906

Shortly after Greg Hathaway became superintendent, he wanted to make an inspection of the western district. I took him in my patrol car, and we headed toward Yuma. We were east of Telegraph Pass and a Greyhound bus passed us like we were standing still. Hathaway looked at me and said, "Well?"

So, we took off after the bus. My old straight-8 Pontiac would top out at 85 miles an hour. I told Hathaway if we rolled up the windows we could get another 5 miles an hour out of the car. We rolled up the windows, but the rear of that bus kept getting smaller instead of larger.

We called ahead and had a patrolman stop the bus. When we got to the bus which had been stopped by the patrolman, we talked to the driver and then we headed up SR95 to US60 to Salmoe and back to Phoenix. Hathaway had inspected his western district.

The next day, Patrolman Lee Shepard, who was stationed in Salome, called and said he needed a new generator, so I picked one up and headed to Salome. Near Aguila, I was flagged down by a man who said he had been sideswiped by a car. I headed after the car. Again, all I could get out of my Pontiac was 85 miles an hour. It was hot and we had no air conditioner in the car, but I rolled up the windows anyway.

Now, at this time. we used Never Leak in our tires. It was designed for our cars that were not used at high speeds. Well, the Never Leak had weakened the fabric of the tire, and all of a sudden, the right front tire blew out. I took out a right-of-way fence and rolled through the desert. Two things in that car were trying to get out. The generator through the back window and me through the right front window.

After Lee arrived and applied some iodine, I was fine. I began to think of what might have happened if it had happened yesterday. The Chief would not have had even a steering wheel to hang on to. (At that time, there were no seat belts).

This was the fourth patrol car I had wrecked in over 500,000 miles. I not only enforced the traffic code, but I believed in the traffic code. I got to thinking that, if I didn't want to be identified by one of those white crosses alongside the highway, I would have to take my problem to a higher authority. Traffic Safety taught us the cause of accidents, but if I couldn't live by it and stop my own accidents, it wasn't good enough. There are circumstances bigger than the jurisdiction of the AHP.

I put my trust in higher authority and drove another half million miles on the highway patrol. The work remained the same, but then it was worse. The numbers became larger on the speedometers of the Oldsmobiles and Fords than on my old straight-8 Pontiac.

Later, I drove a Ford pickup, a '51 Oldsmobile 98, and a '55 Oldsmobile 88, driving over 700,000 miles without a scratch.

TRICKS OF THE TRADE
Colin Peabody #481

Between my sophomore and junior years of high school, my family moved to Ramsey Canyon in the Huachuca Mountains at the end of a one-lane, rutted, dirt road south of Sierra Vista. Back then, Sierra Vista didn't have a traffic light, and businesses were scattered along Fry Blvd for about a mile. Buena High School was at the junction of Hwy 90 and Hwy 92 another mile or so beyond most of the businesses. Very sparsely populated, with the exception of the Army personnel and support folks at Ft. Huachuca.

Traffic was light after dark, and contacts for the local patrolman, Cal Vance, were few and far between. Repair orders were issued by Cal regularly for headlight out, one taillight not working, license plate light not working, and other equipment-related stuff.

Tickets and warnings for speed were hard to come by on those narrow two-lane roads with a nighttime speed limit of 55mph and a daytime limit of 60. One had to develop tactics that would keep the unsuspecting motorist unaware of the presence of Patrolman Vance. The ability to make braking movements to turn on a violator was considered tricks of the trade, and the temporary interruption of electrical energy to the brake lights was often employed, as was patrolling with one headlight temporarily deactivated to confuse the oncoming driver so he wouldn't suspect the car approaching would be a highway patrol car. Once the turn was made, all the lights were restored to working order.

Cal got a '65 Plymouth, and some of those cars had larger top mounts than the previous models had. The lights had large, almost transparent, amber and red lenses, mounted in a thin chrome band. At night, those Mickey Mouse ears were easy to spot from both front and back, so what do you do? Black electrical tape covering the chrome bands, loosen the screws holding the left red light so it could be turned 90 degrees so light wouldn't go through it, but once Cal decided to light you up, he reached up through the window and turned the red light toward the front.

Cal and I became acquainted in that manner over several years of my transgressions. First-name basis and he knew who my dad was, so I became much more observant, but paid close attention to details on Cal's cars. Knowing his duty hours helped! I never got a ticket from Cal, but certainly deserved a few. With his deep voice and Marine bearing, he was not to be messed with, but he was professional in every aspect during his contacts with this kid. I respected the hell out of him.

THE ROLLING FAMILY FIGHT
Tom Ticer #490

My first duty station was Yuma in 1968. I left the Phoenix P.D. after 2 years because I was tired of going to family fights. My desire was to work traffic and investigate accidents.

After O.J.T. and training in Yuma, I was turned loose on my own to work the highways in the Yuma area. I was working the day shift on Highway 95 south of Yuma on a hot summer day southbound toward San Luis when a northbound pickup with a man driving and a woman sitting next to him blew by me at about 85-90 mph. Before I could turn around, another pickup went by me, also at a high rate of speed.

I finally got turned around and overtook the pickups about two miles later. I motioned for them to pull over and they did. The following pickup parked behind my patrol car, placing me in the middle. That pickup only had a woman driving it. Before I could get out of my vehicle, she ran by my vehicle and up to the passenger door of the front truck, jerked open the door, and grabbed the other woman by the hair. She then proceeded to beat her without mercy.

I finally got the fight stopped. Turned out to be a family fight. The woman doing the beating of the other woman was the wife of the male driver. She had caught her husband and his girlfriend doing what comes naturally, and the chase was on. I cited both drivers for reckless driving and sent them away in different directions. Didn't I just leave a department because of family fights??

PATCHES
Paul Palmer #342

I'm going to tell a story on myself about my temporary loss of cool. Normally, I'm fairly even-tempered, except that day in the training division.

I was a police patch collector and went to a lot of work displaying the patches on cloth-covered boards. They adorned three walls of my office in the training division building. When I say I collected patches, I mean thousands of them. I took my favorites and put them on the boards in my office. It took a lot of work, and I was pretty proud of my collection. Whenever I had a visitor come into my office, they were amazed at how many patches I had and would search the boards for different patches.

One morning, I came to work, and my walls were bare. I was stunned! I fumed out of my office and went down the hall to complain to Lt. Dave McDowell. He explained that Marty Dangle had taken them for a presentation he was giving at a local school. Dave said that Marty thought they would be a great addition to his other exhibits.

I went berserk. I began ranting and raving, and Dave sat there looking very serious telling me that he thought I had given Marty permission. I began telling Dave how much work went into my patch display and they probably would come back ruined.

I left Dave's office and walked down the hall leaving a blue streak of profanities. Who the heck did Marty think he was, I ranted, to come into my office and take things. It wasn't enough to rant and rave in the hallway, so I went up and down the stairs to the gym professing my displeasure. In case I left doubt in anyone's mind, I continued my rant outside on the compound.

Seeing my bulging eyes and the veins in my head about to explode, Dave decided to fess up. I took them, he said, to play a trick. I have them in safekeeping he added. It took a while, but I finally relaxed. I even gave a feeble laugh. Dave is a huge guy with arms like tree trunks, and with a guy that big, it is not good not to laugh at one of his pranks.

Dave then retrieved my patches and even helped me put them back up on the wall. I told him I was glad he fessed up because I was about to shoot Marty Dangle. He said he wasn't worried about that because he has seen my scores on the range.

Never a dull moment when Dave is around!

THE GREAT PRACTICAL JOKE
Harley Thompson #6

This is a story that, if I don't tell it now, it may never be told because I am the only one left alive who knows anything about this long-ago happening.

The time of this story is somewhere around circa 1939-40 area. At the time of this story, the highway patrolmen were wearing boots and britches with Smokey Bear hats and full Sam Brownes. Assistant Superintendent J.C. "Jack" Powell was the victim of the joke. He was a patrolman at the time stationed in the St. John's-Springerville area. A local merchant in this particular area was known to be a great practical joker, and no one was immune when he put one of his antics into practice.

On this particular night, there was a dance at the local schoolhouse, and many of the locals were in attendance, including Patrolman Jack Powell and his wife. Jack was in full uniform and had backed his patrol vehicle up against a very large pine tree. Somehow, during the festivities, The

Joker, as I shall call him, and a couple of his cohorts placed a 30-foot long logging chain around the rear axle of the patrol vehicle and anchored it to the pine tree.

The Joker then ran into the schoolhouse and shouted to Patrolman Powell that there was a bad accident about 10 miles west of town. Old Jack runs out, fires up his trusty Ford, and floorboards the gas pedal. The almost instant result was that when he came to the end of the chain everything came to a halt, ripping the rear axle off. Jack hit the dashboard and windshield, and his Smokey Bear was driven down around his ears. No one was hurt, and the culprits were supposedly unknown.

The reason I know about this long-ago happening is because Jack told me and Ray Dahm about it because Ray was going to St. Johns after riding with me during his break-in period, and Jack, then our district captain, wanted Ray to be aware of The Joker.

In later years, The Joker pulled another stunt on Ray, but that is another story.

THE GOVERNOR'S CALL
Dysart Murphy #906

I was in the office one day on the front desk and the phone rang. Every so often, Chief Ed Brastelien's brother, Arnold, would call and he would ask, "Is Ed there?" And that's what this voice said.

I said, "Darned if I know, Arnold. He's around here someplace."

And the voice said, "This is Sidney Osborn. Tell him to call me."

YES SIR! Nothing was ever said about the call.

THE FEDERAL MAN
By Colin Peabody #481

I was working traffic about five miles west of Winslow on I-40 and got a good speeder running about 90 eastbound. I got him on VASCAR and got him stopped just at the Navajo County line going into Winslow. As soon as I got stopped, this guy jumps out of his car and wants to know why I stopped him. I told him I stopped him for speeding and had him at 90 in a 75 mph zone. Immediately he asked if I did a speedometer pace.

"No, Sir, I didn't."

"Did you get me with a stopwatch?"

"No, Sir, I didn't."

"Did you get me with radar?"

"No, Sir, I didn't."

"There is only one thing left. Did you get me with VASCAR?"

"Yes, Sir, I did."

"I want to see it."

I opened the passenger side door, and he looked in.

"I'll be a dirty S.O.B. You got me on the only device that is that good."

"Yes, Sir, that is correct. How do you know so much about VASCAR?" I was thinking he had been stopped for speeding a bunch of times.

"I work for Federal Systems. We manufacture VASCARS, and I sell them." Because VASCAR was such a valuable tool for law enforcement, I told him that, wrote him a warning with VASCAR printed on it, and wished him a good day, only a bit slower this time. He probably had a good story to tell his bosses and future customers after that.

AERODYNAMICS VS AHP RADAR GUN
Colin Peabody #481

We had a newly promoted sergeant assigned to Winslow in late 1972, who had gotten promoted out of Plots and Schemes...uhh, excuse me... Planning and Research, and he had done the study on the effectiveness of our recently issued radar guns. In those days, when you wrote speeding tickets, you indicated if you used radar or VASCAR to determine the speed. You just wrote RADAR or VASCAR on the violation space with the violation code.

Two of us in the area had VASCAR units, and we wrote a lot of VASCAR tickets. The unnamed sergeant wanted both of us to write radar tickets because his studies showed radar was way more effective than VASCAR in clocking speeders. Both George McGuire and I tried to explain the superiority of VASCAR over the radar units, but the sergeant wasn't convinced. His studies were accurate and correct.

One night he told me he was going to ride with me, and we were going to use the radar to get speeders, not VASCAR. I had no choice but to relent to his wishes. We were halfway between Joseph City and Holbrook where I pulled into the median facing westbound traffic. I was holding the radar unit in my left hand, focusing it on the traffic coming towards us. No speeders yet. Where we were parked was just past a curve with a slight downgrade to an overpass for Ortega's Curio shop about a quarter mile away.

A set of headlights came around the curve very rapidly approaching us, and I am trying to get a read from the radar unit but not being successful at it. My right hand was automatically at the ready on the VASCAR, while I am still trying to get a radar reading. No luck. When the car went by, I flipped on the time on the VASCAR and saw the car was a Jaguar XKE, one of the most aerodynamic sports cars built back then, with no flat surfaces that would allow the radar beam to hit and send a signal back to the unit. They had aluminum bodies then, which I suspect may have had some bearing on the lack of a signal from the radar gun.

Once the Jag's headlights cleared the overpass, I shut the timer off and pulled out, hitting the VASCAR's distance switch. By the time I had the distance run in, I had the guy at just under 100 mph. I got him stopped in Joe City and wrote him the VASCAR ticket.

When I got back to the car, I disconnected the radar unit, put it in its case, and tossed it in the back seat. "So much for your precious Radar unit, Sarge." He never bugged me or George about our VASCAR tickets again.

HIGH-SPEED TRUCKER
Jim Berry #2364

My assignment was to District 1 Kingman. I was working I-40 east of Kingman. This was around May 1979 timeframe. I had a Kustom Radar Gun. One of the areas that is east of Kingman on I-40, starts about MP90 and westward down to about MP75, is mountains and significant downgrades. There is an exit at Willow Ranch Road MP87 that is obscured to traffic by a dirt hill.

Back in the day, truckers would always complain about their truck not being able to go faster than their governor on the engine. Well, we knew better. If they were going downhill, the truck would coast above the governed speed, or they put it in neutral and just coasted with the

251

downhill gravity. This is a time before dedicated truck enforcement details.

I had pulled off at Willow Springs off-ramp at MP87 to catch up on my paperwork. It was about 1400, if I recall, and traffic was reasonably light. I had been there about 10 minutes. Incidentally, my patrol vehicle came with a CB installed, and I always had my CB radio on. We used to get Code 34 reports from the truckers, in a time when truckers were actually "Professional". It was before a time of drugs and amphetamines to keep you awake; this being a standard for trucker's these days. Then, the truckers were always the first to stop and help at wrecks before the troopers arrived.

The "Smokey Reports" had lost sight of me. Generally, when I was using radar, I intentionally was usually visible to traffic. This was also the days of the dreaded 55 mph enforcement for "waste of finite resources." Where I was stopped, I had full view of both east and westbound traffic and was actually visible to the eastbound traffic, however, the interstate was separated by a super wide median at that area.

I had my radar gun resting on its side, up on the dashboard, just sitting there operating. All of a sudden, the thing hit 114 mph and locked, BEEP, BEEP, BEEP, it sounded! I looked up, and this 18-wheeler passed my location at a high rate of speed. I reset the gun, and it hit on 114 again. So, off I went and it took me about three miles to make the stop.

When I met the driver, we had the typical driver's license, registration, and log book encounter. The driver actually had the audacity to ask me why I was stopping him??? Like Yeh! Were you asleep at 114 mph? (I also had paced him at 100 MPH prior to the stop.) I informed him that I was stopping him for speeding. He said, "How did you get me? My radar detector didn't go off!" (Oh, so you have a device to break the rules.)

I informed him where I had been parked and that it was after you went by me at 114 mph. He makes this statement, "You mean you shot me in the back." I responded yes.

His response was, "Well that ain't right. The Lone Ranger never shot nobody in the back."

I went through all the babble with him. He was shaking like a wet dog from nerves. After I finished my standard scan of his paperwork, I wrote him out a ticket for 100 MPH" based on my pacing him before the stop. If I remember SOPs, you were not supposed to use the radar from a rear indication. So, I finished the encounter.

This quote: "High Speed Down Hill Trucks," was a standard for this area.

This also happened to be my career high-speed encounter, 114 mph, by an 18 wheeler! It was pretty significant. In hindsight, I should have arrested him for "endangerment." It was a different time.

It was about six months later, at about 2 AM, a 45-foot, single trailer truck had a high-speed rollover at that very location in the median. This was a time when Ranger couldn't get off the ground with the jaws of life and for some reason Ranger was unavailable.

We didn't have a fire department local to the area. A special assistance call for the City of Kingman Fire Rescue was requested. It took Kingman Fire almost two hours to cut and disentangle the driver from the cab as it had rolled over several times and literally wrapped the cab around him like a ball. After they got the driver out, he had relatively minor injuries. He truly was lucky.

THE WHISTLING RADAR
Rick Tannehill - #1235

Another story from the civie side of DPS. Back in '75-'76, the department was simultaneously engaged in upgrading the old simplex VHF radio system to a new UHF duplex (repeater) system, as well as purchasing hundreds of new Decatur X-Band (two-piece) speed radars. I believe, at that time, only Districts 5 and 10 had completed the transition to the UHF radios.

One day, I got a call from a sergeant in Wittman (D-10). He apparently knew I was the engineer in charge of the UHF radio upgrade program and had a story to tell. He said that he was getting strange readings on his new Decatur radar, especially when the UHF radio was transmitting. I didn't know what to make of this, but it concerned me a lot, so I made an appointment the next day to meet him out at an abandoned airstrip in Wittman to run some tests. I also had a car with a UHF radio in it, which was necessary for the tests.

Well, the tests were eye-popping. The high-power UHF radio did, indeed, radically affect the reading on the radar. We were getting readings of 25-60 mph on the radar with absolutely no target in front of his vehicle when transmitting. Worse, I discovered that I could whistle just about any speed I wanted into the microphone! And then it got even worse yet. I ran tests driving away from him while transmitting, and indeed, his radar gave bizarre readings when I was up to 100 yards away. And yet, I could whistle a speed into the microphone of my radio registering on his radar. This is what's known in the engineering world as "RF interference." It's insidious and very hard to cure, especially with a two-piece device with an eight-foot cord between the units that acted like an antenna for stray radio energy near the radar unit.

After getting back to the office, I immediately went into the office of the then-bureau manager, Bernie Flood, and told him what I found. He was quite concerned too and told me to go talk to Col. Pennington, then HPB (Division) chief. I ran next door and walked right into Carroll's office without knocking (We were on a good first-name basis already) and told him I had a bombshell to drop on him.

After explaining the problem and results of my tests, he looked like someone had knocked the air out of him. He asked what I recommended, and I suggested that we immediately take all the Decatur radars off the road and not purchase or distribute any more. He agreed and that solved the immediate problem. We told Decatur about their problem, and they tried to look into it and solve the problem, but they never could.

We changed to buying Kustom single-piece K-band radars which didn't have a problem with our radios but had a warning light in case there was RF interference. As for Decatur, we sued the company, and I believe we sent all the units back and got about half our money back on them in the settlement. A year or so later, Decatur went out of business. I never heard how many motorists challenged their speeding tickets as a result of the problem, perhaps because we tried to keep it rather quiet.

Just for the record: I was NOT the engineer involved in the purchase of the Decatur radars.

201 FLAGSTAFF
Paul Palmer #342

I have heard this story from several people, and I can't swear that it is true. But even if it isn't, it is a great story.

Jerry Deihl #201 was dispatched to an accident north of Flagstaff on 89. When he arrived on scene, he saw that a car had gone down an embankment and the driver and sole occupant was not injured. He was a man Jerry knew quite well. He had arrested this guy quite a few times, and they were on a first name basis.

Jerry had the guy sit in his patrol car, and he put on his outside speaker and went down the hill to investigate the accident. He no sooner got to the car when he heard dispatch call. He went back up the hill and called in, and Radio said they did not have traffic for him. He went back down the hill, and the same thing happened. He climbed back up the hill and called in. No, Radio said, they hadn't called.

This happened three times. After the third time, Jerry headed down the hill and out of sight, circled back, and came up behind his patrol car just in time to see the man pick up his mic and say "201 Flagstaff" then start laughing.

IMPROVISATION
Harley Thompson #6

I used to tell a joke when I instructed a cadet class many years ago illustrating the analogy of utilizing initiative and sound judgement in dealing with a situation that might not be specifically covered by an order or regulation. It was the story of a mortician's helper.

One day, the mortician came to the helper and said, "The wife of the deceased wants us to put a toupee on her husband's head. We've tried everything, but it keeps falling off."

Don't worry, sir," the helper said, "I'll take care of it."

So, on the appointed day, there lay old Sam with a curly head of hair. After the funeral, the mortician asked the helper, "How did you do that?"

"Nails," the helper replied.

On another occasion, they had two funerals to do within an hour of each other and had only one burial suit. The mortician asked the helper, "What can we do?"

"Don't worry, I'll take care of it" the helper replied. Everything went off like clockwork, and later the mortician asked the helper how he did it.

"I just switched heads," the helper answered.

I had to put this into effect one time when the Boss told me we were going to have a couple of high-ranking Army officers from South Vietnam visit, and he wanted to impress them with a shooting demonstration. They didn't speak English, and it was necessary to communicate with them in French. Luckily, one of our dispatchers, Sabine Jourdan, spoke fluent French and was a great help.

Lt. Pat McCollum and I worked out a routine where we would assemble a riot gun, Browning 12 gauge while blindfolded. We would then load the weapon and take off the blindfold and shoot at five targets as different numbers were called out.

I also rigged up an old axe I had, sharpened the edge, and used a couple of coat hangers to make a frame to hold a balloon on either side. The object being to split a .38-caliber bullet on the sharp edge of the axe and break a balloon on either side.

We put on the demonstration, and when it came my turn, I stepped off the prescribed distance, raised the old .38, fired, and broke both balloons. The two visiting officers were amazed and asked if I could do it again.

"No problem," I said, and we blew up two more balloons and did it a second time, breaking both balloons even faster than before.

Later, the Boss asked me, "How in the heck can you do that every time so quickly?

"Easy," I replied, "I used bird shot."

I hope you have enjoyed these stories, and I hope it gives you incentive to write down your stories. It is actually fun once you get started. And that's the hard part, getting started. You have stories. I know you have them because I have heard you tell them. I would enjoy reading them. I'll tell you more later.

THE DUI WHO TURNED HIMSELF IN
Bob Osborn #1159

It was in the mid-1970s when I was stationed in Sunflower. I was working a single-vehicle 961 off the northbound lane of SR87 at MP218. I was parked off the roadway at the driveway to the Sunflower store with just my deck lights on.

I happened to look up and noticed a northbound vehicle coming down the hill toward my location having a problem staying in his lane of travel. I was not finished at the accident scene, as the accident vehicle had not been retrieved out of the depression off the side of the northbound lane.

I had decided to leave the accident scene and chase down this vehicle. However, I didn't have to, as the driver turned off SR87 and parked next to my patrol car. The driver got out and asked if he could help. I told him sure but that I would have to have him do a few tests first. I ran him through some FSTS (field sobriety tests) which he failed. I arrested him, cuffed him, and put him into my patrol car. This was at a time when our patrol cars did not have cages.

I went back to finish the accident investigation. I was doing the tow truck paperwork when the DUI driver was suddenly standing right next to me. He was out of the patrol car with his cuffs now in front of him. I re-cuffed him and put him back in my patrol car.

A short time later, he was standing right next to me again. This time I sat him on my push bumper and cuffed him to it. This is where he remained until I was finished with the accident scene. He was then taken to Mesa and booked into jail.

THE LUNCH THIEF
Paul Palmer #342

Ben Hancock started out on the patrol as a police cadet in Casa Grande. At that time, the patrol office was a couple of miles east of Casa Grande. Ben was always in great physical shape and ran daily.

One day when his car broke down, he decided he would run from Casa Grande to the patrol office. On the way, a mean, vicious dog began chasing him. This dog looked like Cujo on steroids. As Ben lost ground to the dog, he would reach in his lunch bag and throw some of his sandwich to the dog. That would slow the dog somewhat as the dog ate some sandwich. The dog would then eyeball Ben and tear after him once more. Ben would hold out as long as he could, but when the dog's fangs began tearing at his pants leg, Ben would reach in his lunch bag and toss out more sandwich.

The dog was hungry! Ben began wondering if he had packed enough lunch.

Little by little, mile by mile, Ben ran out of lunch. By the time he got to work, his lunch was gone, but he was on time and not bleeding from any dog bites. Ben was happy about that, and the dog was happy and well fed.

Note: After graduation from ASU, Ben left the department and joined the US Marines. He flew Harrier jets and served numerous tours in Iraq and Afghanistan. He was also a Blue Angel and flew the #2 jet. I had the great opportunity to fly with Ben in his F-18 Hornet when he was with the Blue Angels at their winter headquarters in El Centro, and yes, I did throw up. Ben retired from the USMC at the rank of colonel.

STOLEN PATROL CAR?
Paul Palmer #342

After the academy, Ben was stationed in Casa Grande. Being a rookie, he got the best vehicle available, of course. But even rookie's cars break down. Ben's broke down so bad they couldn't fix it in Casa Grande, and it had to be towed to Phoenix.

After a couple of weeks, Ben was told the car was ready to be picked up. On a day off, Ben hitched a ride to Phoenix to get his car and to enjoy his day off in the big city. After a big day in the metropolis, Ben picked up his car, ran it through the car wash, and headed back to Casa Grande. With his FM radio on and his mind recalling his big day, he at first missed the broadcast of the stolen highway patrol car. The second broadcast from the dispatcher broke through his fog.

Ben listened as the dispatcher gave the description and location. *Heck,* Ben thought, *I'm in that area.* Making sure his gun was available, he began looking for the vehicle. What a great opportunity for a rookie to prove himself.

Ben listened intently as the dispatcher described the driver. "The vehicle is being driven by a teenage male," the dispatcher said. "The car was stolen from Danny's Car Wash."

What's the matter with kids these days? Ben thought.

He pulled out a pen and wrote as the dispatcher continued the description. "Blonde hair, wearing a green pullover shirt, eastbound on I-10 near 16th Street". The sunlight reflecting off Ben's green shirt cast a greenish tint on his notepad as he passed the 16th Street exit on I-10. Ben scanned the freeway as he continued eastbound towards Casa Grande.

Once again, the dispatcher broadcast the description which was being given by a driver with a CB radio that was following the patrol car. "Young teenage male, wearing a green pullover shirt, eastbound at 48th street." Just as Ben passed 48th Street, it hit him! The dispatcher was talking about him!

His thoughts of a big arrest and a glowing fitness report vaporized as he picked up the mic and advised the dispatcher to cancel all units. "It's me," he said. He advised the dispatcher that he was in civvies and had just picked up the patrol car and was headed back to Casa Grande.

THE ULTIMATE RIDE
Paul Palmer #342

I had the idea to do a traffic safety PSA with Ben, thinking his ties to the department and now a Blue Angel would make for some neat PSAs. I called Ben in El Centro, and he said that the Navy had approved the PSAs and we could tape them in El Centro. But then he told me that he had arranged a VIP flight and that was mine if I wanted it.

I couldn't believe it! I had a chance to fly with one of the world's greatest pilots in an F-18 Hornet! This had to be a dream. Of course I wanted to fly with Ben, and I told him so. He briefly told me what to expect and what we would do in the air. He said that a video camera would be on me during the entire flight so I would have a souvenir to take home. He told me we would talk several more times before we went to El Centro, and he would give me more information.

During the next month and a half, I had more talks with Ben. He told me about the G's we would pull and how to prepare for them. He said that he would tailor the flight for me, and we would do whatever I wanted to do. But he reminded me that, if I wanted to fly straight and level, I could get a ticket on a commercial flight. He said that, when our flight was over, I would know what it is like to be a jet fighter pilot.

He talked more about the G forces that we would pull. He said that after the flight I would be worn out as if I had just finished a hard physical workout. He reminded me that the Navy Blue Angels were the only military fighter pilots not required to wear G suits. He explained that the G suits were too bulky and restrictive for the movements they had to make in the cockpit. I would also be without a G suit.

The Air Force Thunderbirds wear G suits, but here I was, a non-flyer, about to pull some horrendous G forces without a G suit. I was still thinking hard about this. Could I do it? Would I embarrass myself and the department? I wanted more than anything to fly with Ben, but I didn't want to embarrass anyone. Would I pass out? Would I throw up?

The time finally arrived, and our crew, made up of Ruben Chavez; Sgt. Randy Strong and myself from the video unit; Officer John Adams and Capt. Bob Halliday who would each appear in a PSA; and Sgt. Jeff Trapp from GOHS, our money man, loaded up and headed for El Centro. I knew I was going to be flying in an F-18 Hornet, and I was a little apprehensive. No, I was scared! I had been in the Navy. I hoped that Ben wouldn't hold that against me.

We waited while the team flew two practice flights, then they finally called me in for a briefing and had me sign some release papers. Everything they told me had already been explained by Ben, but still, I paid close attention. When you start to pull G's they told me, tighten every muscle in your body, strain, and grunt the word "hook." Keep grunting the word hook and force out the last letter and then begin again until you have pulled out of the G's. This, they explained, would prevent me from blacking out or suffering GLOC, (G induced loss of consciousness). Some people will pass out at 3 G's, and I would be pulling 7 or more.

Ben had previously told me about the hooking process. He warned me that the people watching the video tape would be laughing at me because it does look and sound funny, but it is the only way to keep from blacking out.

After the briefing, I was taken out to the flight line by the crew chief, Sgt. Jim Driscoll, and climbed aboard jet number 7, a two-seater used by the Blue Angel narrator. There are two F-18s, numbers 7 and 77, which are two-seaters and used as backup jets and for VIP flights. Once seated in the aircraft, for some unknown reason, I was no longer apprehensive. I guess I had used all of that up.

The F-18 is not big on comfort. The metal seat had a little thin cushion, which I was later to learn became much thinner. The cockpit was roomier than I thought it would be, but maybe that has more to do with my size.

More instructions were given, and an endless number of belts were strapped around my body and cinched down tightly. I couldn't have moved if I had wanted to. I was shown two metal handles alongside the cockpit just below the canopy and was instructed to pull on these during the G's.

I wondered if I would leave my handprints on these!

The Blue Angel's photographer was busy taking pictures of me just prior to the flight. I wondered if these were like the portraits taken of our officers by our own photo lab. You know why they update those every three years!

Ben showed up and climbed up onto the plane and asked if I was ready to go. He gave me more instructions, a smile, and a handshake. "Let's go and bend an airplane." What did he mean by that?

We were ready! He strapped in, the canopy came down, and we began to roll. We taxied to the end of the runway and sat talking while we waited for clearance for takeoff. He explained that he would be telling me each move we were about to make and what to expect. "I will say stand by – stand by! The first stand by is to get ready for the maneuver. As soon as I say the second stand by, get ready to strain and hook if you feel it is necessary."

He said we were cleared for takeoff. I leaned back and pressed my head back into the headrest. I hoped that Ben remembered that I treated him with respect when he was just a rookie patrolman assigned to the training division. Is there a chance that he would forget that I was ex-Navy, as Capt. Bob Halliday had reminded him just prior to takeoff? Here I was, strapped into an F-18 Hornet, sitting behind a Blue Angel pilot about to experience something I never dreamed possible. To this day, it is hard to believe.

"Parking brake off. I'll run the engines up to 85%, take one last look at everything. There's 85%. Everything looks good. You ready to go, bud?"

I answered yes, but in my excitement, my voice must have been 10 octaves higher. "Here we go. Off brakes now. Burners ready now." We were rolling down the runway. "Airspeed 100 knots. 130. A little back stick here. Nose up. Here's 150. Gears coming up. Flaps are up. Show minus 50 feet here. (El Centro is 40 feet below sea level). There's 10 feet. STAND BY – STAND BY!"

All of a sudden, the plane shuddered and shot straight up. I was pushed back into my seat, my head was forced back further into the headrest, and I was looking at nothing but blue sky! It happened so fast I didn't even have time to think about hooking. As it turned out, I didn't have to.

Ben told me to look over my shoulder as the earth got further away. I strained against the forces to watch as the airfield got further and further away. We rolled over in a loop and then came to level flight. "OK 4,500 feet. 200 knots. Out of burner." I was amazed at how smooth we were now flying and how quiet the aircraft was. "OK 300 knots, 5,000 feet. We'll level off here." How can this be? Just seconds ago we were rolling down the runway, now we were flying at 300 knots at 5,000 feet!

We flew for a short time, and then Ben let me take the stick. Me fly an F-18 Hornet? No way! This must be a dream!

Ben explained that the Blue Angels fly with a 30-pound spring on the stick. This allowed for precise moves with no slack at all in the stick. As I flew the plane, it was a strain to hold the stick steady as I pulled against 30 pounds. Ben said that, after a couple of hour-and-fifteen-minute training flights or a 45-minute air show, it is quite a workout and physically demanding for the pilot. He then let me fly the Hornet without the spring. What a difference! It was so easy! You could move the stick around with just two fingers. Ben explained that this was how the stick feels on all of the F-18s in the fleet. Ben then took the stick back, and we headed for the Blue Angels practice area.

"We'll start off with a few mild maneuvers, some slow rolls, wingover barrel roll, diamond roll, and an aileron roll or two. I'll let you try one. Okay, 370 knots, 3,200 feet."

Ben had me check the VCR to make sure it was recording. I made sure the Record light was on and scanned the cockpit, looking at all of the instrumentation. This was still so unreal!

Without warning, we did a slow roll. As we began to roll, I started saying the word "hook," expecting some G's. Ben explained that hooking wasn't necessary because we weren't pulling any hard G's. We did the slow roll and were flying level. That was easy! No G's and really very smooth.

"Okay, these first maneuvers you won't even have to strain. Just sit back and relax. They're very low G's and very comfortable." He again explained how to hook during the G forces that we would be experiencing.

"Okay, let's accelerate a little bit, take it down to about 1,000 feet, and do a diamond roll. 360 knots, 1,000 feet. We'll do a nice and easy roll to the left. Here we go, a nice, easy up.

Okay, let's roll to the left here." The plane began a smooth roll. "This is a real mild maneuver, very low G. The only difference is that we do this three feet from another airplane. There we go, put a little speed in the roll, back down the other way." We were back to level flying.

"We got 2.1 G's. Hardly even feel that. Okay, not too bad huh?" It wasn't bad at all. It was very easy and smooth.

I looked down at the multifunction displays in front of me. One monitor showed the G's we had just pulled. This was still so hard to believe. Here I was flying with a Blue Angel, doing the things I had watched many times before from the ground. I knew this was a once-in-a-lifetime experience, and I was trying to memorize the cockpit and digest everything that was happening.

My brain was going into overload! Look at this! Don't miss that! I was glad that the camera was rolling. I would always have the tape to watch over and over and experience again what I had done.

So far, so good. Two rolls and not even sick. I was ready for more. "Let me show you an aileron roll. We're just going to pick our nose up. Now I'll push the stick fully left. Here we go!

Wham! Before I knew what had happened, we had

rolled completely over! It's hard to explain. My head jerked to the side during the abrupt maneuver, but it was so smooth!

"There we go. I'll do one more, and then I'll let you do one. They're easy to do." What? He's willing to let me do an aileron roll in an F-18 Hornet? I thought Ben was smarter than that. I figured he was taking a chance letting me take the stick and fly nice and level.

As we were getting into position for another roll, Ben told me that if I didn't want to do a certain maneuver then we wouldn't do it, and if we did a maneuver that I didn't like, we wouldn't do it again. I told Ben that I wanted to do it all. I wanted to experience what a Blue Angel experiences. I had made up my mind before we took off that, no matter how bad it got, I would not ask Ben to stop.

We set up and did another aileron roll. "Okay, you ready to do one? It's like a big video game, that's all, Paul."

I nervously took the stick. "You've got the stick. Pull the nose up". I eased back on the stick. "A little bit more. A little more." I gingerly pulled the stick back towards me. "A little more. Stop it right there, then roll." I slammed the stick hard to the left. I felt it hit hard when it reached its furthest point. The F-18 rolled over quickly just as Ben had done!

"All right! Nice job!" I relaxed my hand on the stick and the plane wobbled a bit until I brought the stick back to level.

"Nice job. Most people won't be aggressive. They kind of milk the stick over and do a slow roll. That's a nice job."

I felt great! Here was a guy who didn't like to fly being congratulated by a Blue Angel pilot. My mind was racing! Did I actually do that? I was really enjoying myself! We flew for a bit as I sat back and gloated.

"Okay, we'll do a nice little wing-over. We'll pull our nose up. This will be a real mild maneuver. There's 2 G's right there."

"Put our nose up to about 30 degrees and start turning

left. About 45 degrees nose up. 1.6 G's. Real mild maneuver. It doesn't take much to do these."

"Here we go, back over the other way. 180 degrees out. Starting to roll back upright. 45 degrees nose down at the bottom here. 1.9 G's. Very docile maneuver."

It was very smooth. At one point you looked up and saw blue sky, then you looked up and saw the earth. I felt queasy for a bit but it passed quickly. So far, so good. That was great! OK what's next?

Ben watched me through the rearview mirror in his cockpit throughout the flight. He must have noticed my color. "If you have to, use those bags. About 85% of people do. You won't be alone."

"Let's try a loop here. Now, this will be about a 3 and a half or 4-G maneuver. About 385 knots here. 1,400 feet. We're going to start up and do about a 4-G pull. It will get light on top. If you want to go ahead and practice hooking on the way up, you can do that. The G's will lighten up on the top, and then, when we come back down to the bottom, the G's will come back on to about 4 G's."

Oh, no! This is what I feared, the STAND BY part! "So, here we go, STAND BY – STAND BY. Up we go." I was being forced down into my seat. I felt pressure from everywhere all over my body. I began pulling hard on the handles and began straining and grunting the word hook over and over. The pressure was more than I expected.

"Nice job!" All of a sudden, the G's were gone. We were on top of the loop.

"Okay, nice and light here. We'll rest here for a second. This is 1.4 G's here. No strain here. As we come back through here, you'll see the G's start to increase. Passing 8,000 feet, 230 knots."

Down we went, and the pressure began again. I started hooking seriously! I was being crushed!

"There's 4.3 G's. Okay, nice job. All right, Paul, nice job. You kept awake on that one, huh? We'll rest here a little bit, nice and easy."

We were back to level flight, and the G's were gone. Man, those G's were something else.

"If you're interested, I'll let you try one of those yourself." Me try one? He had to be kidding! I was straining as hard as I could, pulling back on the handles as hard as I could, and hooking. As if I had time to fly the plane too! I thanked him but declined the offer. It was all I could do to keep from blacking out from the G's, and here was Ben flying the plane and calmly talking to me throughout the maneuvers. I didn't hear him say the word hook once. Okay, I made 4.3 G's and didn't black out. I felt proud. Shaky, but proud. What's next?

"We'll do something real simple. We'll do some inverted flying. No strain at all. You will feel yourself being pulled away from the seat a little bit. Don't be alarmed about that. You'll feel your butt come off the seat a little bit. This is a fun one. It looks good on tape. You'll love this one. It'll make you a hero back home. Here we go rolling in."

The G's began as we rolled over and then stopped as soon as they had begun. We were flying upside down.

"370 knots. 800 feet." I was hanging by all of the belts with my butt off of the seat and my feet off the floorboard. I looked straight up and saw the ground. We rolled back over, and suddenly, I decided that I would barf!

I asked Ben to fly level for a bit, and he assured me that it was no problem, most people do barf on these flights. I began using the barf bag, but not much was coming up since I hadn't eaten much in the past 24 hours. As I retched, I could hear Ben singing 'Tequila Sunrise'. Ben can fly a whole lot better than he can sing, but at the moment, I wasn't about to tell him so. Ben told me it was harder riding in the back seat than being in front. Maybe he was just trying to make me feel better. It was soon over with, and I began to feel better. I told Ben that I was ready for more. Did I just say that?

"Let's see, we've done aileron rolls, a roll, wing over and loop, and some inverted flying. We're going to try some vertical rolls here in a couple of minutes. That's a real spectacular maneuver. You'll like it, especially with that look-back video."

"What we're going to do is come down low, pitch up; it will be a pretty good pitch up, some G's on the pitch up, you'll have to strain against that. Then we'll unload again like on take-off, only this time we'll have more airspeed hence more G's available as we pitch up vertically. It's about 70 degrees nose high, and then we're going to roll". What have I gotten myself into? "Okay, Paul, you ready to go for it?" For some strange reason I told him I was ready.

"What I'll do before we start up is give you a stand by – stand by. On the second stand by, I'm going to pitch it up." Oh, no! Those STAND BY words again! "So, you want to start straining on the first stand by. Don't wait for the second stand by or for the G's to come on. Start hooking on the first stand by. We'll start this at 300 feet, 400 knots. Okay. STAND BY – STAND BY!"

All of a sudden, the Hornet was standing on its tail going straight up and spinning. I was hooking hard. The G's were unbelievable. I was being crushed, and I could no longer feel the padding on the seat as my butt was putting an imprint in the metal seat. I felt like I was pulling the handles off the side of the cockpit. I was having trouble seeing. The pressure was tremendous, and it felt as though I was being forced through the bottom of the jet. There are really no words to describe the pressure I was feeling.

After a few seconds, I could hear Ben through my grunting. "All right, Paul, relax now." We were going straight up and corkscrewing. No G's at this point. All I could see was blue sky.

"Passing 8,000 feet, 300 knots. One more roll. 15,000 feet." We then rolled over into level flight. I had made it!

"You're going to love that one on tape, Paul. Good job. You know how many G's you got through that time?" I didn't have a clue, but from what my body had just gone through, it must have been a lot. "7.1 G's. Look at the left DDI (Digital Display Indicator). See what it says there?" I had pulled 7.1 G's and not blacked out! I couldn't believe it! "Good job. Good hooking. You have to get with it. You have to work, you have to want it. If you don't want it, you'll black out."

Wow! What an experience! But still, I didn't hear one bit of hooking coming from the front seat, only Ben's calm voice talking to me. How can he stand all of those G's and still be able to move and maneuver an airplane? The pressure of the G's on me was so great, I couldn't have moved if I had wanted to. All I could do was pull hard on those handles.

"Okay, let's go look at the mountain. What do you say?" Ben had told me before we had taken off that we would fly through the mountains near Palm Springs. That would be neat I thought, flying an F-18 around the mountains.

As we flew towards the mountains, Ben pointed out a tower beneath us. He flew over the tower and marked it for a target that we would attack later. He put the information into computer storage as a mark point. The computer would then give him constant information on time and distance from the target.

"Okay, let's go play around the mountains a little bit." After saying that, he talked about the dangers of shadows and sunlight while flying near mountains.

We were flying low and banking sharply around the foothills near the mountains. "Now, this is what Marine attack pilots do for a living. Down here. Carrying bombs. This is the most fun you'll have flying. This and dogfighting with other airplanes."

As we talked, we continued to bank left and right, still flying low. For a while I would be lying on my left side, then lying on my right side as we banked sharply. Oh, oh.

Barf time!

I asked Ben to fly level for a bit as I used the barf bag. He said he would stay in the valley and fly level for a bit and reminded me again that most people do barf on these flights. "Most of our troops go back the proud owners of one or two bags."

Ben made small talk as I barfed and asked me where we had breakfast. Just what I needed, to think about food. Ben laughed as I barfed. It was soon over, and we headed for the mountain. I felt better, but weaker.

"Let's go play a little bit and have some fun."

We headed for the mountain, and we were soon there. We would bank sharply to the left and then back to the right. I would be lying on my left side and then lying on my right side. I would look out the top of the canopy and see canyon walls. We were so close to the mountain and flying at 400 knots! It looked as if I could reach out and touch the mountain.

It was awesome and beautiful. Ben began to sing "Tequila Sunrise" again. This close to the mountain at 400 knots, and to him, it's like a leisurely Sunday drive. This was almost unreal, as if I were not really doing it. My mind was racing. So much to see, so fast! We were getting near some snow-capped peaks.

"We'll take a peek at the snow and then head back to the target. I'm going to show you an attack profile on a target. If you're going to attack something tactically and we're coming in low to do it to avoid being seen, especially by enemy radar and such, this is how to get in and get out."

We could see Palm Springs off to the right. The mountains were becoming more rugged and beautiful. I was speechless. What a view!

All of a sudden, we shot up and the G's came on. I began hooking. Ben rolled the plane over so that the snow-capped peaks would show up on the look-back video. Upside down over the peak of a snow-covered mountain then a gentle roll back to level flight. What an unbelievable experience!

"Okay, let's get to work. We're 41 miles from target."

We banked sharply left and then right, at some points almost inverted. Back and forth, we rolled left, then right. Ben said we would stay down low and use the terrain to mask our approach.

"Okay, target bears 126 degrees, 35 miles out, 4 minutes and 40 seconds away."

Bank left, bank right. The ground was so dang close! "This kind of flying is fun."

"Yeah," I answered weakly. I was starting to get nauseous and felt completely worn out. But I wasn't about to ask Ben to stop. An attack on a ground target from an F-18 Hornet! If I didn't do this, it would be something I would regret forever.

We saw a small ranch down to our right. "We're going to climb above these guys so we don't startle anybody." Up we went and then did a slow roll at the top of our climb and then came back to level flight. "I don't want to get down there too low and startle anybody with the noise. We'll try to be fairly polite if we can.

We flew fairly level for a few minutes at a higher altitude.

"Okay, 24 miles. We'll kind of wind our way over there, not go directly there." We dropped down low again and rolled left and right over the terrain.

"This attack profile is going to have some pretty good G's again, so you're going to have to get on top of it." We were right down on the deck following the terrain, banking sharply, having to climb to get over small ridges.

As we flew, with the sagebrush scraping the bottom of the airplane, Ben asked me questions about my family. We talked about my wife and two sons nonchalantly, for his part anyway, as if we were visiting over a cup of coffee.

We continued flying, down almost to the ground and

banking sharply left and then right, skimming the ridges and mountainsides. It was amazing how smooth the ride was. During the entire flight, even during hard G's and all of the maneuvers and mountain flying that we had done, I felt no bumps or air pockets. At times you could feel the airplane shudder during hard turns and G's, but it remained smooth. I was again looking out the top of the canopy, watching the side of the mountain whiz past.

"We're almost there, bud. Here we go, over the top of this ridge."

We continued to skim along the ground, banking hard left and right. After another wild maneuver, the G's came on. I began hooking. "Little bit of G there. You're doing good, Paul. Keep straining." I continued to hook as the G's pushed me down into the seat.

"Okay, we'll back it off there. Nine miles from target." No sooner had he said that when he said seven miles from target. I couldn't believe our speed.

"Our target will be on the left side as we come past this last ridge. All right, Paul, get ready to work for a living now. Here we go. Remember the target? We're going to see it again. Four miles."

No sooner had Ben said four miles to target when all of a sudden, it felt as if we hit a brick wall, and we went straight up. The G's were extremely hard. I was hooking and straining as hard as I could, but I was worn out from all the previous maneuvers. I pulled on the handles as hard as I could.

"Chaff flares! Chaff flares! Target on left side low!" We did a roll as we climbed, and the G's went away.

"Tally ho!" We were inverted, but soon rolled back over. "Okay, that's 6,000 feet."

We began diving almost straight down toward the target. "Triggers coming on! Chaff flares! Chaff flares! Wait for an in-range cue from the guns and open fire. 500 knots, 2000 feet. Here we go! Triggers on! Triggers on! Triggers on!"

We were diving hard and fast! The ground was getting too darned close! "Coming off."

As Ben said that, the plane felt as if it were going to break in two. The forces on my body were tremendous. I had never felt such pressure, and I didn't think that my body could take much more. I was straining as hard as I could. My vision began going. We went straight up and back as we rolled in a three-dimensional pull away from the target.

At this point, my head flopped back, and my eyes rolled back until only the whites of my eyes showed. The G's had gotten me! I was out!

"All right, we'll come off here. Old Paul went to sleep on that one. We'll go ahead and knock this off. Nice and easy here."

My head fell forward as I faintly heard Ben talking. I was in a fog somewhere between being awake and in a good sleep. I began to think that I had better pay attention to what Ben was saying, but he seemed so far away. I looked around, and my eyes began to focus, and I felt as if I might black out. No pain or sickness, just the need for sleep.

"One G-flight, Paul. Just take your time and come back to and relax." I could hear Ben talking as if he was hundred miles away, but I couldn't focus in on what he was saying.

I told Ben that I thought that I was going to black out. "I think you did, bud."

I heard and understood that. I managed a weak laugh and told Ben that I didn't know that I had been out. "Oh, you were out. You were asleep like a baby in a crib, but don't worry about it." His laugh was almost wicked. Maybe he did remember that I had been in the Navy.

"You did a good job. You were hanging tough. We're going to take it nice and easy and head on home. How's that?" I told Ben that I thought that would be a good idea. This had been fun and a fantastic experience, but at this point, I had had about all the fun I could stand.

"7.3 G's, Paul. Nice job."

Oh, oh, where did I put that barf bag? After using the barf bag, I felt much better.

"I'll try to make this a pretty docile ride back home. I'll tell you what, that was a good aggressive ride. We didn't do it like the MRT (Minimum Radius Turn, an 80-degree angle of bank 7.5-G turn for 360 degree of turn) which is a hard one. It's 7 to 7.5 G's for about 23 seconds. You'll put about everybody out on that one, so we skipped that one. But we did have a pretty aggressive sortie, and you saw a lot of maneuvers, and you didn't give up. Man, that's tough which is good, because too many people get out here and get this one opportunity, and they want to go home in five minutes and then they regret it. Everyone that's done that has wished that they had a second chance because they didn't experience much more than airline flying. If you get a chance to fly in an F-18, well, this airplane is magic, and it will do some great stuff."

I felt pretty good that I had stuck with it during all the wild flying, but I couldn't imagine 7.5 G's for over 20 seconds. I guess that's why they call Ben the 'G Monster'. As I hooked and grunted or groaned, I never heard a sound from the front seat, unless it was Ben talking or singing. It was all I could do to hang on, and here he was, withstanding all of the G's and maneuvering the aircraft through wild maneuvers as if it were a Sunday drive.

We flew nice and level on the way back to the airfield, and I looked hard at everything in the cockpit, knowing that I would never see anything like this again. I wanted to remember everything.

"I want to show you just one more thing." Oh, no! "It's low G. I want to show you just one more demonstration of what a Hornet will do. Slow flight. I'll show you how slow it can get. This is a no-brainer here. It won't make you feel any worse or any better or anything." How about something to make me feel better?

"We'll start it off at 300 knots; we're at about 5,000 feet. I'm going to hold it around 5,000 feet here. We're going to pull the nose up a little bit and hold it there. Passing 220 knots now. The flaps will start to program down automatically. 190 knots now. I'll put the boards up here. Here's 5,000 feet, 145 knots. If you look out on the wings, you can see the flaps are coming down by themselves. Still 5,000 feet, 135 knots, 15 degrees angle of attack."

I started to hear a warning tone, which didn't sound too good to me! "Ignore the tone, it's just a gear tone there. 125 knots."

Heck, I've driven faster than that! Ignore the tone? I don't think so! I've gone through rolls, flips, dives, and G's strong enough to crush a bowling ball, and now I was going to fall out of the sky because we were flying too slow!

"The nose is pretty high here, and the airplane is flying nice and in control. This is important in flight, trying to get behind a guy in a slow fight which is actually kinda suicidal because you might get nailed by someone else because you are so slow that you're a target. This airplane will fly pretty nicely at about 60-80 knots. Most airplanes will not fly at this angle of attack. They stall well before then. Okay, we're about 22 alpha. This airplane will go up to 40 or 50. It's amazing."

We leveled out and picked up speed. "All right, Paul, your ordeal is almost over. I wanted you to enjoy it. I hope you have. I know it's hard going out there and getting sick, that's not fun."

I didn't care. Sick or not, what an experience! I don't know how many times I stood on the ground in amazement watching the Blue Angels perform, never in my wildest dreams thinking that someday I would be up there doing those things.

"We actually got 7.4 G's on that attack."

My mind was still racing, going over the things we

had been doing. Ben was busy talking to the tower as I looked out over the Salton Sea.

"Okay, we got the carrier break looking at us. (The carrier break is a high-G maneuver used by Navy and Marine pilots to set up to land on an aircraft carrier. It bleeds off airspeed and positions the jet for the landing). "It's pretty good G's. I'm not going to put you to sleep, or I'll try not to. That's not the intent, but it will be some pretty good G's to get the thing downwind for the proper abeam distance. This will look good on camera for your friends down there. We don't want to come in on some Mickey Mouse approach. Not in an F-18. I'll get my knots back up here."

We flew for a few minutes, setting up for the carrier break. Some pretty good G's, huh? I got a good grip on the handles and prepared for some bone-crushing G's to begin.

"Okay, that's 800 feet. Okay, here we go, Paul. STAND BY – STAND BY!"

Once again, I was being crushed and pressed down into the seat. I began hooking and straining hard as the Hornet slammed into a sharp bank and turn. The G's came off.

"All right, good job". We leveled off and began lining up toward the runway.

"All right, standard Navy-type approach here, Paul. It's a constant turn. We don't roll out, and there's no straightaway. No sharp turns. You don't go 90 off and all that kind of stuff."

The ground was approaching fast, but we were nice and smooth on a straight approach.

"Okay, we're on the deck." I didn't even feel us touch down. "Paul Palmer has made it! Nice job. Lynn, I'm sorry if I hurt your husband. I didn't intend to." Was that another wicked laugh?

We rolled down the runway. "On deck at 1652, roughly a 50-minute sortie. We got a good jet, and we didn't break it." But did we bend it? "Maintenance will like us."

"7.4 G's. You're a G guy. You were awake for most of it. Just one time you went out there coming off target. That's a pretty aggressive attack profile, but that's the way you train. When people are shooting at you, you don't want to be a stationary, predictable target. You have to move the jet. You have to get back up there away from them and move it around a little bit."

"But that's a pretty aggressive profile for anybody, especially without wearing a G suit. Now, if you had been flying in a regular F-18 in the fleet and been wearing a G suit, it would have been a big difference. A world of difference. You probably would not have gone out at all. It's just unique to the team. It's the way we fly. We never put the suit on."

We continued to talk as we rolled down the runway toward the Blue Angel's hangar. "It's really an honor to take you up." An honor to take ME up? Boy, did he have that backwards. "It's great to have taken someone up from the Arizona Highway Patrol. I finally got a chance to do it when I was here for two years, but I was excited we got a chance to get you up there." He was excited?

We rolled to the hangar area and stopped. It was hard to believe that it was over. I had done something people only dream about. I had flown with the best and will have memories of that forever. I have the video that I still watch occasionally, and I still have a hard time believing that it really happened.

MY EARLY DAYS
Herschel Eaves #399

Having moved around the country as a kid, our family wound up in the abandoned but refurbished military barracks in Poston #2; which was a former Japanese internment camp located about 10 miles south of Parker. Subsequently, I graduated from Parker High School, then went to ASU for a year, majoring in electrical engineering. That didn't work out too well, so it was volunteer draft time and I spent a couple of years in Germany; which was still bombed out some 15 years after the end of WWII. I returned to Arizona looking for a job and spent four years on the PPD.

The Arizona Highway Patrol received a substantial raise at the time, and I joined up. My first duty assignment was Dateland. It was a good group of guys fresh out of the academy (four of us), and it wasn't long before the Triple A Automobile Association red-lined the area with a precautionary travel warning.

Getting called out for an accident was via a "squawk box" located in the state housing closet. Exhilarating when that puppy went off at 3:00 in the morning.

I moved in early July of '67 only to have a senior officer already stationed there shoot down the single power line providing swamp cooler, which was the only cooling to the homes. He had occasion to drink what he described as Stump Blower, which was a concoction of 180-proof whiskey and Tang. He was a poor shot and missed the bird he was shooting at and hit the power line. Poor Major Raymond stopped by to check on the welfare of the now-moving-in families, and he met my mother-in-law. Not a happy first meeting. He retreated back to Phoenix.

Due to my previous experience, I was told to pack my bags and move to Parker. You know the routine. Pick up a U-Haul van and be there in 48 hours, ready to hit the road.

Parker! You've got to be kidding me. But the area had improved. The two-lane road now extended to the Bill Williams Bridge and then turned into a dirt road to Lake Havasu City. There were seven jurisdictions involved: Tribal Police, Parker P.D., AHP, Yuma County S.O., FBI, plus the CHP and Riverside County S.O.. No radio communications other than a low-band frequency radio that enabled an officer to contact the Arizona Port Of Entry station. Our excitement was to hear skip communication out of Georgia with personnel talking about calls they had responded to and even that was infrequent.

SUPPLIES FOR PARKER
Colin Peabody #481

When preparing to head for a Parker detail, supplies were secured ahead of time and loaded into our trucks and trailers for the trip. One detail, two Motors who shall remain nameless, had bikes loaded into the 5th-wheel trailer being pulled behind the fully marked dually. As they were getting a late start, they stopped at the Smitty's store on Grand Avenue and loaded up on foodstuffs and several cases of adult beverages for off-duty consumption. They loaded everything in the trailer and headed out.

Another officer and I had the D-5 wagon with Intoxilyzer, pulling a two-bike trailer. I headed out I-10 to Quartzite and up 95 to Parker. About 20 minutes out of Parker, dispatch called advising I needed to call #57 (Major Mildebrandt) as soon as I got to Parker.

I called the major and was told that two of my motor officers were seen loading beer into a marked highway patrol truck and trailer at Smitty's in Peoria, and I better find out what the hell was going on with these two out-of-control officers. "Yes, sir, I will take care of it right away." What the heck was I going to say?

The dually and trailer were just pulling in, so I confronted the two officers, and they said "But, Sarge, we took off our uniform shirts before we went in the store!"

"Yeah, but you couldn't take the stars and decals of the damn truck, could you?"
Letters of instruction to follow.

The rest of the weekend went without any disciplinary problems; however, the major did show up and rode in the wagon with me for a couple of nights. That in itself was an experience that will not be written about by me, but not forgotten either!

THE JAIL TREE
Jeff Raynor #2392

From 1979 or 1981, when I was stationed in Tonopah, several of the officers from District 10 had to go up to Parker on holiday weekends to augment the local officers. We had to deal with throngs of Californians who came over to party on the river. At that time, La Paz County had not been formed, and Parker was in Yuma County.

There are lots of stories, like handcuffing drunks around a tree in front of the JP's office, and as time permitted, Carl Svob, badge 375, or one of the Parker officers would take them in to see the judge, who would generally ask the patrolman (who had read the report) what his opinion of a suitable bond or sentence would be. I do not remember ever actually seeing that tree, but I do recall arresting a ton of DUIs there.

I SAW IT
Scott Lane #2936

I remember seeing prisoners handcuffed together around the tree in front of the Parker jail circa 1981-1982.

GOIN' FISHING
Mike Denny #1441

Being in old District 10, I got to work the Parker details frequently. These were always fun.

One year, I was assigned to room with Cecil Dallas Waddell. Cecil was a legend at DPS. He had been a Phoenix PD officer, a liquor agent, and a professional boxer. I met Cecil when he was an observer in my academy class.

I checked into my room, and it was clear Cecil had been there. His uniforms were hanging up, and he had food chilling on the A/C unit (there were no refrigerators at the Kofa Inn then). His patrol car was out front but no Cecil.

Several hours later, just before our shift was to start, Cecil came bombing through the door in full uniform. I asked him where he had been, and he explained he had come to Parker early in the day (explaining his stuff in the room) and then hitchhiked back to Yarnell to get his personal truck (dressed in civvies, of course) which he had driven back to Parker.

I asked him why he had done this. He told me was going fishing on his off time and knew it was wrong to drive his DPS car to go fishing!

On the last day of the detail, Cecil reversed his travels and hitchhiked back to Parker just in time for our last shift.

WAITIN' FOR THE WAGON
Mike Denney #1441

I have another Cecil story.

When we were working that same detail, I was driving north near Ah Villa Park when I saw a patrol car stopped, emergency lights on, on the southbound shoulder near a road sign. As I drove closer, I could see a patrol officer apparently struggling with a subject on the ground. I flipped a U-turn and pulled in behind the other patrol car, got out, and ran up to where the struggle was.

When I got there, I found Cecil Waddell handcuffing a subject to the road sign. When I asked Cecil what was going on, he said he had arrested the guy for public intoxication (yes, it was illegal to be blitzed in public). He said he had called for a paddy wagon, and he was securing the drunk to the road sign to await the wagon! Cecil said he was heading back on patrol.

I explained that it wasn't really a good idea since the drunk could get run over. Cecil shrugged, uncuffed the guy, and put him in patrol car. I waited with Cecil until the wagon came and we both drove off for another crazy night along the Colorado.

Cecil was a great guy with a huge heart. Loved working with him.

I WARNED HIM
Herschel Eaves #399

On day one of my familiarization of the Parker Strip, I was picked up by one of two officers anxious to exit their Parker duty assignments. One had an epiphany during his tour and became a minister. The other, well, he was a personable individual who shall remain unnamed.

After about 15 minutes of his giving me the tour, he made a U-turn and headed south. There was a hitchhiker along the road. which the aforementioned officer had apparently made contact with earlier in his shift. The hitchhiker was standing just off the edge of the pavement and didn't attempt to move, nor did Karl (fictitious name) attempt to move the patrol car to the left on the narrow two-lane road.

I heard a whack and saw the guy spin and hit the dirt. More acting than serious impact of his hand with the side rearview mirror of the patrol car.

I said, "Karl, you just hit the guy."

His response, "I warned him not to hitchhike," and on down the road we went.

THAT DAM ARREST
Jeff Raynor #2392

One night, I was north of town and observed an old pickup truck weaving northbound. I turned on my lights, and the driver continued driving slowly northward.

I do not remember where I first saw him, on 95 or the Parker Dam road, but he ended up getting closer and closer to the dam. I turned on the siren, but he continued. I am pretty sure no one else was close because I was the only patrolman on the stop. He continued onto the dam, which really had no place to safely stop, and pulled to the right onto the paved apron just over the dam.

I contacted the driver, determined he was DUI, and arrested him. I recall trying to decide what to do next. I knew I was in California, but if I asked for a California officer, who knew how long that would take. If I told dispatch where I was, there was no turning back. I remember briefly considering asking the driver to drive back to Arizona, but I knew how that would turn out if he crashed doing it.

I called for a 926 "on the dam". The wrecker driver asked if I knew I was in California, and I said yes. He shrugged and hooked the car. I took him to Parker and processed him.

I never heard what happened to the case. It never went to trial. In fact, I cannot recall any Parker cases ever going to trial.

IT'S JUST DPS
Colin Peabody #481

One Parker detail, the night or so before the detail actually got started, several officers wanted to go out for a steak dinner. So, we piled into my unmarked, 4-door Chevy and went upriver to a nice steak house, had dinner, and the guys had a few drinks. I am not a drinker, so I was the designated driver.

When I determined the guys had had enough to eat and drink, we loaded up the car and headed south to Parker. State Route 95 was a narrow two-lane highway with lots of sharp curves and hilly areas between Parker Dam and going into the town of Parker.

After negotiating most of the 20-mile route down past Ah-Villa Park and the residential areas along the river, we made the turn towards Parker. All of a sudden, I hear, "Sarge, you better pull over, I'm gonna be sick"

I pulled over immediately, and three of the four doors opened, and guys were barfing out of each door opening. About that time, a car pulled in behind ours and a set of red lights came on. I knew we were the only highway patrol guys in town at the time, so I got out of the car and an officer from the Colorado River Indian Tribal Police came walking up.

Looking at the sight before him, he stoically commented, "DPS, huh?" turned, got in his car, and left.

THE NAKED PRISONER
T.K. Waddell #803

One night during the Parker detail, John Gantt Jr, badge 718, and myself were driving the paddy wagon, transporting mostly the motor officers' arrests. Business was booming, and we had a full wagon heading towards the infamous Parker jail.

We received a call from a motor (I forget who) needing us to transport a prisoner. We advised we were full, but he insisted we take this guy. We found him and his prisoner in the area of Buckskin Park.

Upon arrival, we saw the prisoner NAKED and freakin' out on something. The motor brought him to the back doors, and Gantt and I opened the doors as the three of us tossed him in and slammed the doors! Wow!! the yelling, screaming, and shouting by the surprised drunken passengers yelli"g "get this creep off "e." He was being tossed back and forth as they tried to get this guy out of their faces.

We hurried, jumping in, trying to drive to the Parker jail. The wagon was rocking side to side as we tried to stay in one lane of traffic. The yelling and screaming could be heard two blocks away.

As we arrived, we backed in at the jail to unload. You could see other officers standing outside, wondering what the heck was going on. The jailers were waiting outside, too, ready for us to unload, a normal procedure.

We yelled out, "Stand by!!!" We opened the wagon doors, and like a floodgate opening, the prisoners gladly jumped out and ran into the jail.

The awaiting booking officers had never seen such eager prisoners and were quite surprised to see our naked passenger. They carefully processed the naked prisoner.

If you've ever been to the old Parker jail, you know none of these prisoners ever want to see that building again. An dats da truthhh.

THE POKER GAME
John Hale #288

I was assigned to several of the Parker adventures and enjoyed many of the same types of incidents previously discussed, except for the "Nude Guy" story. Never had one of those. But with all due respect and gratitude for the statute of limitations, I'll relate a different kind of fun.

Like several others, I always carried a sock full of coins when I was sent on details, perchance to happen upon an after-hours game of quarter-limit-(no limit on side bets) poker in one of the guys' rooms. Just such an opportunity occurred, and after booking my final DUI for the night, I went 10-7 and joined the game.

Among the players (*VICTIMS*) *was* a lieutenant who apparently judged himself a pretty good poker player. Now, I have been playing poker since I was in Korea at the age of 18. I played the entire game with the lieutenant saying how crazy I was but still betting against me as others folded.

When the betting stopped and the dust settled, we remaining intrepids showed our hands. The lieutenant had a pretty good hand, but when I laid out my low-ball Ace-thru-Five Straight, he slammed down his cards and stomped out of the room. But at least he had stopped telling me what a stupid, inexperienced poker player I was. I won about $17.50 in that quarter-limit game.

PRISONER ENTERTAINMENT
Linda Rouillard #963

Back in 1978, '79 or '80, I was riding with a sergeant I will not name in the paddy wagon, picking up prisoners at one of the Parker details. He suggested to the prisoners that it was a slow night, and the poor dispatchers were bored and maybe they could sing a little song to them. It was called "Please Release Me, Set Me Free."

They practiced a few times, and then he picked up the radio and said start singing, and they did. When done, all the officers did the click, click on their radios, except the lieutenant whom I will not name. Also, when we got to the jail and the jailers opened the doors, the prisoners started singing that song to them. It was priceless.

SHE BEAT ME TO IT
Dennis McMillen #2486

Shoot, Linda beat me to the story. They sang really good. They were told if they performed really good, he would let them go.

I WAS THE DRIVER
Greg Eavenson #680

I'm sure the statute of limitations have expired, so I must admit that I was the paddy wagon driver for the night shift. About 10 or 12 prisoners participated in the chorus and sang all the way to the jail.

THE PIGLET
Colin Peabody #481

Sometime around 1976-77, numerous DPS officers were assigned holiday weekend details in Parker over Easter, Memorial Day, 4th of July, and Labor Day, handling excessive traffic problems, accidents, drunks, assaults, and other crimes revelers committed along the Colorado River.

One weekend, Officer Chuck Wright was assigned to Parker and had arrested a particularly nasty and mouthy citizen. He abused Chuck all the way from the time he was arrested through transport to the Parker jail and even when Chuck got him in the cell. He called Chuck every name he could think of, including calling him a pig several times. It seemed to be his main slur against Chuck and police officers in general.

Back in those days, Chuck was not tall, about 5'8" or so, and weighed about 165 lbs., but he was a powerful weightlifter and pretty darn tough. Word has it that, once Chuck was escorting the guy to the cell, he took a good but blurry look at Chuck and said, "Hell, you ain't big enough to be a pig; you're a damn piglet."

It is my understanding that there were no witnesses or bodycam footage detailing this guy's entry into the cell.

WELCOME TO ARIZONA
Herschel Eaves #399

During the holidays, extra manpower was infused into the Parker Strip, and it was like a holy war. All colleges and high schools were let out at the same time It was a no-quarter-asked-and-none-given mentality. The Californian's, etc., would treat the area like it was the outback with the anything goes 'tude. Vietnam was just winding down, and the country was in mental shambles, much like today.

One of our officers, known as the Grey Fox was assigned TDY during this particular Easter vacation. He had backed his patrol car off the pavement between the roadway and the river-doing paper work? It was early evening, and he heard a boat coming upriver toward the dam with the occupants screaming, pig, f--- you, and various other choice words. They continued past, with their profanity echoing off the canyon walls.

Sometime later, they returned downriver with the same routine, cussing, screaming, obscene gestures, going wide open throttle. But what they didn't realize was peak hours of generating electricity was over, and the release of water down river had been reduced considerably. Subsequently, the next thing the Grey Fox said he heard was a whump, whump and cessation of the insulting verbiage and no roar of the boat engine. Now there were screams for help.

They had hit a previously water-covered island of rocks in the middle of the river, and it was now dark enough-drunk enough, they didn't see it. Unhurt, they began swimming to the Arizona side toward the patrol car.

The Grey Fox activated his loud speaker and said, "The first one of you s.o.b.s that touches Arizona soil is going to jail." They all turned around and swam to the California side.

I STILL OWE ON THE LAST ONE
Scott Lane #2936

I had been working Quartzsite/Parker for a year and had done several Parker details. This detail, working evening shift, I had stopped a DUI near Buckskin State Park. The driver was cooperative up until I went to handcuff him. We started wrestling/dancing up and down the side of my '81 Plymouth. My scanner antenna got snapped off, and there were belt buckle marks on the fenders I later had to buff out.

Steve Vildusea stopped and asked if I needed any help. Of course, I did. When we got the driver secured, I asked him why he started resisting. He stated he didn't want to be arrested for DUI because he was still paying off his fine to the Parker JP for a DUI arrest he had received over the previous Easter holiday.

THE HEAD-ON
Jeff Raynor #2392

You never wanted to be that last officer to check 10-7 in Parker. All the out-of-town officers were asleep at the Kofa Inn. That was before cell phones, and I'm pretty sure they didn't even have phones in the rooms at Kofa. No one was on duty in northern Yuma County after 2. If you were the last person out, you took calls until there weren't any more.

I got a call to a head-on crash north of town, north of the Parker Dam turn off, probably milepost 159. I was expecting some horrific scene, but when I got there, things were pretty calm. The Buckskin Fire Department had a vehicle on the scene, but they were just waiting for me to arrive so they could leave.

Both cars could not have been more centered on the roadway. The northbound car was going up a hill and entering a curve in a cut. They met headlight to headlight at what must have been about 20 or 25 miles per hour – fast enough that some radiator fluid was drizzling down the hill. They were both intoxicated and straddling the center line, trying to make it to wherever they were going.

Both drivers were heavy-set females traveling alone in their cars. Neither had much to say. I towed both cars and took the women to Parker.

I remember administering the Breathalyzer (the old Borkenstein one). I vividly recall the needle getting to .40 before the balance needle centered. I reset it to zero and kept turning. I think she blew a 0.43. I remembered having been shown how to do that in the academy, but it was the first time I ever actually had to do it.

I made my note on the little green slip and moved on to the second driver. She too blew over .40. I am fairly sure I called someone to pick them up or maybe I dropped them off at CRIT – it was early morning by then. I never heard what happened to that case either.

THE COUGAR
Bill Whitlow #804

Skip Fink #940 and I were working the evening shift on the Parker detail and were driving the paddy wagon. We would respond to officers making arrests, mostly DUI's. We had a couple of prisoners in the van and were called to pick up one near Sundance.

We get there and put the suspect in the front cage with the others, and the patrolman said that his suspect was the keeper of the cougar used in the Mercury Cougar commercials. Skip went up to the driver side of the vehicle where the cougar was and roared at it. The cougar roared back, scaring the heck out of Skip. The suspect was allowed to put the cougar in the rear cage of the wagon, and we headed to Parker.

On the way, we picked up a couple more suspects, one of which was calling us names and being obnoxious. Skip tells me to stop the van, at which time he exited, opened the front cage, grabbed hold of the suspect, and told him he was going to put him in the rear cage with the cougar if he didn't behave.

We continued to Parker during which time the suspect did not utter a word.

SUSPICIOUS CHARACTERS
John Hale #288

After I had been assigned to undercover Narcs long enough to grow my hair pretty long and get pretty grody, my partner and I were sent to a Parker detail. We were sitting in a booth in a restaurant that was crawling with highway patrolmen. Sgt. George Schuck.......May God Rest His Sweet Soul......later laughingly relayed a comment to me that his waitress had made.

She said, "There's a lot of bad-looking people coming into town, but if I were you, I'd REALLY keep an eye on those two over there." George looked over, and there sat Bob Terry and myself, looking as decrepit as we could.

DOUBLE DUTY
Herschel Eaves #399

At about 1:00 or 2:00 a.m., I had booked a subject for DUI during one of the holidays into the standing-room-only Yuma County Jail. My OLDER brother was assigned to work the Parker Strip on this particular holiday.

After appearing before the judge the following morning, the suspect was released to his buddies. They had arrived in their pickup to take him back to their campsite. The suspect was in the bed of the pickup when my brother stopped the vehicle for a not-recalled infraction. During the stop my suspect kept putting uglies on my brother.

My brother politely asked, "What's your problem?"

The guy replied, "I don't have one, but you have to be the meanest s.o.b. on the river. Apparently, you don't sleep, work 24 hours a day, and arrest everybody you come across."

I'M COMING HOME
Carolyn Barnett, wife of Joel Barnett #571

How fun to read today's Parker detail stories. I wish Joel was here to share some of his stories from his experiences as the Quartzite/Ehrenberg/Parker sergeant working Parker details.

After the first couple of details, he told me he was going to put in a request to go through Motor training so he would know what the Motors were able to do up there. His request was honored and off he went for motor training. At the end of the first day, he called and said he would be home the next day. There was no way he was picking up that motorcycle again! Years later, he had his own motorcycle and enjoyed riding.

Yesterday, my daughter and I drove out to Arizona Mills to drop off dog supplies for Tucson. We had the pleasure of meeting Mike and Christie Denney. Mike shared a few memories of knowing Joel. It made our day.

THE GREAT BANK ROBBERY IN YARNELL
Frank Glenn #468

One morning about 0900, we got a call that there was a bank robbery going on in Yarnell, and the sheriff's office called and was requesting assistance. Of course, this is a federal crime, and the FBI was to show up later in the day. Some of our SWAT team went by car. The chopper landed on the roof of the training building where I was working, so Ed Teague and I went by chopper, a Bell Jet Ranger.

You will have to excuse me, but I know of no other way to express this. It was a cluster #&^% to the nth degree from the beginning. Let me see if I can set the stage.

The bank was on the east side of the road; a café was directly across the road, west of the bank. There was a two-story building just to the south of the bank. The bank had big glass windows in the front and a door with many panes. Along the south side of the building, there were three windows, the bottom of which were about six feet off the ground. There was a back door which was steel with no windows.

When we arrived, we were briefed on the situation, and then I was stationed on the balcony of the building to the south. It seems that, when the sheriff's office arrived, there was a female, one of the robbers, outside the bank, and she was captured. Inside the bank was her boyfriend, the other suspect, along with the bank manager and another hostage. The S.O. wound up trading the female they caught outside the bank for one of the hostages. Now the famous FBI arrives.

At the time, the FBI protocol in these situations was to shut off the telephones, water, power, and other services.

This did not happen! We were all deployed, some to the rear of the bank and me on the balcony.

We waited around forever. Finally, about noon, I caught the attention of the team commander, Mel Risch, our team commander at the time, and asked if I could get something to eat. After a bit of delay, I finally got a hamburger. This same thing was to tick me off for many times to come, not taking care of the troops.

Directly, we heard a chopper land. The bad guy in the bank had called the bank HQ in Phoenix and requested big bucks. This was a direct result of not cutting off the phone service by the FBI. This transfer of money was halted. Now it is about 1300 or so, as I remember, and a request came from the bank which now held only the two robbers. The bank manager had been released earlier.

Along about this time, two FBI agents joined me on the stairwell, one a sniper and one with a tear gas gun. This situation dragged on and on for several hours.

We got word that the bad guy would give up if we gave him 30 minutes with his girlfriend. Now, they did agree to this and you have to keep your word, but 30 minutes is 30 minutes. Well, those 30 minutes dragged on and on for several hours.

About 20 minutes before dark, we hear shots in the bank. Well s___, now everyone gets excited and s___ starts happening. There are only bad guys in the bank and no bullets are coming outside, so what is the rush?

Now, this is funny. Remember the FBI have been across the street for at least 5-6 hours? They shoot tear gas from the café, miss, hit the top of the roof, and it bounces off and starts a fire in the empty lot behind the bank. I said to the guys with me, "Ask them if they want gas from the stairwell."

With some delay, one of the agents does so, no answer. He asks again. Then a withering voice comes across the radio and says, "If I want gas from the stairwell, I will

**%#% tell you." Holy s___, they were cowered to say the least. That was their last transmission!

Now the guy that was shooting gas from across the street shot again and hit the front of the building. It bounced off, and the tear gas was gassing us. They never did get gas into the building.

Now mind you, they had been looking at the building across the street for several hours. After they shot the second gas round, they decided to enter the building from the front and rear. As we watched from the stairwell, the agents crossed the street and started to kick in the door. Now, guess which side of the door they tried to kick in; the hinge side! These guys didn't have the brains god gave a jackrabbit. They did finally enter from both entrances, and as it turns out, the guy had shot the girl and then himself. They were both DOA.

If I had been the girl's folks, I would have sued the S.O. for them letting the girl back into the bank and putting her into a bad situation. They did get a hostage out with the trade but at the cost of the other girl's life.

By the time it ended, it was completely dark. This could have ended much earlier if they had allowed us to gas the place much earlier, after all the hostages were out and nobody but the bad guys in the bank.

1969
Paul Palmer #342

I was working Radio in Holbrook the day Patrolman Paul Marston was shot and killed. We received a teletype about the shooting, and after notifying people in the office about Paul's death, I started to broadcast the information to the patrolmen in the field.

Sgt. John Consoni stopped me and said that Patrolman Pete Perkins was working US66 east and Pete had gone through the academy with Paul. Sgt. Consoni said he didn't want Pete to hear the news over the radio. He said he would drive out and notify Pete and advise me after he had talked to Pete. Then I could broadcast the information.

Sgt. Consoni was a wonderful man who cared deeply about his men. During my time in Holbrook, John became like a father to me. John passed away while I was still stationed in Holbrook. I still miss him.

Note: We picked up this "tradition," if you will, and we try to notify some of our retirees first when we know they had a close friendship or relationship with a retiree who has just passed before we send the information out to our membership. We hope it helps. Colin Peabody

THE BEER TRUCK
Tomie Lee - Pat Lee's 101

According to Pat's account (and his favorite highway patrol story on himself), this is what occurred:

The day before the incident, Pat had reported to his sergeant that one of his back brakes was locking up. (As I recall, his sergeant was on a ride-along and had Pat demonstrate the problem, and the brake did lock up.) Pat was told to take the patrol car down to Phoenix the next day for maintenance. Pat always said that was what saved his backside (actually he said "butt").

The next morning, as he was heading down to Phoenix for the maintenance on his patrol car, he was dispatched to an "incident" on SR188. There was a man who was disoriented and didn't know the whereabouts of his friend or the pickup truck the man had been in as a passenger.

The old SR188 was part dirt and part gravel, narrow and curvy with several steep embankments (drop offs). Pat said the rear brake grabbed/locked up as he went around that particular (steep) curve. The patrol car went off the road, landing upside down well below the road. He was seat-belted in and was hanging upside down. He released himself with the usual results, climbed out of the vehicle, and hurriedly climbed up the embankment to the road, afraid the vehicle would catch on fire.

The old (he called it the Broderick Crawford) siren continued to blare and no smoke was visible, so Pat climbed back down to his vehicle to turn off the siren so it wouldn't short out and cause the vehicle to catch fire. He then opened the trunk of his upside-down vehicle for his first aid kit. Again with the usual result, everything came tumbling out of the trunk to the ground. Pat picked up his first aid kit and climbed back up on the road for the second time.

The first vehicle on the scene was, indeed, a beer truck, which Pat flagged down. Pat said the driver was a young man, shocked at the sight of a dust-covered patrolman standing along the road and below a wrecked patrol car laying on it's roof ("kid's" eyes were big as saucers and his mouth was hanging open). The young man gave Pat a ride to the site of the reported accident. Pat said, surprisingly, there wasn't much conversation on the way.

At the site of the reported accident, Pat found the passenger of a pickup truck that had also rolled off the road and was upside down below the steeply sloping embankment. The passenger said he was asleep when the accident occurred and didn't know how the accident happened and could not find his friend. The driver was found where he had been thrown out of the truck, which then landed on top of him. The accident was a one-victim fatality.

The passenger had also been thrown from the vehicle and, although disoriented, had otherwise suffered minor injuries.

Pat said he had made a DUI arrest the previous night and had the evidence in the trunk of his vehicle which had fallen out along with everything else when he opened the trunk for his first aid kit. (A partial bottle of whiskey and some beer cans) While he was at the fatal accident scene, the ADOT road crew showed up. They got Pat to the side and quietly told him they had found "his" bottle and beer cans at the site of his accident and had thrown the bottle and cans off into the brush below the wrecked patrol car.

Pat found that hilarious and always thought that was the best part of the incident. Pat and that ADOT crew became good friends, and the incident became an inside joke. Pat always laughed harder at that part of his telling of the whole incident.

I hope you will be able to clean this up, make it more readable, and will use what you think is pertinent to the retelling of the incident. Pat never hesitated to laugh at himself and was always able to find humor in all but the most tragic incidents in life. I never heard Pat make excuses for himself professionally or in his personal life. In my experience, it is rare to consistently see that characteristic in a person.

US66 REDLINE
Harley Thompson #6

In late November 1949, I was transferred to Holbrook. At that particular time, there was a lot of confusion and transferring going on in the area. Both patrolmen stationed in Holbrook had just been promoted to captain along with two patrolmen from US66 stations. From

Holbrook, Captain Bob Cochran was transferred to Williams as district commander. Captain Dick Whitlow went to Phoenix, Captain Dick Raymond went to Globe as district commander of District 2 and Captain George Stinson went from Kingman to Phoenix as Central Area district commander. I was the only patrolman in Holbrook, and there was another patrolman who was stationed in Chambers, who was very shortly thereafter transferred to Tucson. It wasn't until early January 1950 when Patrolman Billy Sorrells was sent to Holbrook.

Our accident situation along old US66 kept Billy and me running day and night. It seemed like we were having an accident someplace almost every day. This was starting to tell on us both because we were working ungodly hours all of the time. Finally, about the middle of February or so, I told Billy we had to do something about this situation and told him that I had a plan.

Billy said, "Well, what do you think we should do?"

"Well," I said, "the way to impress people, in this case motorists, is through action, not words. Courage is a career commodity, and we have to have the courage of our convictions. What we should do is start putting pressure on the violators to the extent that the word will get around not to violate laws along US66. I'm sure that our predecessors didn't put too much emphasis on tourists in the past, and when they were cited to appear, the majority of them never were heard from again. So, what we will do is write everything that moves out there, and instead of citing violators to appear, we will take them immediately before the judge."

Billy said, "That sounds good to me, but what about at night and on the weekends?"

"Well," I replied, "we'll just get the old judge out of bed, and he can hold court at night or whenever."

"That's gonna piss them off a whole lot," Billy said.

"That's what I'm counting on," I said. "Perhaps we'll get some pretty stiff fines."

So, this is what we did. Hardly any warnings. Mostly citations and lots of them! Billy and I wrote more activity than all the rest of the Northern Division put together, and we did it month after month.

About the first of June, Inspector Riley Bryan came up to Holbrook and wanted to know what we were doing up here. I said, "Inspector, whatever do you mean?"

He said, "You two guys are making a lot of the other patrolmen upset because of the amount of activity being written up here."

I replied, "Inspector, we just write what we see, and we have not lost a case in court or had an appeal in the past four months, so we must be doing something right."

Inspector Bryan agreed with us, and after I pointed out that we were starting to have a reduction in accidents also, he said, "Well, keep up the good work."

A short time after that, Assistant Superintendent Jack Powell brought Superintendent Greg Hathaway up to the Northern Zone for a tour, and they stopped off in Holbrook and met with Billy and me for lunch. Hathaway asked what we were doing up here that was different than what seemed to be going on in other adjacent areas. We explained our little program and the progress we had made, from an accident almost every day to one or two a week and that it seemed to be working for us as we tried to concentrate our efforts in those areas where we had experienced a number of accidents before. Superintendent Hathaway seemed pleased with what we had accomplished and said to keep up the good work

By late fall, we began hearing little innuendos about some names some of the locals were calling us, i.e., Ticket Thompson and Citation Sorrells, so we knew that the word had already gotten around about our increased activities. The Board of Supervisors was very pleased with increased revenues as was the judge, since they gave him a raise.

There were some other side effects also, such as the redlining of US66 by AAA. AAA would provide travel folders for members with maps etc., to assist in the members; travels. On the maps provided that included travel on US66 in eastern Arizona, the route would be highlighted in red, indicating excessive traffic enforcement. This was designed to warn their members to be careful when going through this area.

In 1951 Billy and I both took examinations given for the new rank of lieutenant. We both passed and were promoted in May. Billy was assigned to Wickenburg, and I was sent to Globe to work with my old friend, Captain Dick Raymond. We hoped that the "Halo Effect" would work for a while after we were gone.

GOIN' TO JAIL IN STYLE
Colin Peabody #481

When I was assigned to Fugitive Detail in the mid to late 80s, I was also assigned to SOU, so I carried a lot of equipment in my undercover 1-ton Chevy van, affectionately known throughout CI as "The War Wagon." During a prisoner transport, a motorist rear-ended it one day, so it was in the shop for some body work, and I needed a swing car capable of carrying a lot of "gear." Fleet gave me the biggest passenger car they had, a seized Mercedes Benz 500, a beautiful and very fast luxury sedan, to use until the van was back.

We were searching for a DOC escapee, and Steve Hinderliter and Larry Verdugo (RIP) had tracked him to 35th Avenue and Lincoln. The escapee was a known Aryan Brotherhood member, so we weren't taking any chances with him. He came out of a small store and climbed into a

Ford Bronco, at which point he made us and took off down Lincoln, with us in hot pursuit— me and Larry Troutt in the lead in the MB, Steve and Larry Verdugo right behind.

He pulls up into a driveway and starts to rabbit on us, but was not successful in his endeavor. We cuffed him, and up and into the rear seat of the big Mercedes he went. As we pulled out, heading for the DOC Alhambra intake on east Van Buren, he was looking around and said, "What the hell kinda car is this?" I told him it was a Mercedes Benz 500.

He replied, "Man, the guys ain't gonna believe DPS caught me, and I'm in a @#$&*#@ #$&@% Mercedes Benz, goin' back to prison in style!

THE FERRARI
Bill Whitlow #804

Patrolman Ellie Salyer was in the Black Canyon City 103 doing paperwork. Gus Stallings, owner of Stalling Imports, was out on a drive in a Ferrari and stopped by the office and asked Ellie if he would like to go for a drive. Ellie got into the passenger seat of the Ferrari and off they went.

They were moving right along when a car with Oklahoma plates passed them and moved into the right lane. Ellie told Gus to pull alongside, and when the driver saw Ellie's highway patrol patch, Ellie motioned for him to pull over.

They pulled up behind the vehicle and approached the driver. He got the driver out, and the driver was taken back by the Ferrari. Ellie explained why he stopped the driver. The driver asked if the Ferrari was his police car? Ellie said yes and that he had a driver also.

You've got to know that the driver went back to Oklahoma and told this story about the Arizona highway patrolman in a Ferrari with a driver.

A HELLUVA GUNFIGHT
Colin Peabody #481

In the mid-80s, the Fugitive Detail was tracking another DOC escapee, a huge Hawaiian guy, and had tracked him to a house in east Phoenix. Steve Hinderliter and Larry Verdugo were closing in on him when he fled from them, heading for 24th Street. Steve and Larry were behind him, with me driving the War Wagon close behind. Randy Oden was riding "shotgun" that day, and Louie Mannheimer was in the back.

The bad guy had another guy with him, and as he tried to evade us, he turned west on Buckeye Road. We had been calling in the pursuit, and Phoenix PD had alerted some of their units, a couple of which were at 16th street and Buckeye. Our Hawaiian saw them, did an abrupt U-turn, and headed back towards 24th street.

Steve and Larry got turned around and were quite a ways behind the bad guy. This entire area was under road construction, making things more difficult. I stopped in the westbound lane of Buckeye Road in a curve in the detour, planning our next move. I had a PPD car on my right with a PPD motor behind him. There was enough open space in the eastbound lane for the guy to avoid us but give me enough room to maneuver.

Our escapee was coming right straight at us, with me planning to violate policy and ram the guy, when, all of a sudden, a loud explosion went off in the van, and my windshield cracked. Now it had a hole in it about the size of the muzzle of Randy's .45.

Needless to say, we didn't ram the bad guy's car but continued after him, advising Radio of shots fired. We were effectively taken out of that part of the chase then, but Steve and Larry continued on and, with the assistance of Steve Lump, later that afternoon captured the guy in Glendale.

The person firing the shot was Randy Oden, who was sure we were going to die when he cranked off a round from his Sig Sauer P220. He did not hit the bad guy's car.

Lee Patterson was in SIU, and he searched but couldn't find any traces of a bullet strike at all. So a decision was made to take the War Wagon down to the PPD range and have DPS firearms criminologist Bill Morris set up about a dozen paper targets in frames all the way around the front of the van. He then fired Randy's .45 at each of the targets through the rest of the windshield to determine the trajectory of the bullets when they passed through the glass. Not one round struck any of the targets! A lesson to be learned!

I got the van back late that day and the next morning took it to the glass shop at I-17 and Thomas for a replacement windshield. The guys at the glass shop took a long, hard look at the windshield and asked what happened. I told them, "It was one helluva gunfight."

X MARKS THE SPOT
Gamble Dick #1743

When you described the war wagon, I was reminded of this.

In the early 1980s everyone knew about Otis Thrasher, the narc who liked to bully people. I was in

Narcotics and had the misfortune to be around Otis a lot. He did his thing unmercifully. Although I was a rookie, I was also on SWAT.

One day the narcs were at the range shooting our cute little "snubbys," and Otis waited until he had a bit of an audience before he struck.

"Gamble, you're on SWAT, aren't you?"

Yes.

"Do you have your gear with you?"

I always have my gear with me.

"Well let's see you shoot."

No.

"C'mon, you're supposed to be hot s—t.

No, I don't want to have to clean it.

Finally, after several more go arounds he said what we all knew was coming.

"What's the matter, you scared?"

I got the .243 out of my trunk with one round and squatted on the firing line. Otis had a couple of guys take a silhouette target out to 250 yards.

I waited for their return, sighted in, and squeezed off the shot. Otis and his audience started down range while I put the rifle back in the trunk. When I got to the target, things were quiet, and nobody was razzing me. I figured I must've made a pretty good shot.

I looked at the target and saw that my shot had pierced the "X" dead on.

Otis wanted me to do it again, but I said no.

I couldn't duplicate the shot because I had a cold barrel zero, and my second shot wouldn't be as accurate because now the barrel was hot.

He accepted that.

Turns out that I earned his respect that day, and we've been good friends ever since... and a man couldn't ask for a better friend.

DEAD BATTERY
Bill Chewning #41

Back in 1953, I was stationed in Benson. Capt. Harley Thompson was the district commander and Sgt. Ray Dahm was my sergeant. Sgt. Dahm's squad was nicknamed the "Dahm Yankees." It was part of my patrolling routine to meet Officer Bill Raftery at Mountain View on I-10 for a bull session.

One day when I arrived at Mountain View, Raftery was sitting in his usual spot, but this time, the hood of his car was up. Raftery asked me if I had happened to see a black car headed west on my way to meet up. I said that I had, and Raftery related his story.

He had stopped the black car for speed and wrote the driver a ticket. When he had completed the ticket, he got in his car, and the car wouldn't start. The speeding driver walked back to the patrol car and asked what the problem was. Bill explained that the battery was dead.

The speeder said, "Are you sure? Do your headlights work? Try it again" Officer Raftery assured him that the battery was dead, but to humor the speeder, he tried with no success to start the patrol car, figuring the good citizen would give him a push.

After determining that the battery was indeed dead and the car couldn't be started, the speeding driver said, "Yep, your battery is dead," then turned around, got in his car, and drove off.

THE STATE LINE
Steve Gendler #1064

This took place near Window Rock on the reservation in 1980 and involved DPS officer Leo Holmes, who certainly did things in a unique way.

As the newly promoted district commander in Holbrook, I naturally wanted to get a feel for the territory and meet the officers where they worked. Throughout my career, I had heard stories about the way things were done on "the reservation," so I thought I'd start there. It was 1980 and "Pow Wow" time in Window Rock, so I arranged a ride-along with Leo Holmes, a veteran officer who I was told "marched to the beat of a different drum"….that was an understatement.

I met Leo in Ganado, and we proceeded to patrol SR264 east toward Window Rock when he said, "There's something we have to take care of first," as we drove past Window Rock toward New Mexico.

We pulled over on the side of the road where a cement "pillar" (like one of the supports they put under a mobile home) was sitting with "Arizona" embossed on one side and "New Mexico" on the other.

"Come with me," Leo said as we went around back of the patrol car and he opened the trunk. "Put that in the trunk," he said, pointing to the cement pillar.

After loading the state line marker, I asked him how we will know we are in Arizona if we make an arrest. Leo said, "With that marker in the trunk, anywhere we stop someone is in Arizona." Who was I to argue with that logic?

PS: We did put the state line marker back in the "vicinity" (about a quarter mile east) of where we found it at the end of the shift.

THE BOT-FLY INCIDENT
Harley Thompson #6

One of the cadets, I don`t remember which one, was assigned to take his OJT (on-the-job training) in the Safford area. While he was there, he made contact with a friend who worked at a local research laboratory where the primary task was to submit the eggs of bot-flies to radiation, thereby making them unable to reproduce. So when bot-flies mated with other similar flies, those flies would not be able to reproduce, thereby eradicating the species, or something like that.

Just before the cadet returned, he acquired several boxes of the eggs that were nearly ready to hatch. On the first day back to work, the cadet made arrangements with one of the counselors to get the duplicate keys of Sergeant Wentzel's new Dodge patrol vehicle, and they put these unhatched eggs in every conceivable cranny and crevice in the vehicle, literally thousands of eggs, or so it later seemed. They rolled up the windows, making the vehicle very warm, and the flies began to hatch all day long until the end of the workday.

When the good sergeant came out of the training building ready to go home at the end of a long day, the old Dodge was literally humming with very large bot-flies.

PICTURES THAT GET TO YOU
Bud Richardson #62

One of the most troublesome photos of my career was a fatal accident west of Benson on US80.

When I was called out, all that Radio told me was that it was a fatal accident. Upon my arrival at the scene, I found a drunk man with minor injuries and a small, towheaded girl about six years old impaled on a guard rail.

The story was that the man was en route to Benson after drinking most of the day. He was on his way to pick his wife up from work. It was late at night, and he put his daughter in the car and took her with him. Being drunk, he lost it, ran off the right side of the highway, hit the guard rail, and the rest is history.

This really got to me for a long time, as I still reflect on it when I see my daughter. She was a blonde towhead at the time of this accident and about the same age as the victim.

A CLOSE ENCOUNTER
Jim Daugherty #2176

Sometime around 2006 or 2007, while assigned to the School Bus Inspection Unit, I was rechecking a bus I'd previously placed out of service for faulty air brakes at a school on the Gila River Indian Reservation.

Rolling under the bus on my creeper to check the rear brakes, I came nearly nose to nose with a sidewinder rattlesnake who appeared to think I was invading his space.

He struck at my face and actually hit the bill of my cap and sort of ricocheted off my forehead.

I doubt many professional athletes could have matched my speed coming back out from under the bus that day. After taking a moment to collect myself, I instructed a driver to pull the bus away.

So, in keeping with my **self-image** as a "rogue officer", I immediately took the law into my own hands by appointing myself as judge, jury, and executioner. After a fair but speedy trial, the accused was sentenced to death for trespassing on school property.

Thinking more about avoiding unnecessary paperwork than any inherent danger of firing multiple shots with my handgun on school grounds, I grabbed a fire extinguisher off another bus that was just a few feet away. After a few blasts with the extinguisher, the snake was stunned enough for me to pin and remove its head with my official DPS buck knife.

To commemorate my narrow escape from a painful demise, I sort of wanted to keep the snake's rattles for a souvenir. But since it was technically tribal property, I ceremoniously surrendered the corpus delicti to tribal transportation employees.

MY TROPHY ELK
Herschel Eaves #399

When I was stationed in Parker, I arrested a major local drug dealer for DUI and booked him. Sometime later, he waved me down near Blue Water and I stopped. He flashed a $100 bill and began a routine. 'I can leave this money on the hood of your car, drop it on the ground, and if you pick it up, it's yours'. He didn't want me to show up for court.

I turned the money over to the newly created C.I. Bureau of DPS. They wired my phone with a tape recorder, etc. Several weeks later, a neighbor advised me someone had been in my yard during the late evening hours the night before, and light bulbs were seen going off, and a car and physical movement was observed.

I called Rayburn Evans, who was a deputy for Yuma County in Parker, and he came to the house. We observed the tire tracks, so he mixed up a batch of Plaster of Paris and made a mold of the tire tracks, etc. I was ready to go to war.

During the time frame between the above arrest and the flash bulb incident, I had gone elk hunting in Colorado. I bagged a spike elk. Certainly not in the trophy category but I was satisfied. Good meat but I had left the head of the animal in the yard to dry out for a possible mount.

During the next issue of the Highway Patrol Digest, I observed a picture of the head on the front page (maybe the second page). The rascal (then Sgt. Larry Thompson) and I believe Bob Pierce and/or others had slipped into my yard and taken pictures of my not-so-trophy elk head.

Embarassing but funny. So much for the tire molds. They were destroyed, and the bribery suspect pled guilty.

THOSE ARE MY CARS!
Paul Palmer #342

John Christie ran drivers training for a time, and he had this great fleet of cars that he would park in the lot just east of the compound, east of 20th Avenue. He was proud of those cars! He would back them up against the fence so that they were facing the Encanto golf course, and you would have thought he used a laser beam to line them up. You could look down that line of cars, and there wasn't a fraction of an inch difference in their positioning. To hear John talk about them, you would have thought they were classics. (They were actually fleet cast-offs.)

The director's office used to be on the second floor of the building which makes up the east portion of the compound. Now when Hoy would walk out of his office into the hallway, instead of looking out of the large windows and seeing the Encanto golf course, Vern saw John's wrecks. They ranged from 1970-1975 model Dodges, Ramblers, and Chevys with a rainbow of colors. Beautiful blues, bright-yellow mustard, rust, and green. Vern did not like looking at the cars.

One day John asked me to help him load the drivers training truck with tires, and on the way over to Fleet, I could tell that John was in a really bad mood. He wouldn't say much, and his sullen mood continued as we backed the truck up to the tire barn to begin loading tires.

I asked John what was wrong. He said that Director Hoy said that his fleet of classics looked like a junkyard, and he wanted them moved and stored at Fleet so that he wouldn't have to look at them every time that he looked out the window.

That's what John said, but it went more like this. "If that #%#^&%^* director wants those $%$^%$ cars moved, then he can move the $^#&%^%$ cars himself. Those are MY $#%^$^$ cars, and I'll park MY $#^$^%$ cars where I want to park them. Who does he %$&%& think he is telling me to move MY *%*%*#@ cars? He can just @#%&^$%!"

As he was ranting on, Director Hoy was walking up to us from behind John. I've never been one to interrupt a good rant and rage, so I didn't say anything to John as the director stopped behind him. I let John rant a little bit more about the director's heritage, and then I said hello to the director. Hoy acknowledged us with a nod and walked away.

The color drained out of John's face and he said his career was over. John made sergeant and later retired from the department. Maybe Hoy didn't hear him.

THANKS, ROOKIE
Bruce Moody #613

I had worked as a Glendale police officer in 1968 and part of '69 until I took the AHP test and passed. I began cadet class training in August of 1969 (1st DPS cadet class) under direction of Sgt. Jerry Wentzel. We were the first class to get firearms training (Sgt. Johnson) and carry sidearms on our OJT. Not only that, we were the first class to be sworn in by Gov. Williams at the Capitol before graduation. This was due to the fact the Phoenix PD and MCSO pulled out of working the state fair (one week before) since they said we were now "STATE POLICE" and this was "STATE PROPERTY!!" Lucky us, we marched from the compound to the fairgrounds every day of the fair. We worked in pairs, me and Mike O'Brien, 10-hour shifts with a half hour for dinner.

After the fair, it was duty station assignments, our own vehicles, and time to drive to our duty stations to arrange for a place to live. I was assigned Tucson, and on the last Saturday before final week, I traveled to Tucson and secured a place to live. Upon returning to my residence in Glendale, I was stopped at a red light at 55th Avenue and Glenn Drive in my BRAND NEW 1967 Dodge, fully marked patrol car when a vehicle going the other direction runs a solid RED LIGHT. The guy next to me looks at me as if to say, "WELL, whatcha gonna do now, kid?"

I pulled the vehicle over, only to find four drunken subjects. I took the keys and told them (those that were not passed out) to stay in the vehicle. My radio in my patrol car had District 8 and State frequency. I switched to State and called Phoenix. "Phoenix, 479 on State."

She came back and said, "WHO?" I requested back up from Glendale PD and a unit off of Grand Avenue.

An officer from GPD (who I knew) arrived within minutes. We had all the subjects out, cuffed, and lying face down when my Grand Avenue unit arrived. It was Gary Zimmerman, who I knew also from working GPD.

The subjects were transported to GPD and booked for 28-692 and three counts of 13-379 (D&D). I started to do the paperwork and asked Gary if he wanted the driver or passengers. He looked at me and said, "YOU GOT THEM ALL, ROOKIE!"

I wrote till my hands cramped (report writing 101); then he took credit for all five arrests. GOTTA LOVE AN EXPERIENCED HIGHWAYPATROLMAN. Thanks Gary!!!

TWO FER ONE
Greg Eavenson #680

Ever arrested two DWI's out of the same vehicle? I had occasion to do that one day in '72 south of Quartzsite.

A southbound sedan blew through the stop sign on 95 in Quartzsite at about 90 mph. I caught up about 5 miles south and got the driver's attention. As he pulls over onto dirt, he leans right as female passenger leans left and slips in behind him and drives another 200 plus yards till they run into a shallow wash and stopped. Both blew double rings on the Mobat.

Judge Hagely got a good laugh about the story.

WILLIE
Ralph Shartzer #220

A new service station – café – convenience store had recently opened two miles south of the Utah-Arizona border on I-15 at Black Rock Road. There was no telephone, radio, or other means of communications for the people working the station. In my mind, they were a prime victim for robbery or anything else, and I always checked on them whenever I was in the area.

On a cold, windy night in November 1979, I was patrolling southbound on I-15 and took the Black Rock Road off-ramp. I observed a vehicle stopped at the stop sign facing east, toward the station on the other side of the overpass, with his lights on. I observed motion outside the passenger side of the vehicle and also that the driver was smoking, and the cigarette had a cherry about one inch long (indicating a very nervous person).

I utilized my speaker and spotlight and asked the driver if he was okay, which he ignored. I couldn't see the person on the passenger side even while using the spotlight. I again hailed the driver on my speaker, and this time he just pointed toward the service station but I could see no one. I turned, drove past the car, and U-turned behind it. I still couldn't see anyone anywhere near the car other than the driver. Now I'm getting nervous.

Working out of St George, Utah, I had my DPS radio, a Utah Highway Patrol radio, a Nevada Highway Patrol radio, and a Washington County Utah Sheriff's Office radio, plus a CB. My patrol car had so many antennas it looked like a tuna trawler. Since DPS radio communications was spotty in this area, I ran a check through Utah Highway Patrol radio, and the car came back stolen.

I informed UHP of my location and informed the driver via speaker to step out of the car, facing forward, with his hands up. He did as instructed, and as he was bending over to lie face down on the ground, I observed a large spot of blood on the butt of his pants. Bleeding hemorrhoids flashed in my mind, but too much blood and the dark color indicated probably not.

After cuffing his hands behind him, I raised him to his feet and asked him if he was hurt, to which he said yes. I asked him how he was hurt, and he replied "I cut myself.' I placed him in the rear of my vehicle behind the screen. The wind was blowing, it was colder than hell, I still can't see what made the motion on the passenger side of the car, and this guy is giving me short answers and I'm on edge!!

I shined my flashlight in the car and saw that it was crammed full of boxes of clothes and various camping gear, including the passenger side of the car, so I assumed he was alone. There was a blood-soaked newspaper on the driver's seat, so I went to the back of my vehicle and asked him how he had cut himself, (I will now clean this up for you) and he replied, "I tried to cut my penis off." I asked him why he had cut himself, and he said that he was impotent and, since it was useless, he might as well get rid of it. Now I am worried!!

I called UHP dispatch requesting a wrecker. A local UHP officer asked if I would like assistance, to which, I replied, "Oh, please." I have a bonafide crazy who tried to whack his willie off and he's bleeding.

I transported him to the hospital in St. George, and the doctor who stitched his penis back on said that he didn't slice it, he sawed on it!! He was known by me thereafter as "WILLIE THE WIENER WACKER."

Four days later, he caught a flight back to California. It was a rental car, and the rental company didn't want to prosecute.

BOMBS AWAY
Paul Palmer #342

In 1990 I had an idea to do a traffic safety PSA where a Harrier Jet would pull over a traffic violator. I ran the idea by the commanding officer of the Marine Corps Air Station in Yuma, and he said he thought it would be a neat PSA. We made arrangements, but about a week prior to us going to Yuma, I got word from the commander who approved the taping that he had run the idea past his general who said, "Not with my $^%$% jets." We were invited to go ahead with the taping, but the jet and the vehicle had to be stationary during the entire taping. A disappointment, but we went ahead with plan.

We arrived in Yuma and had a meeting with the base commander and the pilots we would be working with the following morning, and the commander again said the car and jet must be stationary. We agreed, but the pilots gave each other a quick look and smile and the meeting ended. We went to a local Ford dealer who agreed to loan us a Mustang convertible for the taping and picked up the car.

The next morning, we met the pilots and were taken to an unused section of runway. They said we would tape the PSA as originally written. Don't worry about the general. One pilot told us he would be the LSO or landing safety officer, and he would cue me when to start down the runway. The Harrier would land behind me, and I would pull over with him taxiing behind me.

I was a bit nervous as the LSO cued me to start driving down the runway. I saw Ruben Chavez standing quite a distance away with the camera set up in the middle of the runway. But what I really saw was this Harrier behind me screaming towards me. I lost my nerve and sped down the runway. Way too fast.

No problem they said' let's try it again. Don't worry, the Harrier won't run over you. Take two. Take three. On take four, I started off when the LSO cued me and managed to stay at the speed I was instructed. The Harrier landed behind me and made a "traffic stop." It looked great!

We had taken Patrolman Bob Stein with us to act the part of the pilot patrolman pulling me over. Once on the ground we would shoot a close up of Bob in the cockpit pointing at me to pull over.

We had taped a DPS door decal on the side of the jet under the canopy. One thing we had not calculated into the plan was Bob's size, 6'5" if I am not mistaken. A little large to fit into the cockpit of a Harrier.

As Bob was getting ready to climb into the cockpit, he was warned not to touch anything that was yellow, like the ejection handle that would be positioned between his legs. Or a few other yellow items. Don't forget about the explosive charges in the canopy.

Bob gingerly climbed in and squeezed in between all the yellow items. The canopy was lowered, and Bob's Smokey was barely below the top of the canopy and those explosive charges. But it worked, and the PSA won national awards.

Afterwards, after talking to our pilot, Lt. Gross, whose handle of Smells was given to him by fellow pilots, the lieutenant told us he would soon be deploying to be a part of Operation Desert Storm. We gave him a DPS patch decal and asked him to put it on one of his bombs that he would be dropping.

We hadn't thought too much about it until one day I received a letter from Lt. Gross, and he had included two photos. One was of him standing by his Harrier next to a bomb that was tucked under a wing. The other was a close up of the bomb. He had stuck the DPS patch decal on the bomb and written, "Hey, Saddam. Paul, Bob, and Ruben of the Arizona Department of Public Safety say Buckle Up For Safety."

He also said the bomb was a canister bomb filled with hundreds of "bomblets." After he released the bomb at a prescribed altitude, the canister would open, and the bomblets would fall away. The canister would then fall to the ground. He told us that the canister would lay on the desert floor for years and that we should be alert for anyone wearing a turban knocking on our doors.

THE REST OF THE STORY
Paul Palmer #342

After telling the Harrier story, I got to thinking of other videos that the video unit produced. The DPS video unit was in a class of its own. We were far ahead of other police video units across the U.S. Thanks to the work of Gary Josephson, Bill Burkett, and Bill Smerdon, other police video units followed our lead. Our training tapes were in demand across the country.

Our slightly-out-of-focus videos were well received, and I don't know how many times I was asked how I got away with it. It worked because no one was safe. I took shots at myself as well as management, and there were never any personal shots taken at anyone. I just happened to be in a position to say things a lot of you wanted to say.

Soon after SOOF started, Bill Burkett, Bill Smerdon, and Dave Smith came up with the idea for Buck Savage. Who can forget Buck Savage, the bumbling, macho (in his own mind) patrolman. The segments were not only funny, there was a training message in each segment.

After Dave retired, we kicked around ideas for another training series that was humorous but also had a training message. Along came Officer Chuck. Chuck Torrie played the part of a kind, big-hearted patrolman that always tried to do the right thing but always seemed to make a mess of any situation. Just the opposite of Buck Savage. After each foul-up, his standard line was, "Sometimes it just ain't easy." We did two segments which we thought were fantastic, and then we were shot down by management. Go figure.

Okay, that didn't work. So along came "Down The Barrel." This series starred Frank Glenn and Ron Cox. Since they worked in the armory, we figured they could come up with firearms messages.

We shot it in a desert setting with Frank walking through greasewood and cactus, speaking in his slow drawl and down-home country manner. He would start with such lines as, "When the dawn breaks and the cock crows," and merge into a firearms safety message. Ron Cox was in the background strumming "Do Not Forsake Me Oh My Darling" or some other country classic on his guitar.

We did two segments and then were shot down again. I'm sorry if you never got a chance to see Officer Chuck or Frank Glenn and Ron Cox. You really missed something.

But they did let SOOF continue. It ran from 1980 to 2006, and we had a blast.

TRAINING VIDEOS
Anonymous

When we were first issued pagers, another unnamed narcotics officer and I signed out on his pager a couple of times to watch "training films." One was Cheech and Chong in *Up in Smoke*. The other was a Chuck Norris movie, but I can't recall the name. *Up in Smoke* was funny because there were two crowds in the theater—cops and dopers. You could tell who was who by which parts they laughed at.

ORIGINAL STOP STICK
Larry Thompson #148

The guys out in Salome got some "cotton picker" blades and welded them to a delineator post. When properly placed, this was the first ever "spike strip."

Phoenix found out about this and wanted to test this new device. The test was scheduled for the parking lot at the coliseum. Jim Eaves was very good about signing out on the location board and was doing so to attend this test. After making several attempts at "coliseum," he scratched it all out and wrote "fair grounds." (You had to see it to appreciate it.)

You know that the social separation has a negative effect on old AHP stories – we can't lie to each other and remind and remember the old days. Things like the day Jim Eaves was my admin sergeant. His office was next to mine, with our desks facing a mutual wall between us. He swatted a bee, and all my pictures, calendars, and memorabilia flew off the wall and were scattered over the office. What made it worse was when he laughed out loud!!

TOO DRUNK TO GO TO JAIL
Dennis McNulty #1959

I believe it was in 1983 that DPS switched over to the Intoxilizer 1000. I was working the late shift one night out of Winslow. After 2 am at closing time, all the drunks left the local low-life establishments like the White Cafe, the Brown Barn, and other dives to drive east out of town on old 66 to the intersection of SR87 to go north over I-40 to the sand pits, where they would park and continue drinking the night away (lots of fights and the odd homicide).

I would park just east of the intersection on the road to the Minnetonka Trading Post and watch for the worst driver to screw up the left turn to go north, then pull out and try to get him stopped once they crossed I-40. I got this car stopped, and out of it stepped the tallest Hopi Indian I ever saw. I'm 6 feet and I was looking up at him, plus he had me by at least 30 lbs. Very drunk but very happy.

The first FST was tilt your head back and touch your nose. He tipped his head back and promptly fell to the ground. Okay, you have failed your FSTs, and 'you're under arrest. After he got himself up and was leaning on his car fender for dear life, he said "not goin' to jail tonight, John Wayne."

He took one step towards me and fell on the ground again. It took two sets of cuffs to get him secured and about 10 minutes to fold and stuff him in the back of my unit. After the tow truck arrived, it was off to the Winslow 103.

We had just gotten certified on the Intox 1000, and he was going to be my first customer. I got the machine set up and had him blow into the mouthpiece until the printer clicked. The B/A showed .40%. Must have screwed up the sequence, so I waited the prescribed 20 minutes, reset the machine, and had him blow again until it clicked. B/A was

.42%. This guy was still going up. I had never seen a B/A that high and had only heard of it in training, and the warning was that anything this high was a probable medical issue.

Not wanting to book him into the Winslow PD drunk tank (just a concrete box with a drain in the floor) with a chance of him dying on me, I stuffed and folded him back into my unit again and off we went to the PSH (public safety health) Hospital in Winslow. I got him into the ER (the guy was walking under his own power) and showed the triage nurse both intox printouts. She said, "Yeah, we're gonna keep him, make sure there's no alcohol poisoning or liver shut down."

I left him with a citation to Judge Cub Culbertson's court. He was gone the next morning, and as I recall, the citation went to warrant. Fun times in District 3.

AN INTERESTING LUNCH
Gamble Dick #1743

In the early 80s, I was lucky enough to be a sergeant on the ditch. Great squad and a great job.

At any rate, one day I was in Bureau Headquarters around lunch time. I was just getting ready to leave when Major Mayes came out of his office and asked if I wanted to go to lunch with him. I said, "Sure." He explained that he had to be back by 1 pm for a meeting, so we decided on the Ramada Inn Coffee Shop just down the street.

We got to the coffee shop, and the hostess seated us in the middle of the restaurant. We were both in uniform. It took less than a minute before the major said, "What's going on here?"

I said, "I think they're having a lingerie show. Do you want to go someplace else?"

He said he didn't have time but let's move to a small table by the window where we may be more unobtrusive. We ordered lunch and seemed to be escaping notice. After a minute or two, I looked over the major's shoulder and said, "Brace yourself."

He turned to look, and we saw an absolutely stunning brunette in a bikini sashaying toward us. We were both looking at our napkins, and she did a pirouette and started her routine, "My name is whatever, and I'm wearing this very attractive bikini from Dillard's, blah, blah, blah . . ."

I looked at her and said, "I know you."

No doubt she thought it was a pick-up line and insisted she didn't know me, and I told her I just met her this past weekend. She said no. I said, "Think about it. We met Saturday night."

"No way," she said, "I was at a concert and didn't meet anyone."

I said, "Well, you met me. I was the cop who threw you out of the MEN'S ROOM at the .38 Special concert."

She turned a color that Mayes later described as strawberry and sat down at the table and started talking to us. She asked how I recognized her after such a brief encounter, and I told her we were cops and we remember stuff. Besides, there isn't a man alive who, once he's seen those eyes, would ever forget them. She became a darker shade of strawberry. We finished our lunch, bid our adieus, and headed for the car. On the way back to the office, Mayes asked, "How do you do that?"

"What?"

"That thing with women."

I said, "I think it was the eye thing." And he agreed that she did have gorgeous eyes. Every day on patrol is different, and some are better than others.

DEJA VU
Bill Hansen #2055

This story is called "Déjà Vu" and is a compilation of the memories of retired Motor Officer Bill Hansen #2055, retired Motor/Polygrapher Officer Dave Schroder #1176, and retired Sgt. Colin Peabody #481 and in honor of our fellow Motor Officer/Sergeant, Larry "Rocketman" Kenyon #2068, and retired Sgt. Larry Capp #596, may they both rest in peace.

Officers/Sgts:

Ofc. Larry Kenyon 2068
Ofc. Dave Schroder 1176
Ofc. Bill Hansen 2055
Ofc. Ramon Figueroa 3081
Sgt. Colin Peabody 481
Agent T.K. Wadell 803
Agent John Gantt 718
Agent Otis Thrasher 642
Agent Gene Babcock 458
Sgt. Larry Capp 596
Asst. CA Jerry Landau

Suspect #1 Todd Ballenger
Suspect #2 Billy Kaites
Suspect #3 ????

During the spring of 1982, Phoenix Night Motors partially consisted of Larry Kenyon, Dave Schroeder, Sgt. Colin Peabody, and Bill Hansen. During this time, Cadet Ramon Figueroa #3081 was finishing up on his FTO with Bill Hansen in a marked patrol car.

At some point one-night, Larry had come into contact with an occupied stolen Datsun (now called Nissan)

280Z when the driver ran a stop sign at 7th Street and the I-17 frontage. The arrested driver had all of his personal property contained in a large "man" bag which was retained by Officer Kenyon. In the bag was evidence of other criminal activity. Inventoried items of interest included stolen credit cards, a CB radio, personal belongings from victims, and pictures of other vehicles, including a Lincoln Continental. While processing suspect #1, in looking at the pictures, Larry concluded that the backgrounds in the pictures, some taken up on South Mountain Park, showed that other vehicles were involved, including the Lincoln parked at a hotel in the area of 24th Street and Buckeye Road near Sky Harbor Airport.

Later that night, at approximately 2300, toward the end of their shift, Bill Hansen was taking Ramon Figueroa back to D-5 (The Old Pepsi Plant) so we could finish up on the daily FTO PPR entries. All during the day it had been lightly raining in Phoenix.

While stopped at Van Buren on the NB frontage road of I-17, both of us observed a Datsun 280Z (with a CB antenna) stopped, facing westbound on Van Buren. The driver of the "Z" was waiting for the traffic signal to change so to proceed westbound on Van Buren. When the traffic signal turned green for westbound traffic, the Datsun drove west and then turned south onto the SB I-17 frontage road.

At this time of night and because of light traffic on Van Buren, Hansen was able to pull onto Van Buren and then southbound on the frontage road without using his top mounts and come up behind the "Z" car and then, with top mounts, performed a traffic stop. I told Ramon in the car to pay attention as this might be something related to the other stolen cars.

As we walked up to the "Z," I said out loud, "After we write him for his broken taillight, we'll go have coffee." (This was an oral "bluff" in attempt to not alert the driver.) I could see the driver looking at me in his side-view mirror

(Caucasian adult male, blonde hair). I think he had observed me unholstering my weapon and hiding it behind my leg as I approached.

About the time I walked up to the left rear area of the car...the driver fled. We quickly got into our vehicle and, with Ramon on the radio announcing, we were in pursuit. Because of the light rain, we were able to slowly catch up to the suspect vehicle, but because the driver had nothing to lose (and he had a 280Z), he soon lost us as we backed off of the pursuit. Since Phoenix OpCom had notified Phoenix PD, it was only a few minutes before the car was found abandoned in south Phoenix with the engine still running, the windshield wipers running, and the lights on.

During the pursuit of the second Datsun 280Z, Sgt. Peabody had Assistant County Attorney Jerry Landau riding with him and began checking the motels around Sky Harbor Airport for a Lincoln Town Car. He found a Lincoln Town C that matched the description of the Lincoln in the photos and ran the plate. The plate came back registered to a Ford sedan.

So as to not arouse suspicion at the hotel, Sgt. Peabody made contact with Auto Theft Detail Sgt. Larry Capp and told him what we had. Sgt. Capp advised to maintain surveillance at the motel. Since we were in an unmarked car, it was not difficult to do. Sgt. Capp mustered his troops and advised our participating Motors to change into civilian clothes and meet as soon as possible at the motel without raising any suspicions to potential suspects.

After we helped Larry Kenyon process the second 280Z vehicle and book his first suspect, we went to the hotel and met up with Larry Capp and his squad. Larry Capp and his squad had checked into the hotel and had rented a couple of rooms to set up surveillance on the stolen Lincoln, waiting for a suspect to emerge. It should also be noted that the Lincoln also had a CB Radio installed.

About 8 am the following morning, two suspects emerged from their motel room and got into the Lincoln and headed out of the parking lot, with several DPS undercover vehicles behind in a loose surveillance mode. The Lincoln travelled to a local gym on the frontage road south of Buckeye Road noted for alternate-lifestyle individuals and dropped one subject off. That suspect was subsequently taken into custody by some of Sgt. Capp's troops.

The Lincoln then continued back on the freeway, exiting at Van Buren, then going north on 43rd Avenue, still with DPS units in a loose surveillance mode. The Lincoln's driver seemed to be getting hinky and pulled into a Circle K at 43rd and Thomas and went inside. Several DPS officers covered the rear, and several of us went in the front door and made the arrest of the Lincoln driver. The clerk behind the counter made a remark to a Pepsi delivery driver that he hoped these guys were cops. The delivery driver was a former DPS officer named Bob Terry, who replied, "Yeah, they're all cops. I know them all."

As we exited with our prisoner, I said "Hi Bob, how are ya doing!"

Within the next few weeks, we were in Maricopa County Superior Court (Judge Cecil Peterson's court) for suppression hearing with suspect #1, Todd Ballenger. While waiting for the proceedings to commence, Larry Kenyon, Dave Schroeder, and myself were directed by the bailiff to the judge's chamber.

As we entered, seated was Todd Ballenger, his public defender, and Jerry Landau. Just as we sat down the judge's desk phone rang. For approximately 15 minutes the judge spoke on the phone, and from the one side of the conversation, it seemed Todd's father was speaking to the judge. In a quiet voice, Todd leaned over to us and said that his dad had passed away, and the judge was actually speaking to suspect #2, Billy Kaites.

After the judge hung up with the caller, Todd shared with the judge what he had stated to us. The judge was really put off on the impersonation and immediately postponed the hearing. All parties were excused, and suspect #1 Ballenger was put back into the custody of the Maricopa County Jail.

Jerry Landau was able to persuade the public defender to allow Todd to give us all of the pertinent info for Billy Kaites. It was determined that Billy Kaites had outstanding criminal warrants from various jurisdictions in the Midwest. A warrant was issued for his arrest and was signed by Judge Peterson.

After the case was concluded in Superior Court for Todd Ballenger, all of us thought the case was closed. It wasn't long afterwards that, during a squad meeting, Larry Kenyon informed all of us that he had received a phone call from the Kansas State Highway Patrol. It seemed that a trooper attempted a traffic stop on a reported stolen sports car. The driver failed to yield and led the KHP on a long high-speed pursuit. The pursuit continued until the driver of the sports car lost control, left the roadway, overturned, and the car burst into flames. There were no survivors. The KSP trooper reported to Larry Kenyon that the driver of the stolen sports car was Billy Kaites. The sports car was, you guessed it, another Datsun 280Z.

The final tally — two recovered Datsun 280Z's and one Lincoln Continental in Phoenix and a burned 280Z in Kansas. Two suspects spent time in prison...and one in the cemetery.

It's hard to believe that this case happened "40" years ago…. how can that be?

I OBJECT
Ron Bruce #2048

This was in '79 or '80, as I recall. I'd arrested a typical low-life marijuana smuggler with 40-50lbs of weed. I'm in Justice of Peace Judge William Gastelum's court for the prelim hearing. Bill was a retired Casa Grande PD sergeant and a good judge, meaning troopers got a fair hearing.

I'm on the stand presenting my case, while my deputy county attorney is pretty asleep at the wheel. The doper has a high-end drug attorney out of Tucson, who was rumored through DEA to take a lot of his fees in cocaine. Anyway, when it came time for the cross-exam by the defense, I'm getting butchered on the stand. I kept trying to get the DCA to object and get me some slack cut. It was not working. I finally paused after a vicious attack by the defense, turned to my right, looked at Bill, and said, "Your Honor, I object!"

The defense attorney went ballistic, screaming loudly at Bill that "he" (me) cannot do that!!! Bill raised a hand and said the court would take a ten-minute recess. He told the DCA and me to adjourn to his chambers, which we did. Bill proceeded to rip the DCA and told him he'd best wake up and do his job or the state was going to lose its case. He then looked a me and said, "Bones, that was funny as hell but don't do it again!"

Court was back in session, and I was able to get the case bound over to Superior Court. There, of course, a "deal" was cut, but the doper still went to prison for 3-5 years.

FRIED FRENCH
A. Whitney #1410

There's no particular reason anyone would know this, but I happen to be one-half French. Heck, I even have a dual citizenship and was once sent a draft notice from the French Army. Really. Since I ignored it, I may well be wanted there...

Anyway, from the time I was about six months old until age five, I lived in Paris. Not Texas, but France! So naturally, when I came back to the USA, I was a little French kid. (It's complicated; Dad was an Air Corps pilot who met my mom in France in '45. But that's too far off-point to get into here.)

Everything went well until I started school. Seems I was the only Francophone anywhere in sight attending Mrs. Pirchbarker's Grand Rapids, Michigan, kindergarten class. (Dad had gone to work for his friend, Bill Lear, who, at the time, was manufacturing avionics equipment there.) Naturally, the other kids made fun of me. Naturally, I clammed up with the French and learned American. Naturally, the French went away.

So. Once I had the opportunity to stop a carload of fellow Frogs for speeding on one of Arizona's highways. I tried to communicate with them is English, and they attempted to make themselves understood in French, complete with the appropriate hand gestures. We got nowhere.

Finally, in desperation, I told them, "Je ne' parle pas bien Francias," which means, "I don't speak French well." The only problem was, that I said it in perfect Parisian French!

My attempt at communication did not turn out as intended.

CITABRIA - BOMBS AWAY
Ron Cox #1101
Jim Heflin #1983

I don't recall the case except to say that a surveillance was taking place somewhere between Phoenix and Casa Grande. Jim was driving the Citabria. I was NOT the spotter in the plane. A much taller member of CI was handling that job on that day. The vehicle being followed had ended up somewhere in a sparsely populated area as I recall. During all of this, the ground units were on car-to-car radio frequency. Apparently the Citabria wasn't since Phoenix dispatch could hear its traffic. There were discreet blips coming from the spotter, indicating, to the trained ear in such circumstances, that the observer/spotter was in dire need of a porta-potty and there were none available for him in the aircraft. Jim took over the mic, which left us with the impression that the spotter was preoccupied. Try and picture in your mind, a 6'+ narc in the back seat. With a full bladder. Squirming around to relieve himself in a barf bag. I know; some things are difficult to unsee if you have that mental picture by now. After his completed chore of emptying his bladder, he comfortably sat back down. It was quite common to fly in that little bird with the windows open since it was so slow. Soon we hear, "Bombs away!" Meaning the said barf bag, now full, had been ejected. And I understand that a vehicle, possibly the one being followed, was the target. Some of those details have faded over the years. Whether or not the "bomb" hit anything or not, we'll never know. Surveillance ended and we all went back to Phoenix. When I checked out at the office, the dispatcher asked if I could call her. I went inside our office and called her. She said, "I've figured out a lot of the things you guys try to code while on surveillance, but what does Bombs Away mean?"

I asked if she had picked up on the fact that the spotter had to find a restroom. She said no. I told her that he did, and that he had utilized a barf bag, and the Bombs away was launching it out the plane window. She thought that was quite humorous.

20 IN 20 OUT
Paul Palmer #342

After hearing the story from Ron Cox about the Citabria Bombs Away, it brought to mind the time when we also had the same narc in the car with us and he was having the same problem. Like Ron, I will not use his name.

One day a narc came down to the video unit and told us that the CI division wanted us to video tape an upcoming narcotics raid. We were told not to tell a soul about the assignment and said there was a potential for a confrontation and someone getting injured on this raid. There were also vicious dogs to contend with. The raid was to take place southwest of Prescott in the middle of nowhere and it was to go down at day break. The narc said that he would be assigned to be with us.

Several days later we got the word and headed to Prescott.

After an evening briefing at the motel we called it a night and as I recall, rolled out of bed at 3:00 AM. We went to another briefing and downed way too much coffee, then hit the road.

We didn't know where we were going. Just follow the taillights of the car in front of you our narc said. We were tail end Charlie. We weren't gone all that long, heading down the White Spar towards Yarnell when the narc told us to pull over. He had to pee.

If you're not familiar with White Spar, it is a narrow highway with sharp turns and not many spots at all where you could pull off the highway. I said there was no place to pull off and besides, we had to keep the taillights in front of us in view. He kept saying over and over that he had to pee. Finally he gave up and we heard the distinct sound of liquid going into a Styrofoam coffee cup. 20 in 20 out he said and you guessed it, bombs away!

We continued on down the White Spar and turned off onto a dirt road somewhere near Yarnell. The CI caravan is now roaring down this dirt road and the dust is so thick we can barely see the taillights ahead of us. The narc in the back seat tells us again to pull over because he has to pee. I again explain that we can't because we will lose the caravan. He continues to tell us to pull over and finally says IF YOU DON'T STOP NOW I WILL SHOOT YOU. I have known this guy for years and I had no reason to doubt him. We stopped and it seemed like it took him 10 minutes to complete his business. I imagine that runoff made it all the way back to Yarnell. He hops in and we are off again, but now the dust has settled and no taillights in sight, Finally we see all of these cars parked and narcs standing next to their cars relieving themselves. It sounded like a summer monsoon storm.

We finally get going again and when we near the secluded house with the bad guys, we cut the headlights and quietly drive up onto a small airstrip just north of the house. We barely had time to set up when this earsplitting noise filed the air as a Blackhawk helicopter roared in and hovered over the house with its blinding lights illuminating the house and yard, its loudspeaker giving commands to the house occupants. The noise was not just loud, you could feel it! It was awesome, just like in the movies!

The raid went down as planned and the bad guys gave up without a fight. We drove down off the air strip and pulled into the yard where all the narcs were finishing up the arrests. As we were standing around, the "vicious" dogs were going up to everyone and licking their hands.

When it was all over, we made it back to Prescott. This time with no pee stops.

NARCS VS COYOTE AND DOGS
Ron Cox #1101

Word was that there was an underground drug lab on the property. The owner had mean dogs, supposedly. There was a short dirt airstrip on a small hill overlooking the house and outbuildings. I believe this particular raid involved all 5 SOU squads, along with a hoard of other folks. What little I can remember is as follows:

At dark thirty, a very long convoy headed out of Prescott toward the property, which was a couple miles off the highway. Squads came in from about every direction, on foot, and pretty much surrounded the property until the bust was given at dawn. I believe Sgt Tony Melendez, Neal Hanna, and myself were given the opportunity to walk in on the main dirt road and position ourselves with scoped rifles, on the airstrip overlooking the house. As we 3 were doing our very best to be as quiet as possible, probably at about the halfway mark, a coyote no more than 10' to our right started barking. Very loudly, and very close! I believe it was actually screaming. I can tell you, with some amount of certainty, that it scared the crap out of all 3 of us. But no rounds were fired, proving that none of us had our finger on a trigger.

We were all laughing so dang hard we couldn't keep very quiet. I know, that to this day, that coyote got some mileage out of that story! So, on we went. We got to the airstrip and scattered out along it to cover the front of the house. I think Tony had a DPS M16 with a night scope on it, but not positive. There was a porch light on by the front door. Getting close to daylight, a man comes out with a dog. Don't recall if it was a Rot or a Dobie, but it caught a whiff of something strange up towards the airstrip (3 narcs) and starting barking and starting up the hill. The owner started shouting and cussing at the dog profusely! The dog is trying to tell the guy that there's strange folks in the area, and he actually called the dog by name and said "you dumb SOB, get back down here. There's nothing out there!!" It was also at this time that about half of DPS and I believe a US Customs Blackhawk converged on the property.

I heard a car coming towards me on the airstrip (with lights out) and I looked over my shoulder and had to move my legs so they didn't get run over. I found out later that Bill Reutter was driving Col. Milstead in to get a good view of this guy's world falling apart. Bill told me later that he didn't see me until I moved my legs, due to my camo clothes and low light. For what all was found, if anything, I can't say. It was fun, and I think the dog and the coyote both had the last laugh.

THE RAID
Colin Peabody #481

I was on that raid, in the Blackhawk, when the tail wheel made contact with terra firma, I bailed out of the bird's open door, which was still about 6 ft off the ground and the main gear hadn't made contact yet. Larry Troutt was right behind me. We had about 100 yards of open ground to cover to get to the trailer. I was equipped with my issued Uzi and a large fire extinguisher to be used on the dogs without hurting them. They were Rotties, but more scared of us. We hit the trailer house and then the dogs headed for the back of the place. They were no problem, and the fire extinguisher wasn't used. Once the property was secured, those of us who arrived in the Blackhawk got back in and departed. Not sure how much contraband was found.

MY FIRST DAY AS A NARC SERGEANT
Colin Peabody #481

In March, 1983, I had been in the Criminal Investigations Bureau about 6 months when I was transferred to the Air Interdiction Squad as their former sergeant was retiring. I had 6 guys, Mike Stevens, Charley Ruiz, Bill Daily, Jim Paden, Ron Cox and Mike "Maddog" Taylor. This squad was assigned the task of intercepting aircraft smuggling narcotics into the State of Arizona and the United States. My first day, I came to work at 8 AM and got re-acquainted with the guys, as I had known them all for quite a while. I got my new vehicle, a fairly new Chevy pickup and with that, it was time to go to Sky Harbor Airport to meet the federal side of the crew, the guys from US. Customs, who had about 5 guys, a pilot and a Cessna 210 plane and a Supervisory Special Agent based out of the old Terminal 2.

Once we got introduced, it was suggested that we go out to Rainbow Valley south of Buckeye and look for planes flying in to the area that afternoon. Little did I know that the Customs guys had their Cessna in the air down along the Mexican border looking for aircraft. We climbed up a medium sized rocky hill and sat down to take a breather. The pilot of the Cessna called and said he was behind a low flying

Cessna that had crossed the border from Mexico and was maintaining a heading that would take him close to our location.

A few minutes later, the plane appeared at an altitude not much higher than where we were sitting and we could see the pilot in the plane! One of the guys was able to get the "N" number off the craft and found it was out of Cottonwood, AZ. Several of us scrambled down off the mountain and headed for our vehicles. I had Bill Daily with me and the other guys were tailing along. We headed in the general direction of Cottonwood and were kept up to date by the Customs pilot on the location and activities of the suspect aircraft.

That pilot made numerous evasive moves to try to shake the Customs plane and this lasted for a couple of hours as we drove north at a high rate of speed. By now, it is starting to get dark and the customs pilot was getting tired of this other pilot trying to shake him off his tail and a couple of times tried flying into box canyons in an effort to crash the customs pilot. At one point shortly after dark, the Customs pilot reported the plane had landed somewhere north east of Cottonwood on a dirt road.

We were now in the Cottonwood area and found the dirt road the plane had landed on. Once past the cattle guard on the right of way fence, this road was nothing more than a cow path. We continued on several miles up a hill to a more level area and our headlights shined on the tail of an aircraft. We approached it very carefully, but there was no one around it, but it did have a couple hundred pounds of marijuana in the back.

Once the evidence was collected and photos taken, the problem of what do we do with the aircraft? We couldn't leave it sitting out there and it wasn't going to be flying anywhere. One of the Customs guys was a pilot and offered up that if we could turn it around we might be able to drive it out of there and get it to Cottonwood. WTH??? Well, that was the plan and we got the plane turned around with several of us pushing down on the tail empennage of the plane and spinning it on its main gear tires. It fired right up, so the next couple of hours was spent with Bill Daily and me in my truck, lighting the way, guys walking alongside the plane kicking rocks out of the way, so the plane could slowly make its way without damaging the propeller, engine and landing gear. After what seemed like all night, we got it to the highway from Sedona to Cottonwood.

By now it was about 1 AM, and there was no highway traffic, so we continued our escort into Cottonwood, and made the turn up the highway to the Cottonwood airport. We had managed to make the lone traffic light and hadn't met up with any drunks who would swear they saw an airplane driving down the street.

The plane was secured at the airport, sealed and we headed back to Phoenix. By the time we got back to our office if was nearly 8 AM and we still had paperwork to do. My first day as a Narc was a real eye opener.

THE BIG MOTOR
Travis Qualls #3751

First things first I want to honor the men and women that came before me!!!

Now for the good stuff...

I started out as an officer trainee in district 10 under George Elias. Actually, an explorer scout prior to that with Terry DeBoer. During my acclimation to DPS I was blessed to work for Larry Thompson, Bob Kircher, Leo Villapando, Jim Eaves, Greg Evanson, Coy Johnston, and many others... I wish I could list all. I went to the ALETA and was assigned to district 10 again. Now for the good stuff... I transferred to METRO. I spent some time with Tom Elias. A great teacher. Once released and on my own in metro I felt that I had arrived until I met Gary Zimmerman #424.

It was a swing shift. I was out with a 961x2. I was in control until this motor officer arrived on scene. I want to say again I was in control... The motor officer who I never met walked up to me and never asked how I was... never asked can I help you... never asked basically anything, except, here it comes... GET ME A TOW TRUCK BOY as he takes my paperwork from my clipboard. Remember I spent time in HP Bureau... I knew how to pick battles. I gave that BIG MOTOR my paperwork and did what he said! As I left the scene, I thought to myself what an A HOL@#$%^&.

My second encounter with #424 was during a pursuit. When the pursuit ended, I saw said MOTOR pulling an individual out through a wing vent... Probably hurt? So, I continued my life in metro until one goofy decision. I told my better half that I want to be a motor officer.... Yeah me! It was the boots...

I applied and went through the scrutiny of my work. WOW! I was accepted. Yeah Me! Motor school, by the way, was run by no other than ZIMMERMAN #424. @#$%$#@!#%. I made it the first time. I made it through field training. I was on my own in a car squad as a motor. I was special...I thought.

To my surprise, District 17 was created, and Col. Thompson allowed Sgt. Zimmerman to have his own squad. I was assigned. HELP! I went home to my better half and told her my life was over, my career was over, etc.

For the next 10 years I worked for #424 Sgt., LT., and friend Gary Zimmerman. He was the epitome of what a highway patrolman should be! From him, I learned what a patrolman should be!!!

I have other stories where people wanted to complain on me and asked for my supervisor. I told them that was not a good idea. I was never in the complaint after that. Yay me.

I want all who came before me to know I respect you, I truly care about our history & our future, and most of all, thanks to you! Even more importantly, thanks to the families and their sacrifices! They are the true heroes: the wives, sons, daugherts, brothers, sisters, friends, etc. Thank you!!! MATTHEW 5:9

THE LITTLE RUN AWAY
Ron Mayes #225

My duty station from June of 1967 until June of 1969 was Globe. This was when the mine strike was going on, and to say the least, there were a lot of discontented miners. Most of them were unhappy with the times, a good number spent what money they had on drinking, and they certainly didn't like being stopped by the Highway Patrol. A common first comment was usually, "Why are you harassing me? Why aren't you fighting in Viet Nam?"

Late one night in 1968 while patrolling westbound on US-60 as I entered the Miami town limits, I came up on a very slow-moving Oldsmobile, traveling about 10 MPH, weaving and the right side tires bumping against the curbing. An obvious drunk driver, or so I thought. I turned on my top lights, no reaction by the driver so I beeped the siren and pulled up beside the vehicle, which eventually slowed to a stop. I turned on my spotlight, got out my patrol car and approached the driver's side door. As I got closer, all I could see was a very small head looking straight ahead, peeking over the dash and through the steering wheel.

The first thing I said to him was "how old are you?" He replied, "nine". Then the surprise responses to my questions began. He didn't know where he was going, he was just running away from home. Home was in San Manuel. I was aghast! It was about midnight and he had driven up SR77 in the dark on the narrow two-lane beyond Mammoth to Winkleman and on up the mountain on one of the most curvy, mountainous highways in the state, and the old highway which back then wound around through downtown Globe. He had driven a total of seventy-five miles.

For the trip, he had brought his guitar and he had a nickel and four pennies in his pocket. I called Miami PD dispatch and had them send an officer to drive the vehicle to their department. I drove the little guy to the PD and made a phone call to his father in San Manuel. I told his dad what was going on, he wouldn't believe it, he went and checked the boy's bedroom and then, where he had parked his car. He was in shock but said he would get his wife out of bed and they would borrow a car and would drive to Miami and would be there in a few hours. I told him that his son was in safe hands and where the PD was located.

It was a very rewarding night, the little guy was very polite, and I think somewhat relieved, as I imagine that he had bit off more than he could chew. And above all, I didn't have to book a DUI and listen to a bunch of B.S. Incidentally, I checked with the PD the first thing the next morning and everything went well, the little runaway was safely back home.

A MORENCI MEMORY
Colin Peabody #481

When we were assembling in Safford, I shared a room with two of my Narc squad, Jim Paden and Mike "Maddog" Taylor, who hold the record for loud snoring.

No sleep for me, as it sounded like two semi-trucks using their Jake brakes to slow down. I threatened to kiss them both to keep them awake and not snoring.

Rest in Peace 617!

On one of our return trips from Morenci to Safford in the back of a ANG deuce and a half, Dick Richey was sitting across from me. I heard "Hey Sarge" then BANG! Holy Sh... Batman! Dick popped a cap at a crow sitting on a fence post and missed, scared the crap out it the two Guard guys driving the truck and the rest of us as well.

I could only respond with, "Dick, do you know how much paper we are going to write?"

When I was standing tall in Reutter's office on Monday morning, he asked "Did he hit the crow?"

"No!"

"Then give him a day off!"

I think he wound up with two.

Rest in Peace my friend! One of the good guys!

A FREE DINNER
Rich Richardson #188

I remember a story that Dick Raymond used to tell in the academy about Harley Thompson. Maybe you heard the story, as best that I remember:

Raymond said that he and Thompson were in Seligman back in early patrol days. That old 1949 Ford in one of your pictures you sent to me may have been like what they were driving in those days.

Anyway, Raymond was driving through Seligman and observed a patrol vehicle parked at a café. He believed that it was Thompson. A sneaky idea hit Raymond. Why not drive past the café fast?

The café was on a twisted portion of old US 66. The speed resulted in squealing the tires and drew the attention of Thompson.

Apparently, Thompson didn't know it was a patrol car making the noise.

As the story goes, Thompson ran out to his car quickly and went in pursuit of the speeding car. What Thompson didn't know was the speeder had turned off the street onto a side road. Thompson headed west to catch up with the speeder and never located the suspect car.

In the meantime, Raymond parked his car near the café and entered. He observed the food on the counter that belonged to Thompson and commenced to eat the food.

When Thompson returned empty-handed to the café, he saw Raymond seated at the counter. Raymond asked where Thompson had gone, leaving a nearly full plate of food.

Apparently, Thompson didn't put two and two together and thought that the speeder got away and didn't know it was Raymond pulling the prank.

Sometime later, Thompson did find out it was Raymond. I suppose Thompson had to finally admit that Raymond got the best at that time.

I could just see Thompson's facial expression once he found out what happened that day in Seligman.

During my time with the patrol, I served in Yuma, Seligman, Flagstaff, Holbrook and Show Low, all during the first 12 years in uniform.

I transferred to the Narcotics Unit in Phoenix for a year, and then to the Intelligence Unit for another four years. I then transferred to my final duty station in Tucson, working the Intelligence Unit.

After retiring during 1982 in Tucson (Criminal Intelligence Unit), I became a DPS Reserve officer #9791 from 1982-1985 in Tucson. During the last six months before leaving the reserves, I did work for the AZ Dept. of Motor Vehicles as an Inspector in Tucson.

THE HITCHING POST
Bev Jones, daughter of Jim Phillips #36

Dad related the following story to me many times. Each time I heard it, I knew he would never forget that night. It was 1957, when he was a patrolman stationed in Mayer.

I was able to pull over a car just out of Prescott that had been weaving all over the road. He saw my lights and finally stopped after driving into the empty parking lot of a bar that was closed. The guy was obviously very drunk.

As I was preparing to handcuff him and put him in my patrol car, a call came in advising there was a bad accident between Cordes Junction and Camp Verde.

I was, of course, the only patrolman on duty and I couldn't take him with me. Neither could I just release him, for fear he would wander off and get hit by a car. I only had a short time to make a decision.

I realized there was an old hitching post right there in front of the bar. I knew my only choice was to handcuff him to that hitching post, trusting I would not be gone very long.

I assured him I would be back, and we would then deal with his DUI.

I investigated the accident, and indeed it was a bad one.

After several hours at the scene, I headed home, forgetting all about the drunk gentleman handcuffed to the hitching post.

I got home and practically fell into bed, exhausted. I was nearly asleep, when suddenly I remembered the drunk!

I'm pretty sure I broke a speed record putting my uniform back on, and speed limits, too, as I raced back toward Prescott, praying for the poor guy the entire way. I pulled into the parking lot and there he was, still handcuffed to the hitching post waiting for me.

I felt terrible. I had some blankets in the car, put the "little more sober" fellow in my car, and drove him to a café.

I made sure he started with some good hot coffee, followed by the best breakfast my money could buy (at that particular café).

I left his car in the parking lot instead of calling for a wrecker and drove the gentleman home. I told him I wasn't going to arrest him, and that later he could get a ride back to his car.

He was relieved to be spared the DUI charge and now had a full stomach, clear head, and would hopefully not ever drive drunk again!

Sometimes, back in the day, with no back-up or cages in the patrol cars, the choices we had to make on the spot were unusually difficult. This was one of those.

Everything must have worked out all right, though, because I never heard from him or received a disciplinary letter. My prayers were answered!

MAKE ME BARK LIKE A DOG
Colin Peabody #481

When I was assigned to the DPS Fugitive Detail in the mid-1980s, one of our primary functions was tracking down escapees from the Arizona Department of Corrections (DOC). On one of those adventures, a DOC inmate had been brought to the Maricopa County Hospital off 24th St. and Van Buren in Phoenix to be treated for an illness.

A practice then was for the "patient" to have his handcuffs and leg irons removed while being treated. The DOC guard would be stationed outside of the treatment area.

During the treatment, this one inmate managed to escape without the guard noticing it for several minutes. When he realized the inmate was gone, he sounded the alarm to DOC, who in turn notified Phoenix PD and the DPS Fugitive Detail.

Phoenix PD searched the local residential neighborhood the rest of the afternoon, as did our detail with no results.

The next day, we did a canvas of an older residential area about 2 ½ blocks from the hospital. One of the neighbors told us they had seen an unfamiliar male in the house across the street, and that the old lady who lived there didn't have any relatives that would have been there.

We responded across the street, and after identifying ourselves, spoke with the lady who said she didn't have any visitors that she knew of. She was extremely hard of hearing. She allowed us to "clear the house," but we didn't see anyone hiding.

What we did find, was a door in the kitchen near the back of the house that had steps leading down to a partially dug out dirt basement and a crawl space under the rest of the house. There were remains of food that must have come from inside the house.

We went down there and saw where the dirt had been disturbed, and towards the front of the house, we could faintly see tennis shoes showing in the darkness. Our flashlights could barely illuminate that far into the dark in detail.

We knew this was our escapee. We called his name several times but got no response from him at all. We weren't planning on going back there in that small space to negotiate with him. Plan "B" went into action.

One of my squad officers was Joe Mulcaire #904, who had been on my Motor Squad a few years earlier. Joe is a very talented individual, one being the ability to make sounds that mimic a large dog.

I whispered to Joe to get ready to do his dog imitation. I hollered at the escapee that we were going to send our dog in after him if he didn't come out. No response.

"Joe, go outside and bring the dog in! OK. Sarge!"

Joe makes noise going up the stairs and, in a few moments, we hear a large dog barking, yelping, ready to go into action.

Joe comes partially down the steps, still barking.

I yell at the escapee, "OK," we are sending the dog in and you aren't going to like the result, so get your ass out of there."

"OK, I'm coming out."

He was backing himself out of his hidey hole and the "dog" was still barking. I told Joe to take the dog outside. He finally got to where we could reach him and drug him out of the space where we stood him up, searched him and cuffed him.

We took him upstairs and outside in the light. He was looking around for the dog.

Joe was standing behind him and let out a huge bark. The inmate nearly fainted, until Joe came around him and barked once more.

"Here is our "Dog", I told him.

We had the old lady come out and we showed her what we found under her house and that she was now safe from this escapee. She couldn't believe her eyes! Not only did we capture a dangerous escapee, but we potentially saved an old, helpless woman from harm, all thanks to an alert neighbor and a dog named "Joe!"

ABOUT THE ARIZONA HIGHWAY PATROL COALITION

The Coalition of Department of Public Safety Retirees, Inc. is a non-profit organization with several hundred members, with both sworn and civilian members and it proudly presents this book for you reading pleasure.

The retirees of the Arizona Highway Patrol/Department of Public Safety served the state of Arizona honorably and richly deserve their retirement days. These officers patrolled Arizona highways from the urban freeways and cross-country Interstates to the narrow two lanes in remote areas of the state. Some areas so remote that the only housing available for their families was in an adjoining state. The families sacrificed the niceties of big city life to follow their patrolman spouse to remote tiny towns and communities; towns tucked away on Indian reservations. They experienced different cultures and learned to do a lot with less. They are the forgotten heroes.

These are true stories from patrolmen who lived them. Some sad, most funny, some unbelievable. It is a must read for anyone in law enforcement.

Paul Palmer and Colin Peabody are the coalition members who put this book together, compiling our retiree stories. Paul and Colin are longtime friends who began their friendship in 1968 when Paul was dispatching in Holbrook and Colin was a patrolman in Winslow. Paul is an Arizona native and Colin says he wasn't born here, but he got here as fast as he could. He was 7 years old when he arrived in Arizona. Both do all they can do to preserve the history and legacy of our department.

CPSIA information can be obtained
at www.ICGtesting.com
Printed in the USA
FSHW021832070721
82847FS